THE VORTEX MADE ME DO IT!

THE MYSTERY AND HISTORY OF

DESERT HOT SPRINGS

BILL EFFINGER

New Century Publishing 100 E. San Marcos Blvd.

Suite 400 San Marcos, CA 92069

Copyright © 2011 Bill Effinger

For information: Address New Century Publishing

100 E. San Marcos Blvd. Suite 400, San Marcos, CA 92069

First E-Book edition October 2011

Produced in the United States of America

Effinger, Bill (2011-10-30).

The Vortex made me do it!

ISBN:13-978-0615470207

Dedication

This book is dedicated to all of the people that have lived in, are currently living in, or are planning to live in Desert Hot Springs when the book is published

It is my sincere wish and hope that one day the city and its residents will be able to enjoy the normalcy of a balanced and financially sound community without strife, fear or angst about their future, in a relative calm and serene atmosphere, suitable for raising and educating their children in safety, or when retired, to fill out the remaining period of their lives in peace and tranquility.

It is also my sincere wish and hope that Desert Hot springs will one day be looked upon as a good neighbor to all of the other cities in Coachella Valley, and in doing so, legitimately earn he title of:

"The Shining City on the Hill

Bill Effinger

Acknowledgements

I could not have completed this effort without the help of my number one Editor and wife, Diana. My youngest son Brian not only did some editing, for the book, but also contributed a few of his more erudite observations of Desert Hot Springs as he watched through the wonders of cyber space and print media, as well as during our very frequent evening exchanges via Microsoft Live Messenger.

I also want to thank Google for providing me and the world at large with great research tools for finding long forgotten news articles and web postings.

A special thanks to Stephen Yerxa who provided me with the Yerxa family tree dating back to the year 1746 and sharing his life path with me that so closely followed my own when we discovered we were both born in Duluth Minnesota, lived ten miles apart and came to California under similar circumstances and timing. It is truly a small world.

Additional thanks to the Desert Hot Springs Historical Society; Cabot Yerxa Museum; Desert Local News, Desert Sun; Press Enterprise; City of Desert Hot Springs staff and members of the city council and all of the city's citizens who consented to being interviewed and allowing me to publish their comments which were extremely important in helping me shape the city's history and resulting stories.

Contents

Introduction

The narrative profile of Desert Hot Springs shown below is how city hoteliers, spa owners, merchants and many residents presented the city of Desert Hot Springs to those living outside its borders during the summer of 2011.

Disclaimer:

*The narrative, logos and spa ads on the following five pages are contained on, and are the property of the web site: **www.deserthotsprings.com.** The Author uploaded this information from Google web pages and accepts no responsibility for the content or authenticity of statements made herein.*

Welcome! To *"California's Spa City"*

The City of Desert Hot Springs:

MSWD
Mission Springs Water District

DESERT HOT SPRINGS
CALIFORNIA
CHAMBER OF COMMERCE

Welcome to the City of Desert Hot Springs, famous throughout the world for our natural hot mineral waters, award winning municipal drinking water, clean air, vista views, plus easy access to world class events and attractions in the Coachella Valley region and Joshua Tree National Park.

Just by clicking on the icons above, illustrations at the top, and banner ads on the right, we will take you directly to the attractions, hotels, spas, and other information you may need to enjoy the Desert Hot Springs area.

Whether you're coming to play, relax, or make Desert Hot Springs your home, you'll be impressed by our town's atmosphere and hospitality. Our hotels and spas offer an incredible variety of massages and treatments to soothe and rejuvenate visitors from as far away as Europe and Asia who seek out our remarkable waters. For a wonderful weekend getaway, or a beautiful place to live, you'll discover something special in Desert Hot Springs, *"California's Spa City"*.

Europeans have flocked to hot mineral springs spas for centuries to experience the restorative and curative values of the mineral waters. The practice of "taking the waters" for therapeutic purposes is as popular today as it was in the days of the Roman baths. Within Desert Hot Springs exists one of the greatest thermal water areas in

7

the world. These natural hot springs have been compared to the famous healing waters of Baden-Baden, Vichy and Evian. The very word "spa" means a place providing therapeutic mineral springs but while the number of spas continue to grow in the United States, very few offer the real nature of a spa... the healing restorative powers of the mineral water.

The health benefits of mineral-rich, hot springs have been well documented over the years. From early indigenous peoples to current day health enthusiasts, mineral waters around the world are famous for their healing attributes. While stress is relieved by the natural heat, the minerals absorbed through the skin rejuvenate the body. Used for years to relieve sore muscles and treat the stiffness that accompanies arthritis, the water in Desert Hot Springs is also especially rich in silica leaving the skin soft and smooth.
- *The Cornell Study on the Spa market*

"The mineral water here is some of the best in America..."
- *Travel & Leisure Magazine 2001*

"Every sickness, every disease, every ailment can be traced to a mineral deficiency."
- *Dr. Linus Pauling, two-time Nobel Laureate*

"The analyses of the waters in Desert Hot Springs, I have not found the like in any country I have explored. What has surprised me most is the mineral content of the water. It is a pronounced curative agency. It would appear to have qualities far superior to any waters known to me. Desert Hot Springs could be an important health center."
- *Dr. Broue, Australian geologist and physicist*

"Take your minerals" was the old adage in the early part of the century. Minerals have been viewed as the key to heath and, in deficiency, the cause of many illnesses. The list of illnesses caused by mineral deficiencies is endless. From dry hair to arthritis to depression, lethargy, cancer, fibromyalgia, muscle pain, memory loss, weight gain, headaches, attention deficit disorder, loss of libido, cramps, and on and on.

However, in the United States, most of our water has been stripped of valuable minerals. Our water has been treated and processed and essentially turned into "white bread". Additionally we've viewed water with minerals as undesirable "hard" water and done our best to remove those minerals in favor of spotless glassware. As a result, our water is dead. We're drinking what is left after all the minerals have been processed and treated out. Our bodies need minerals. It is conceivable most Americans are suffering from some kind of mineral deficiency.

Voted the best Tasting Water... in the World!

The rich pools of water beneath Desert Hot Springs are both hot and cold. The hot mineral water comes from fissures in the earth and vary in temperature and mineral content.

The cold water in Desert Hot Springs is a separate aquifer but it is also high in minerals. This is the region's drinking water. There is absolutely nothing done to this water. Nothing is added and nothing is taken out. The water in Desert Hot Springs is consumed in its pure and natural state... just as it comes out of the earth. This is almost unprecedented in the United States.

Desert Hot Springs water is so delicious it has been voted "The Best Tasting in the World" in a large number of competitions, most recently by the International Water Tasting Competition in Berkley Springs, West Virginia.

Discover the miracle healing waters of Desert Hot Springs. We know you'll be glad you did!

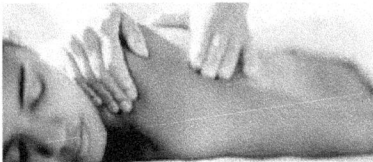

Not to be outdone, the city's web home page makes the following statement to its visitors, further extolling the virtues of its renowned drinking and mineral waters:

City of Desert Hot Springs Home Page

With its elevated views of the Coachella Valley and thousands of acres of gorgeous mountain preserves, Desert Hot Springs is one of the fastest-growing communities in Southern California. Minutes from an international airport, golf, shopping, renowned restaurants, major sporting events and more, this spa destination city beckons visitors and resort recreational developers.

Desert Hot Springs is built over one of the world's finest natural hot mineral water aquifers. Naturally occurring mineral waters bubble and percolate to the surface in this get-away-from-it-all destination. Not surprisingly, spas rule in Desert Hot Springs. You can calm and renew in polished marble resorts, retro-hip motels or ultra-exclusive celebrity retreats. The city also boasts pure and delicious award-winning municipal drinking water.

For a wonderful getaway, or a beautiful, affordable place to live, visit Desert Hot Springs. You'll see why it's "Clearly Above the Rest."

****

Now, please sit back in a cool place with a comfortable chair, and take yourself back in time to the year 1876; one-hundred and thirty-five years ago, and enjoy the history and mystery of Desert Hot Springs, as President U. S. Grant signs an executive order establishing a checkerboard pattern of designated Indian Reservation Land for the Agua Caliente Band of the Cahuilla Tribe along the Coachella valley floor where it all began.

Ulysses S. Grant

"It was my fortune, or misfortune, to be called to the office of Chief Executive without any previous political training".
December 5, 1876

Prologue:

Scholars have said that truth is stranger than fiction. Nothing could be proven more true than what you are about to read.

Since living in the city a relatively short time and moving away a few years ago, I contemplated writing the unusual history of Desert Hot Springs, and was finally jolted into doing so with this news headline:

Former Desert Hot Springs Mayor Alex Bias' wife faces charges in two bank robberies Desert Sun (2:02 PM, Feb. 23, 2011)

"Carol Jean Bias, 69, has been charged with robbing the Bank of America at 5601 Ramon Road on Feb. 3, and the Bank of America at 588 Palm Canyon Drive around noon Wednesday."..................

After pleading not guilty Mrs. Bias was remanded to jail, released on Bail and a hearing was set in Riverside..........

Now if that wouldn't make you jump out of your chair, not much would. It did me. I was a supporter of Alex's bid to become mayor, and met with both he and his wife Carol on many occasions. She was quite small in stature, had a mouth like a truck driver, but I would never have taken her for a bank robber. When that Energy Vortex gets you, it just won't let go. After sharing the article with my wife Diana, we decided the curious story of this community had to be told.

14

Desert Hot Springs is a historical place in the Imperial Desert of California resting high above the floor of Coachella Valley. The area, was once roamed by the Cahuilla Tribe's Band of Agua Caliente Indians, and the Morongo Band of Mission Indians. During 1913 the area became home to one of its earliest and most famous residents, Cabot Yerxa, whose adobe house still stands as a museum and monument to the pioneering spirit of America. It is also a place where local lore and some enthusiasts believe there is an "Energy Vortex" in the center of the city creating mystic powers for residents and visitors.

What follows, is 103-years of that history; starting with Jack Riley in 1908, purportedly the first white man to set foot in the area and then Hilda Gray in 1910, the area's first known white settler/homesteader; followed by Yerxa in 1913.The scientific explanation of the many geological, meteorological and mystic mysteries within this desert oasis containing rare cold pure drinking water and hot mineral springs, exposes two juxtaposed natural phenomena creating a mystery of nature for the curious to experience and ponder the reasons and meaning of it all.

It is also a place where local lore and some enthusiasts believe there is an "Energy Vortex" in the center of the city creating mystic powers for residents and visitors.

Most early settlers of the area were homesteaders, who qualified and secured their 160-acre parcel ownership by constructing the required one-hundred square foot "home" as established by the Homestead Act of the U.S. Government and signed by President Abraham Lincoln in 1862. The law took effect on January 1, 1863.

Now, the city within its boundaries is financially, and infrastructure challenged. There is a small but very active constituency of citizens working as volunteers on civic projects throughout the city, many of whom believe the "natural wonders" of the medicinal quality of "miracle hot spring waters"; the pure drinking water and the "Energy Vortex" will bring prosperity to the city. So far, this hasn't happened.

Approximately twenty-seven-thousand residents are living in Desert Hot Springs today, many of whom are retired. Those that are working, travel outside the city to other cities in Coachella Valley or west into the city of Riverside and Orange County. There are very few jobs in Desert Hot Springs to be had. Commercial and industrial activity is extremely limited. As a result, most shopping by the city's residents is outside the city as well. The latest published figures state 52 percent of all purchases are made outside the city, draining badly needed sales tax revenues.

Cabot Yerxa: Early Settler

Cabot Yerxa is pictured above riding his faithful mule, Merry Christmas, and no doubt hauling building materials with his burro following, on his way to building his rambling, Pueblo style home on "Miracle Hill" in Desert Hot Springs. I found the following information on Yerxa while doing research for the book, establishing his birthplace as being North Dakota:

Cabot Abram Yerxa, Pioneer
Born:June 11, 1883
Hamilton
Pembina County
North Dakota, USA

Died:Mar. 5, 1965
Desert Hot Springs
Riverside County
California, USA

Cabot Yerxa was known in his lifetime as "The Father of Desert Hot Springs." Born in Sioux territory at his parent's trading post, he was guest of Mexican president Porfirio Diaz at the Castillo de Chapultepec in the 1890's, member of an Inuit household during the heady years of the Alaska gold rush, importer of Cuban cigars following the Spanish-American War, political appointee of Theodore Roosevelt, citrus baron, desert homesteader, discoverer of the aquifers that have made Desert Hot Springs a world-renowned health center, soldier in WWI (where he attained the rank of sergeant with the 345th Battalion Tank Corps), student at Academie Julien in 1920's Paris, world traveler, city father, Impressionist painter, newspaper columnist, mystic and builder of Desert Hot Spring's only museum - an epic monument that is an much a sculpture as it is a building. Cabot Yerxa held dozens of jobs in as many fields – everything from postmaster to carnie. It is said that he visited all 50 states. At times he was wealthy, mostly he wasn't. He was largely self-taught; "home schooled" is the term used more frequently these days, and throughout his long life he would thoroughly research any topic that interested him. He collected things obsessively, and recycled virtually everything. He loved all aspects of nature; animals, plants, geology and the starry night sky. He saw UFOs. He was a Theosophist and a Freemason. He traveled the world. He married twice and had a son. He immersed himself in the cultures of indigenous Americans. When he finally "settled down" at the age of 60, it was to build his masterpiece, a sprawling 5,000 square foot, four-story structure inspired by Hopi pueblos and said to contain 35 completed rooms and 150 windows. This structure was primarily designed to be his "castle," but Yerxa also intended it to house a trading post / art gallery and to function as an artist's colony. This structure, which Cabot referred to as "the castle" or "Miracle Hill" in his personal dealings, was named "Cabot's Old Indian Pueblo" for the public. He had a "trading post" and gave tours of his domicile to tourists out for a day trip. The story of Cabot's pueblo might be considered to be as strange and wonderful as the story of Cabot himself. It is now a museum and is substantively unchanged from 1965; a slice of local history and desert lore.

****

The above information from the published Yerxa family tree differs with some of what is contained in the Desert Hot Springs Historical Society archives, but I felt the additional information was important enough to be included here.

Further research turned up this article published in nearby Morongo Valley by the Morongo Historical Society during the Spring of 2010:

Cabot Yerxa: The Man, His Pueblo Home & Folly

Visionary
Artist
Globe Trotter
Architect
Philanthropist
Scavenger

**As published in the Morongo Basin Newsletter;
Spring 2010**

By Carol Sanders

The desert has long attracted those some would call eccentric, others visionary, men who have built structures that embody their visions.

Consider George van Tassel and the Integratron in Landers; consider Leonard Knight, still at work on Salvation Mountain near Niland. And, consider Cabot Yerxa and his Old Pueblo Home, now Cabot's Pueblo Museum in Desert Hot Springs.

In the case of Cabot Yerxa, his combination home, art gallery, work-shop, museum, and trading post is as colorful and expansive as his life story.

The pueblo began as a one-man project in 1941, and was still a work-in-progress at the time of Cabot's death in 1965. Inspired by Hopi Indian architecture, the 5,000 square feet structure consists of some 35 rooms, with 150 windows and 65 doors. Construction material includes adobe bricks made by Cabot himself, with a cup of cement added to each brick. He seldom bought new materials; instead, Cabot scavenged the desert as far as the Salton Sea for used timbers, masonry, glass and wood. He was said to have taken nails from abandoned cabins, straightened them, and incorporated them into his pueblo. The front door is recycled from an old wagon.

The pueblo's exterior presents a flat, irregular façade broken by windows and projecting beams. Irregularity was a deliberate part of Cabot's construction plan. He shared the In-dian belief that evil spirits dwell in symmetry, and so purposely left walls somewhat un-even, floors not perfectly level, doorways aslant.

The pueblo is now a museum, one of the most fascinating in the desert area. What were the trading post and personal living quarters of Cabot Yerxa occupy the ground floor. "Ground" is an appropriate word, because the living room floor is dirt. The room is dominated by a huge stone fireplace, and tucked beside it is Cabot's tiny bedroom. A kitchen, dining room, office and storage space take up the remainder of the first floor.

An apartment suite built for Portia, Cabot's second wife, occupies the second floor, which also has an area to showcase the art work of Cabot and his friends, and his collection of curiosities accumulated through the years.

The third floor consists of one large room with many windows, affording views of the nearby mountains. The room was once used as a classroom for metaphysical and theosophical studies that Cabot and Portia pursued.

The life of Cabot Yerxa is almost as fantastic as the design of his sprawling pueblo. He was born in 1883 in Hamilton, Dakota Territories, and spent his early years on the Sioux Reservation where his parents ran a trading post. The family left there for St. Paul, Minnesota, where they ran a store. The elder Mr. Yerxa next took the family to Mexico where he taught his merchandizing skills and developed a taste for cigars, at least for making them. The family next settled in Seattle, and soon young Cabot decided Alaska was his land of opportunity. Lured north by the gold rush, Cabot drove dog teams and a stage coach in the area of Nome, then set up a store specializing in selling cigars to the gold miners flocking to the area.

He became interested in the culture and language of the Inuit, enjoyed their hospitality, and compiled a 320 word vocabulary of their language which he sold to the Smithsonian Institute. Cabot set up a mobile grocery business in Alaska, going to different areas and taking orders which were filled at his father's store in Seattle and shipped to the clients. It was while engaged in this enterprise that he met then Vice-President Theodore Roosevelt and main-tained a long-time friendship with him.

Cabot's father next sold his General Merchandising com-pany and moved the family to Cuba, where he built tract houses outside Havana. Political developments in Cuba forced the family to move to Florida, where they manufactured cigars in Key West.

Next Cabot headed West. He married, fathered a son, Rodney, and was divorced. Cabot joined the Yerxa family in moving to Riverside and investing in a promising citrus ranch. They lost their fortune in the freeze of 1913.

Cabot then homesteaded near the desert area which later became Desert Hot Springs. At first, he lived a rugged life, sleeping outdoors and cooking over a campfire. Then he built a 10 by 12 foot cabin out of one inch wide boards. He used his artistic talent to create post cards of desert scenes which he sold to train passengers at the nearby rail stop of Garnet, outside Palm Springs.

One of the first items Cabot obtained was a burro he named Merry Christmas in honor of the day he purchased her. He credits the burro with saving his life during a sand-storm near Whitewater, 16 miles from home. Cabot flattened himself against the animal's back, protected his eyes from the blowing sand, and told Merry Christmas "Take me home." She did. A newspaper account of this adventure appeared in the *Riverside Enterprise*. The burro was also known for her eclectic eating habits. Cabot shared what-ever he was eating with her, in gratitude for her saving his life, and she reportedly ate anything, and even drank water from a bottle and chewed tobacco.

With her aid, he built his first permanent shelter, which he called Eagle's Nest, a one-room cabin situated in a hole Cabot excavated on what he later called Miracle Hill. The most pressing problem was a lack of water. Cabot and Merry Christmas hauled water from Garnet, a fourteen mile round trip, several times a week. Then, Cabot dug a well, the first of the hot water sources that later became the basis for the city of Desert Hot Springs. He dug a second well about 600 yards from the first and discovered cold water. This unusual result occurred, Cabot later learned from geologists, because each well was located on the opposite side of the San Andreas earth-quake fault. In honor of the different water temperatures, he named the site Miracle Hill.

The U.S. entered World War I, and Cabot joined the Army in 1918, leaving behind Merry Christmas. One story claimed he left her to roam free; another said that he left her with a friend. In any case, when he returned a year later, she had disappeared into the desert.

Cabot next went to Furtilla California, now a ghost town, near Indio, and ran a grocery store and the post office there. Some time later, he went to Europe to travel and study art in Paris, but again returned to California where he ran a grocery store in Moorpark. By 1941, he'd returned to the desert and helped found the city of Desert Hot Springs. He continued his painting career, specializing in works depicting the Cahuilla Indians.

In 1945 Cabot Yerxa married for a second time. His wife, Portia Graham, was known for her work in metaphysics. Both she and her husband shared a belief in the probability of the existence of other life in other worlds and welcomed contact with those beings.

At age 82, Cabot Yerxa died of a heart attack in his home, the pueblo he had worked on for more than twenty years. Widely recognized for the unique structure he built, Cabot was also known for his good deeds and philanthropy. The city marked his passing by lowering flags to half-staff and closing City Hall. More than 400 mourners attended his funeral.

After Cabot's death, the structure was nearly destroyed but his friend, Cole Eyraud, literally held off the forces of destruction by standing in the path of a bulldozer, shot-gun in hand. He then bought the property, helped restore it, and, when he died, left it to the city of Desert Hot Springs as a museum and art gallery.

Visitors today are struck by the sprawling structure's marriage of folly and ingenuity. Cabot Yerxa's legacy stands as a monument to the spirit of adventure and creativity, inspiring and attracting many who answer the call of the desert.

****

As before, there are conflicts with parts of this article between the Family Tree and the Desert Hot Springs Historical Society information. Without much ability to confirm which of the differences are correct, suffice it to say that we have a fairly accurate portrayal of who Cabot Yerxa was and the many experiences he encountered in his varied life.

The mention of Yerxa's second wife Portia being involved in metaphysics and that Yerxa believed in the existence of outer-world beings seems to set the stage for the existence of many of the other proclaimed mysteries in the area meshing with the Energy Vortex theories.

****

Once again using Google as my research tool, I found the name Stephen Yerxa, clicked on it and he appeared on my LinkedIn site. Lo and behold after sending him an e-mail asking if he was related to Cabot, the response came back in the affirmative. We met for lunch the following week and Stephen brought with him a detailed family tree. The information he has on the Yerxa family dates back to 1746 and far too complex to place in this manuscript. The result of our meeting however is a study in "it's a small world". Has the Energy Vortex leaped all the way to the coast and enveloped me and Stephen Yerxa in its power? You be the judge.

Stephen Yerxa lives about ten miles east from me in the neighboring city of Escondido, we discovered we share many of the same friends and business associates, we were both born in Duluth Minnesota five-years apart, lived about ten-miles from one another and the similarities in our lives are almost too unbelievable to discuss including our stints in the U.S. Navy. Needless to say, we agreed to continue our relationship which I look forward to with great anticipation. The world's mysteries take many forms. Surely there are outer worldly powers at play here.

———

For me, having been born in 1930 as I was, the year 1913 isn't that long ago in some ways. But when we think of Cabot Yerxa coming from the state of Minnesota to California Gold Country through Alaska in 1913, and then pioneering the California desert four-years before Arizona became a state; it does put things in a different perspective.

Living in Desert Hot Springs even for a relatively short time as Diana and I did, we were there long enough to gain a respect for the fabulous Fall Winter and Spring climate with its balmy evenings under the star-lit skies that are mostly invisible in the big cities, and cool clear, see for ever mornings. But I admit, when summer rolled around, bringing with it the almost every day over 100 degree heat, it was hard for us to imagine Yerxa working in that heat, day and night hand-digging his wells and building his home.

We come pretty tough from Minnesota and Michigan where Diana was born, but we're built for the cold weather, not the heat of the desert. When I first came to California at age 16, I wore shirt sleeves all winter when others were wearing overcoats. Yes, after a few years my blood thinned out like everyone else, but I wasn't in the desert and I wasn't digging wells.

Back to Cabot Yerxa: Once his adobe home was livable, Yerxa coaxed his wife to come and live with him with their new-born child Rodney, but she was no pioneer, and only lasted a short time before leaving to return to her family in the East.

Yerxa's former home contains much of the pioneer's writings and photos of his early days in the desert and other explorations of California's gold country and Alaska. Thousands of tourists visit the site every year, which is a state-registered Historical Site.

Cabot Yerxa

One: Early History

Desert Hot Springs is a place on the map with very unusual characteristics; some are scientifically confirmed and recorded; others are somewhat mythical or mystical. You can be the judge of which are mythical and which are mystical. I will use only first names for characters not otherwise identified through news articles or previous publicly published documents in city or county records. Some are our good friends, others casual acquaintances, and others relative strangers.

Since the city's official formation in 1963, the city has had a colored past relative to its government and economy; mainly recognized in early years as a haven for those seeking physical regeneration from the "miracle" underground mineral hot springs generously rushing to the surface and into the forty or more spas sprinkled across the landscape.

As you read the accounts of political upheaval and the struggles put forth by the Desert Hot Springs townspeople, try to visualize yourself, living in the steaming desert, attempting to make a life for you and your family, and what you might have done to improve upon the living conditions of this "Shining city on a hill" as it has often been referred to by the city's more optimistic residents.

Now let me take you through the years of the community from its first discovery in 1908 to the year 2011 and help us make some prognostications for the future of Desert Hot Springs.

Researching and documenting historical records is a relatively difficult task. One must rely on what is first presented as fact, then attempt to cull any fiction from the information presented. Presumably, I have managed to produce a reasonably factual account of the community's history.

Absorbing the records and then attempting to project how the past will impact the future is another thing altogether. I have gathered past information of Desert Hot Springs and its leadership from several sources. Records were sketchy at best, but between piecing together bits of information from the Historical Societies of Morongo Valley and Desert Hot Springs, the Chamber of Commerce, City Administration and members of the public at large, I have assembled a fairly accurate depiction of the first one hundred-three years of Desert Hot Springs.

What follows, is a mix of documented historical background information and reprints from various news sources coupled with relatively current first-hand experiences of my having lived and worked in the community.

Author Joseph Wambaugh in his humorous 1986 fictional book "Secrets of Harry Bright" characterizes Desert Hot Springs as a place that: *"There's little sand left, it's been blown clear to the Salton Sea. The wind can make it rain pebbles and stones like a desert hailstorm and cars with their windows left down, need to be pick-axed."*

Wambaugh pokes fun at Desert Hot Springs in many different ways in his book, much of which is quite close to the truth, but exaggerated as is his paragraph on the wind. To be sure, the wind is strong and the dust does blow, but not quite to the extent characterized above.

Unlike Wambaugh's fictional story, this is a true story of the city and its people, some of whom seemingly made a wrong turn on the road to a better life, and having to live it while hoping for change. Reading at times like a fictional B-Movie with high crime, political corruption, illicit sex and bank robberies, mixed with violence, mystery, myth and Indian lore, it is somewhat laughable at times in a tragic sort of way, but true never the less.

Profiling many of the city's people and their experiences, projects an abject lesson in perseverance, faith and determination as they struggle to overcome adversities in their chosen city, further proving that truth is stranger than fiction.

I have great respect for those who have stuck it out, casting their fortunes on the hopes and dreams of a city that has tremendous unrealized potential for one day actually becoming the "shining city on the hill" in Coachella Valley.

Fortunately as Americans, when we are unsatisfied with our current working or living environment or both, we are free to change them by seeking new opportunities. When finding them, we can move on. Those who are willing and able to make the change, do so.

Living in California, most of us think of mountains and oceans and being close to them both. So if you are already living near the ocean or mountains and you want change, where do you go? The Desert of course. On the other hand, if you are living in areas of the country with long cold and snow-blown winters, the warmth and constant sunshine of the Desert sounds pretty good to you.

From my observation, it looks like that's what most of Desert Hot Springs' residents did—at least the people in this story.

Starting with the founder of the community and continuing with the people I am introducing (including my wife and me) we were looking for a change. Change in life style, geographical location, job or other motivations relative to our state of being at the time. Desert Hot Springs residents were and are products of environmental and circumstantial occurrences that brought us to the point of wanting to make that change.

This then is the story of those of us who took the plunge for better or worse. It is not my purpose to offend anyone in this manuscript, but to tell the story as it has unfolded, to the best of my ability. I believe it is a story that needs to be told, which I trust you will agree.

We will leave it up to you to determine what you may see as the future for the community and what role it will play in the evolution of Coachella Valley. After all, geographically it is the gateway to the valley and possesses the greatest assemblage of undeveloped commercial and industrial acreage in the entire valley and ripe for development.

———

The Beginning

We start with the community in its earliest and most meager beginnings; a wide strip of windblown earth in the Imperial Desert, gently rising to a height of approximately fifteen-hundred feet from the valley floor to the foothills of what is now Joshua Tree National Forest.

The region was home to the Agua Caliente Band of the Cahuilla Indian Tribe and the Morongo Band of the Mission Indian Tribe. Agrarian by nature they governed some 2,000 square miles of ancestral land in the Palm Springs area until 1876.

The Agua Caliente Band web site states:

The members of the Tribe lived in several well-established communities in the canyons and surrounding mountains and desert floor.

The coming of the railroad had a dramatic impact on the lives of tribal members, especially when the Federal Government gave all the odd-numbered sections of land in the Coachella Valley to the Southern Pacific Railroad in 1860s.

When President U.S. Grant established the present Agua Caliente Indian Reservation by Executive Order in 1876, only the even-numbered sections were still available, thus creating the present Reservation in a checkerboard pattern.

To encourage economic development, the Federal Government allocated the bulk of the Reservation land to the individual members of the Tribe in a process called "allotment" that lasted until 1959. In the same year, and for the same purpose, Congress authorized this Tribe and its members to lease their land for up to 99 years.

Much of Palm Springs and adjacent Cathedral City, Rancho Mirage and unincorporated Riverside County is built on land allotted to individual Tribal members and leased to developers in this way. However, under the Tribe's Constitution, adopted in 1955, and federal law, the Tribe maintains primary control over the use and development of all land on its reservation, including those parcels included in cities located on the Reservation.

The activities of the Agua Caliente Band of Cahuilla Indians have multiple economic impacts on the Coachella Valley, stemming not only from the last 10 years of its casino operations, but also the extensive holdings remaining in the Tribe's historic land base, underlying much of what is now the Cities of Palm Springs and Cathedral City, and portions of the City of Rancho Mirage and Riverside County.

Today, much of the Tribe's original Reservation of 31,500 acres has been highly developed into a modern desert tourism center, plus extensive upscale retail and residential uses. The Reservation includes billions of dollars worth of valuable real estate as well as critical desert and mountain habitat.

****

Jack Riley is reported to have been the first white man to set foot in what is now the city, somewhere around 1908. The first white person to actually live there, arriving around 1910, was Hilda M. Gray; a woman described as a diminutive, feminine, hard working and rugged pioneer. Her homestead was just south of what is known today as Two Bunch Palms. Gray homesteaded for close to four years and then moved to resume her career as a legal secretary in Arcadia about a year after Cabot Yerxa arrived In 1913.

As word spread of Yerxa's discovery of the healing mineral waters, other homesteaders began to trickle into the area, laying claim to their 160 acre parcels, creating a patchwork of scattered ownerships.

The Valley gets a name:

COACHELLA. The name for the desert town and valley was coined from Coahulla and Conchilla (Spanish, meaning "little shell") with the "I" of Conchilla changed to "e". Why and from what names "Coachella" was coined makes a long and complicated story.

In the beginning , the valley was shown on the 1856 Map of Public surveys as "Coahuilla Valley", the name U.S. Deputy Surveyor John La Croze used in May of that same year when he was surveying desert townships and sections. Mindful of his instructions to describe land for its possible uses, he commented that "good water can be obtained by digging 15 or 20 feet anywhere" in "Coahuilla Valley" and that "the land.....I think only requires rain or seasons to produce excellent crops of grain" (RCRD Bk. 56 p. 165, Bk. 57 p. 27). It is not known whether La Croze had seen the 1856 map or if he had heard the valley called by this name by others in reference to the Cahuilla Indians who were the sole occupants at that early time.

The 1857 Britton & Ray Map showed "Couvilla Valley" stretching from San Gorgonio Pass to Cabizones", old, old Chief Cabezón's village near the north end of what is now the Salton Sea. The 1857 Map of Public Surveys showed "Coahuilla Valley" and " Cabezon's", the terminology used thereafter for that map series.

Bancroft's 1868 map showed "Cohuilla Valley", which was changed back on the 1873 von Leicht-Craven map to "Coahuilla Valley" and there the matter of spelling remained, as far as maps go, until after the turn of the century. Miners and travelers had their own names. In a letter written by a miner to the Los Angeles Star and published on July 19, 1862, reference was made to "the Cabazon Desert", while Clarence King, who rode muleback from the Colorado River to San Bernardino in early May 1866, called it "Chabezon Valley" (1875 pp. 13, 22) for some unexplainable reason.

Oscar Loew of the Wheeler Survey reported in 1878 on the "millions of minute fresh-water shells (*Amnicola thryonia*)" that littered the floor of what he called "Coahuila Valley", "Coahuila (Cabezon) Valley", or "Cabazon Valley...also called Coahuila Valley" (1876 pp. 177, 193, 217, 224).

Loew's indecision as shown by his use of the two names for the valley was a foreshadowing of what was to come when settlers, anticipated by John La Croze in 1856, began to arrive to farm the land. In 1900, Frances Anthony made a trip through the desert (identifying it only as "Colorado Desert") by horse and buggy and was fascinated by the "hundreds of acres of tiny grayish-white shells covering the ground like dirty snow. They varied in size from a pinhead to a small grain of rice: here and there were spots of others as large as kernels of corn, and some mussel shells two inches long" (1901 p. 22). At about that time, A. G. Tingman, Indio pioneer, railroad man, merchant, miner, and generous grubstaker of prospectors, had also been thinking of the myriads of little shells and, having developed a genuine liking for the name of "Conchilla" as a descriptive, as well as beautiful, name, was promoting it in place of "Coahuilla" (Nordlund 1979 p. 68). The date was never recorded, but at some time before September 1901, the land and water company that was developing a townsite at the Southern Pacific Company's Woodspur siding held a Sunday meeting to decide on a name for the new town.

There could not have been many in attendance, as the population was sparse at that time. Of those who came to the meeting, no one liked the name of Woodspur, but there were some who favored "Coahuilla" and others who favored Tingman's "Conchilla". There is said to have been a spirited discussion that ended in a compromise, which was "Coachella" (Stelle 1978 p. 2; Norlund 1979 p. 68).

The development company then took the name of Coachella Land and Water Company, the first issue of *The Submarine*, a weekly newspaper, published in Indio on November 27, 1901, referred to "The people of the whole Coachella Valley", a post office was established at Woodspur siding with the name of Coachella on November 30, 1901, with George C. Huntington as first postmaster, and the townsite plat for Coachella, dated January 2, 1902, was filed on the following June 5 (RC Map Bk. 4 p. 54).

Tingman is said to have exclaimed in disgust, "They have given our beautiful valley a bastard name without meaning in any language!" It is not known whether or not Tingman, backing "Conchilla", or the backers of "Coachella" talked to the various U.S. Geological Survey teams assigned to the general area from 1897 on into 1904: however, the U.S. Geological Survey San Jacinto Quadrangle was issued in September 1901, with the general San Gorgonio Pass-Palm Springs area shown as "Coachella Valley", while the same government agency issued Southern California Sheet No. 1 in December 1901, with the name "Conchilla Desert" shown for the San Gorgonio Pass-Palm Springs area.

Coins must then have been tossed in Washington, for the U.S. Geological survey issued the 1904 Indio Special Map showing the town of Coachella, but in slightly larger letters Conchilla Valley in the area between the Southern Pacific Company's railroad siding of Myoma and the outliers of the Santa Rosa Mountains, and in still larger letters CONCHILLA DESERT for the area to the north, bounded by San Gorgonio Pass. According to Ole Nordlund (1979 p. 68), it was not until January 6, 1909, after the Rand and McNally Atlas and the U.S. Postal Guide were found to be using "Coachella" that the Board on Geographic Names approved of it for what is now called Coachella Valley. Still, as late as 1913, "Conchilla Desert" was shown on General Land Office Maps and was used in the location description on the township map that accompanied the request for Snowcreek post office (National Archives RG 28).

There has been no dearth of stories (apparently originating with those who had favored "Conchilla") claiming the name of Coachella to be a mistake. George Wharton James (1906 p. 5) said, "Strangers unfamiliar with the name (Conchilla) and unacquainted with the Spanish tongue, mispronounced and misspelled the name". James Smeaton Chase (1919 pp. 114, 115) believed that "by some error the name got upon the maps as Coachella, and the blunder has been retained, until it is now signed and sealed beyond hope of correction".

Brown and Boyd (1922 I. p. 586) called it "a printer's mistake...and the mistake was permitted to stand". George Law (1925 p. 26) claimed "the word was misspelt[sic] upon the map and misspelt[sic] in general usage until the error became too well established for correction".

Elmo Proctor, who clerked in Tingman's Indio store "as a kid" from 1896 to 1899 and whose name has become regionally famous because of his statements concerning the origin of the name, was said by Randall Henderson in *Desert Magazine*, April 1938 (p. 36), "to have lived in Conchilla Valley at the time when a clerk in Washington misspelled the word and changed the name to Coachella as it is known today".

Erwin G. Gudde, who also quoted Elmo Proctor (1974 p. 68), believed the government cartographers misread the name of "Conchilla" and showed it as "Coachella". Washington always seems to be blamed when some citizens are dissatisfied. On the other hand, the triumphant coiners of the name were well pleased, having produced a name that has been called "unique, distinctive, and euphonious" (Gudde 1974 p. 68).

-Date Published and Author Unknown

****

Geology & Meteorology makes the difference:

The geological information contained in this reprinted chapter from Eugene Singer's book: **Geology of California's Imperial Valley**, explains why and how the phenomenon of Desert Hot Springs two types of water, (hot mineral water surging to the surface from 105 degrees to 155 degrees and cold, pure drinking water that consitantly wins awards for its purity).

Imperial Desert & Desert Hot Springs Geology Explained

Why and how there is both hot mineral water and cold pure drinking water

Geology of California's Imperial Valley (As posted on Google)

A Monograph by Eugene Singer

CHAPTER 10
VOLCANIC ACTIVITY IN THE IMPERIAL VALLEY

VOLCANIC ACTIVITY in Southern California is not something one thinks about very much. With earthquakes carrying such a high priority in our concerns for public safety, the thought that other Perhaps it is just as well, for while the valley contains a remarkable selection of volcanic

This might become more clear if we describe the East Pacific Rise as a tear in earth's crust, and that sea floor spreading is opening the gap as a zipper would separate an opening in a garment, in this case from south to north. Off the west coast of Central America, deep submergence vessels, most notably the *Alvin* of the U.S. Navy, have extensively observed and documented startling undersea volcanism, including smoking vents, ore formation and pillowy lava formations.

Progressing north to the Imperial Valley, geophysical evidence suggests that the crust is very thin and that a large mass of super-heated rock exists just below the surface.

All this is characteristic of a zone of sea floor spreading where new crust is being formed as molten material is brought to the surface of the earth. As the combined Gulf of California/Salton Trough structure is a transition zone between continental crust and oceanic crust, it follows that some magmatic intrusion and regional metamorphism is going on with concurrent volcanic activity. But surprisingly, it is limited. Possibly the great thickness of recent sediments in the basin act as a thermal barrier, confining the incipient volcanic activity and insulating the surface from its effects.

Even so, the limited volcanism present in the valley includes a variety of phenomena, from hot springs to recent volcanic eruptions.

The Heat Source

Volcanic activity of any type requires a heat source close to the surface. Geophysical studies of seismic activity, of heat flow in the earth, and of magnetic anomalies in the area around the south end of the Salton Sea all suggest that active igneous and metamorphic processes are now going on associated with an intrusive mass that lies below the sedimentary cover.

The intrusion under the Salton Sea is thought to be a pluton, an arm or protrusion from a deeply buried molten magma.

This intrusion is parallel to the axis of the Salton Trough. It is about 20 miles long by four miles wide, and is at least one to two miles thick. It lies within the upper 10,000 feet of the crust, and possibly as close as 4,000 feet from the surface. It is centered beneath the community of Niland, at the southeast shore of the Sea.

This pluton is acting upon the sedimentary fill, altering the rocks into a low grade metamorphic series under low-temperature/low-pressure metamorphism. Associated with the metamorphism of the rocks, chemical analysis of hot brines brought to the surface by deep thermal wells in the Imperial Valley and Mexico show that active ore formation is probably taking place around the pluton. This involves the concentration of sulfides of iron, lead, zinc and copper.

Hot Springs

The Hot springs within the valley were known and used by Indians for centuries. The first commercial development in the area dates from the turn of the century, when a therapeutic spa was opened in the foothills of the Chocolate Mountains near Bombay Beach, on the east shore of the Salton Sea. This spring is still in use, and is unusual for its high water temperature, ranging from 135 to 180 degrees Fahrenheit.

With few exceptions, the hot springs are concentrated in a linear pattern along the

Eastern side of the valley. The line of springs extends from Desert Hot Springs into Mexico, and the arrangement strongly suggests that the warm waters are reaching the surface using fractures of the San Andreas fault system as conduits.

There are some exceptions. At a natural spring at Miracle Hill, east of Desert Hot Springs, warm water rises to the surface along the Miracle Hill fault, a north branch of the Mission Creek fault. The hot spring in the City of Palm Springs is another exception.

The warm springs in the Coachella Valley are largely confined to the city of Desert Hot Springs and its immediate vicinity. Desert Hot Springs is on the Mission Creek upland, an alluviated surface created by the coalescing alluvial fans from the east base of the San Bernardino Mountains merging with the western Little San Bernardino Mountains. The upland is a sandy plain sloping to the southeast toward the valley center.

There are more than 50 wells in a rough linear pattern from the city center southwest, following the Mission Creek fault trace. The wells deliver thermal waters at an average temperature of about 120° F. with some wells as high as 200° F. Temperature is highest in the wells located in the city, consistently decreasing southward. Desert Hot Springs waters are high in calcium and magnesium salts, primarily the sulfates, and are alkaline.

Well depths are between 20 to 340 feet into three aquifers, with the lowest being the best producer.

As there is no evidence of recent volcanic activity in the area, it is assumed that the hot waters are cool meteoric water that has traveled downward in the aquifers, there to become heated, then rising from depth along lines of fractured and faulted rocks.

Beliefs regarding the therapeutic value of natural hot springs have been popular for centuries. Since the days of the Roman Empire, mineralized hot springs have been a mecca for people afflicted with a variety of disorders. Exploiting these disabilities, zealous promoters have often used vivid imagination to lure prospective bathers. For example, early in this century the hot springs near Bombay Beach were claimed to be "veritable fountains of youth offering comfort and health-giving properties to the bathers . . .finding relief from arthritis and rheumatism." In recent years, the popularity of mineral spas has waned, as the medicinal values of the waters have been largely discounted, but the natural springs have retained some popularity as outdoor hot baths.

There are many warm springs in The San Jacinto Mountains. These are situated along the San Jacinto fault zone from Gilman Hot Springs, in Hemet Valley, south to Borrego Valley.

Agua Caliente Spring (Palm Springs)

The area that is now downtown Palm Springs has been a center of human activity for centuries. Agua Caliente Spring, located on the present Spa Hotel property, was important to the early Indians. For many years before western man came to this valley, the spring was an oasis of palm trees, saltgrass and other vegetation in profusion. It was a natural water source in an otherwise hostile environment, and the Agua Caliente Indians still attach great cultural significance to the spring.

The spring has had a long history of various mineral bath operations using the water. For more than a century, bath houses have been built on or around the spring for commercial purposes.

In its natural state, and before construction of the current hotel buildings, the spring flowed from a low mound that rose a few feet above the ground surface. In its natural development, located in the central part of the spring mound, the orifice deposits are light-gray highly permeable fine sand. This appears to extend to depth, and is the vertical conduit through which the spring water rises to the surface. Surrounding the orifice, and making up the bulk of the mound is an impermeable mass of fine-grained clay-like material.

Prevented from lateral migration by the clay, the spring water rises through the washed-sand conduit of its own making. Flowing water brings sandy material to the surface, where the fine silty material is washed to the margins of the mound while the sandy material remains in the orifice. The structure of the spring, then, is a sandy permeable flow channel surrounded by a silty, clay-like, nonpermeable confining chimney.

It is probable that the spring is very old, and has slowly extended this structure upward for centuries, with the rate of building equal to the rate of deposition of alluvium on the valley floor.

Agua Caliente Spring water is of unusually high quality. It differs markedly in chemical quality from the groundwater pumped from nearby city water wells. It is a sodium bicarbonate type, with low dissolved solids and is very soft. It has a high pH, or slightly alkaline, and is high in sodium and fluorine. Natural groundwater, pumped by the local water company for domestic water, is of the calcium bicarbonate type, has low dissolved solids and is soft to moderately hard. These differences suggest that the spring water rises in its natural conduit from a depth substantially greater than the depth of the domestic water wells.

Emission temperature of the spring water is about 107 degrees Fahrenheit, and the flow rate is about 25 gallons per minute.

The circumstance of the spring is its association with the Palm Canyon fault and the unusually thick 1,000 foot sequence of sedimentary beds at the mouth of Palm Canyon.

West of the fault are the high San Jacinto Mountains, with substantial precipitation at the upper elevations. The granitic rock mass is intricately fractured, and water readily flows in the fractures. This rainwater seepage appears to follow a parabolic path under gravity and convection. It flows vertically in the rock fractures to great depth, is heated in contact with a deeply buried heat source, then, being hindered from flowing laterally by the buried fault, rises to the surface along the fault plane. It ultimately finds its way to the valley floor by the sandy vertical conduit the spring itself has made in the coarse alluvium.

Geothermal Resources

There are several experimental geothermal developments in the Imperial Valley, extending from the south shore of the

Salton Sea into Mexico. The Salton Sea geothermal field is the largest and the hottest of the several fields in the Salton Valley, and has the longest history of development.

Across the Mexican border lies the Cerro Prieto geothermal field near Cerro Prieto Volcano. It is a large field and is economically productive.

The geothermal waters are the result of a complex subsurface heat transfer system.

Convection within the mantle is a continuously renewable source of heat. The heat is transferred by conduction through the thinned crust. Surface waters migrating downward are heated, then dissolve chemical compounds from the rocks undergoing metamorphism, and rise by convection through the water-saturated sediments to the surface.

The potential for the development of geothermal energy resources was first recognized in the mid-1920s. However, it was not until 1961 that the first commercial well in the Imperial Valley was drilled. It reached a depth of more than 4,700 feet.

The energy crunch of the 1970s spurred renewed interest in commercial development, and several wells were drilled to depths of 5,000 to 8,000 feet.

In the Salton Sea geothermal field, typical brines are produced at wellhead temperatures up to 600°F. During extraction, the high temperatures and reduced pressure in the drill holes cause the superheated water to flash into steam, thus bringing in a mixture of steam and hot water at the wellhead.

The steam/water solution is highly charged with chemical salts, principally sodium chloride, calcium chloride and several metallic compounds. A unique characteristic of the brine is the high concentration of dissolved rare elements, including Lithium and Potassium. The brine is slightly caustic, and severe corrosion and scaling problems complicate the

43

production of clean turbine steam. Although the resource is large, technical problems and cost factors associated with processing the hot brines are a continuing constraint to large-scale commercial development.

Important unresolved secondary problems inhibiting commercial development are (1) a means of disposing of the spent brines without contaminating the surface or the ground water systems, and (2) a source of a large quantity of fresh water for coolant.

By contrast, the wells of the Cerro Prieto development just over the border in Mexico are producing relatively clean steam, and commercially important quantities of geothermal energy are generated.

The natural resource is extensive and valuable. The technical problems can be solved, with the principal question being the economic viability of large-scale commercial development. The opportunity is not being overlooked, as the steam resources are estimated to be adequate for the power requirements of a population of four million people indefinitely.

Volcanoes

Volcanoes? In the Imperial Valley? At the south end of the Salton Sea, southwest of Mullet Island, are five small volcanic domes. They are oriented along a northeast trend, or perpendicular to the trace of the San Andreas fault system. The domes rise 100 to 150 feet above the valley floor, and collectively are known as Obsidian Butte. They are extruded into the Quaternary alluvium and are thought to be fewer than 20,000 years old.

Their composition is rhyolite and pumice, with subordinate obsidian.

Obsidian is volcanic glass. It is a volcanic rock that forms when the lava is cooled very rapidly. Mineral crystals do not have time to form in the molten lava, and the noncrystalline mass

becomes a glass when it is subject to sudden cooling. Obsidian is often found associated with pumice, often in layers as at Obsidian Butte.

Pumice is the hardened residue of volcanic froth, or very liquid rock highly charged with gases. If the gas content is high, then the bubbles "frozen" in place upon hardening can give some buoyancy to the rock. It is commonly thought that pumice rock floats on water. Sometimes it does; usually not. Pumice boulders, because they are light and easily handled, are used extensively for landscaping.

The Cerro Prieto volcano, 15 miles south of Mexicali, is a rhyolite dome that is the product of a single eruptive cycle in the late Pleistocene.

The marked lack of erosion of the cone attests to its youthful age. Young volcanoes at Cerro Prieto are apparently part of the same suite of volcanic activity, all being associated with the East Pacific Rise.

Carbon Dioxide

From 1933 to 1954, carbon dioxide was produced from a small field near Niland. The gas was recovered from pockets 200 to 700 feet deep and was converted to dry ice for refrigeration, with much of the output supplied to the railroad for icing of refrigerator cars. The project was abandoned in 1954, a victim of refrigeration technology.

The rising water level of the lake in the early 1980s has since flooded the area, and nothing remains except a few timbers sticking out of the water.

Mud Pots

Mud pots were once a popular sight near Mullet Island. The island, originally an arm of land extending into the sea, was also submerged by the rising water.

The mud field was a dark-colored mass of lacustrine silt mud. Large bubbles of steam, some the size of a football, formed and burst, spattering wet mud into the air. Principal gasses ejected by the field were steam, carbon dioxide and hydrogen sulfide. Similar to other volcanic phenomena, the mud pots are the result of surface waters percolating downward through the sedimentary layers to the proximity of the magma body. The heated water then rises to the surface, flashing to steam as the confining pressure is reduced.

****

Adding to the geological makeup of Desert hot Springs, is the fact that a major fault line crosses diagonally from the northwestern most corner to the southeastern most corner of the city limits at Highway I-10 which is further described in the article below:

The Desert Hot Springs earthquakes and their tectonic environment

C. F. RICHTER, C. R. ALLEN and J. M. NORDQUIST (As posted on Google)

CALIFORNIA INSTITUTE OF TECHNOLOGY,, PASADENA, CALIFORNIA

Abstract

The Desert Hot Springs earthquake of December 4, 1948, was one of the larger recorded earthquakes of southern California, and its aftershocks have continued into 1957. The assigned epicenter is $33°56'.4N, 116°23'.1$W; origin time, 15:43:16.7 P.S.T.; magnitude 6 1/2. Arrival times at local and distant

46

stations are consistent with existing travel-time curves, except for anomalous S – P intervals at very near-by temporary stations; these unexplained anomalies cannot be attributed to varying depth of focus.

Epicenters of the 72 aftershocks that have been accurately located are concentrated in a zone 18 km. long, parallel to the Mission Creek fault trace indicated by older scarps, but 5 km. north of it. Aftershock activity is markedly concentrated toward the two ends of this line. Location of the main shock suggests that fracturing started near the southeast end and progressed northwest-ward. The ground surface was not broken, except by landslides.

Offset of the line of seismic activity from the trace of the Mission Creek fault suggests that the fault plane dips north. This attitude is substantiated not only by field observations, but also by first motions at stations within 6° of the epicenter, which require a combination of thrust-slip and right lateral-slip on a fault dipping north less than 66°. Inasmuch as this fault is not parallel to regional San Andreas trend, such oblique displacement is reasonable and is consistent with the tectonic pattern of other faults in this region.

Five groups of earthquakes represent more than 85 per cent of the total strain release since 1933 in the 3,000 sq. km. area surrounding Desert Hot Springs. These earthquakes, in addition to the Desert Hot Springs shock, are: Morongo Valley (1947), Kitching Peak (1944),

Covington Flat (1940), and San Gorgonio Mountain (1935); all are associated with known faults. The Morongo Valley earthquakes probably represent fracturing on the segment of the Mission Creek fault adjacent to that broken during the subsequent Desert Hot Springs shock.

****

Then of course there is the lore of the former Indian inhabitants, expanded and promoted by subsequent believers in the supernatural existence of special and powerful forces at work in the area due to its location and combination of the unique geological and meteorological structure.

One can take these beliefs and declarations with a grain of salt, or read into them an explanation for what seems to be a continuum of unexplainable results for the past and present members of the Desert Hot Springs Community. As you continue to read the history compiled within these pages, you can reach your own conclusions. Apparently Cabot Yerxa had some belief in these mysteries according to what his writings have shown.

Energy Vortex: Fact or Fiction?

Is Desert Hot Springs an Energy Vortex? [You Decide]

By: Roger Sunpath

Energy vortex, what the heck is that? I knew you'd ask me that, so here it goes. In the case of an Earth energy vortex, it is a location where several Earth powers converge. Vortexes are power spots where a greatconcentration of energy emits from the planet. Some experts feel that these power points are themselves only surface manifestations of an energy infrastructure within the planet. There are two types of energy vortexes. Positive vortexes expand and perpetuate energy. Negative vortexes dissipate energy. I'll have more to say about negative vortexes later.

In the extraordinary case of Desert Hot Springs, there is a convergence of five energies. Earthquake faults, geothermal underground water, mountain peak alignments, wind, and Sun energies. The map included here (you can click on it to see a larger version) will help you understand the location of these energies and their relationship to one another. First, the green line running from bottom right to top left (from Southeast to Northwest) is the Mission Creek fault line. This fault is a break off from the famous San Andreas Fault, which is South of the city. The blue circled area is the location of the underground hot water lake. The blue dashed line running through the lake is the mathematical mean of the lake's position. The red line with the circles is the line connecting the peaks of the rim of the Little San Bernardino Mountains. These mountains border the city to the Northeast. Notice that these three lines are almost parallel to one another. This means that their energy fields are in alignment with one another. This is no accident, for the underground lake is held in place by the fault line and the mountains provide the water runoff for the lake. This is another example of nature in harmony.

The important thing to know here is if you are standing facing the Northeast you are putting your body in alignment with these positive energies. You may have even found yourself standing in this direction and rested or meditating and not really knowing why. Maybe you just found it comfortable. It's like sitting in front of your fireplace at home. We all like to sit directly in front, not off to the side, so we can feel the warmth and see the dancing images in the flames.

It is unfortunate that the founding fathers of the city were unaware of this energy alignment. If they had constructed the city streets on a Northwest by Southeast axis, the general population would be calmer.

In addition to these energies we have strong wind energy, from the common therapeutic breeze to the sometimes ferocious storms. The wind is an energy of purification. Could you imagine the trouble we would be in if our wind didn't blow and ground the smog that enters our valley from the West? Many of us Native Americans can listen to the wind and hear it talk. It sometimes tells us about the conditions from where it came; sometimes it will tell us about the weather that is coming.

Finally there is the wonderful Sun energy for which this area is famous. As the Sun transits from the East to the West, it bathes the valley with all its power, brightness, and healing energy.

So what is the significance of a place that is an energy vortex? Ancient peoples made pilgrimages to these locations because they were believed to be sacred sites. These early people would come to these places to do ceremonies and ask for healing. Over the centuries the knowledge of these sites was passed down from generation to generation. In the Native

American culture these places were in the care of medicine men. Many of the ceremonies performed in these locations involved the four elements-Earth, Fire, Water, and Air. These medicine people knew that communion with these elements could bring forth healing.

So what can you expect when you enter into an energy vortex? If you wish to derive the fullest possible benefit from the energies, you must concentrate your awareness, quiet your mind, and tune your entire being to the energy broadcast of the power point. Here we have the unique ability with the natural hot waters to immerse ourselves in a pool or jacuzzi and have full communion with one of the powers directly. In general, people are drawn to energy vortexes and power spots in search of enlightenment and inner peace; they are attracted by some invisible force and its therapeutic effects.

As I mentioned earlier there are positive and negative energy vortexes and that Desert Hot Springs is on a positive vortex. Vortexes are like a magnet in the sense that one end is positive and the other negative. The negative side of the energy vortex in this area is located in the vicinity of Palm Drive and Highway 10. If you drive that route regularly you may notice that there is almost always a car broken down along the road. This is because machines that are in marginal running condition will fail when passing through a negative energy vortex. Remember negative vortexes dissipate energy. So if your car is already not running very well, it's best to pass through these areas as quickly as possible.

Hopefully, now you can understand a little more about these Earth powers. During your visit to Desert Hot Springs you should bathe in the natural waters, take a hike up to our mountains, lean into a therapeutic breeze and s oak up some of that Sun energy.

If you have any information or experiences you would like to share with me about the Desert Hot Springs energy vortex write to me: Roger Sunpath, P.O. Box 3367, Palm Springs CA 92263 or email me hawkspirit@earthlink.net.

Update: December, 1999

Recently, I had the opportunity to watch, and consult with, Sandy Jack who is a Geologist/Geophysicist with a company called GEOVision. He was here in Desert Hot Springs with a large drill rig taking core samples. His research was part of a seismic study relating to the special geology here in Desert Hot Springs.

His team drilled to depths as far down as 330 feet. They used special electronic imaging equipment to chart the geological patterns surrounding the core-drilling hole. The results indicated that the geology is composed of sand, similar to the top surface sand, all the way down to the 330-foot level where they hit the water table. Sandy said that the interesting thing about our geology is that we have a low gravitational field because of having mostly sand under the terrain. If we had rock under us we would have a higher gravitational field.

I found this to be another interesting element that has to do with the Desert Hot Springs energy vortex. I'm not sure at this time what interpretation to make about this phenomenon, but we can be assured that in Desert Hot Springs we can all walk with a lighter step!

**** ****

For Vortex believers, there is more. Just a few miles North West, and on up into the high-desert area of the Mojave, there are two one-of-a-kind objects; one man-made and one an unexplained, single boulder of astronomical size, to which the local Indians of the area have long attributed supernatural powers.

The man-made object is the "Integraton" shown on the next page, along with an explanation of its origin and purpose.

My wife Diana and several of her friends paid a visit to the Integraton, in 2009 in an effort to experience the "powers" of the Vortex in conjunction with the Integragaton's powers. While there, Diana and her friends say they felt the energy pulses as they placed their bodies directly under the center of the Integraton's roof opening, which purportedly is a concentration of the Vortex's energy directly into the Integraton.

Since her visit, I have noticed no substantial outwardly change in Diana's appearance or demeanor. She is still the lovely, calm, totally organized and pleasant person she has always been. We are not aware of any bodily changes she or her friends have experienced since the visit, but there is still time.

The Integratron

The Milky Way over the Integratron by Wally PacholkaThe Integratron is an acoustically perfect tabernacle and energy machine sited on a powerful geomagnetic vortex in the magical Mojave Desert

Bill Effinger

The Integratron is sited on a magnetic vortex

The location of the Integratron is an essential part of its functioning. Its placement was chosen based on a complex set of theories involving the earth's magnetic field and the Integratron's relationship to the Great Pyramid in Egypt and Giant Rock, the world's largest freestanding boulder. In 1947, Van Tassel began operating the Giant Rock Airport three miles away from the Integratron, and in 1953 initiated communications with extra-terrestrials after a physical encounter at Giant Rock. He subsequently hosted 17 Spacecraft Conventions there for UFO enthusiasts.

According to Van Tassel, the Integratron is located on an intersection of powerful geomagnetic forces that, when focused by the unique geometry of the building, will concentrate and amplify the energy required for rejuvenation and healing. In 2005, a geophysicist measured the earth's magnetic field for up to 15 miles in every direction from the Integratron and then inside the dome. She proclaimed that there is a significant, unexplainable spike in the earth's magnetic field in the center of the Integratron.

Today, visitors from a wide variety of disciplines are drawn to experience the Integratron's enhanced energy fields. They agree that an overnight at the Integratron is equivalent to a relaxing vacation and that a Sound Bath results in waves of peace, heightened awareness, and relaxation of the mind and body.

From Wikipedia, the free encyclopedia

The Giant Rock near Landers, CA

Giant Rock is a large freestanding boulder in the Mojave Desert near Landers, California, that covers 5,800 square feet (540 m²) of ground and is seven stories high.

In ancient times it was considered sacred by the Native Americans of the Joshua Tree, California, area. In the 1950s it was a gathering point for UFO believers. It is located on land which was at that time leased by George Van Tassel, a purported flying-saucer contactee and organizer of UFO conventions.[1] Van Tassel also built the nearby Integratron and a small airport in the vicinity, which he operated from 1947 to 1975. A single large room, which was subsequently filled in, was dug beneath the rock and resided in by a prospector named Frank Critzer during the 1930s and early 1940s. Critzer, a friend of Van Tassel's, perished in a self-detonated dynamite explosion in this room on July 24, 1942, while being investigated by local police.[2] Shortly after the turn of the 21st century, Giant Rock fractured in two, revealing an interior of white granite. The entire exterior surface of the rock is now reportedly covered in graffiti.[3]
wickapidia

****

Energy Vortex claims are not exclusive to Desert Hot Springs as the information on the next pages will show. Sedona Arizona lays claim to four Vortexes within close proximity to each other and identified in the following article which contains pictures and mapped locations for the Vortexes, preceded by this explanation of what a Vortex is:

What is a Vortex?

A vortex is the funnel shape created by a whirling fluid or by the motion of spiraling energy. Familiar examples of vortex shapes are whirlwinds, tornadoes, and water going down a drain. A vortex can be made up of anything that flows, such as wind, water, or electricity.

The vortexes in Sedona are swirling centers of subtle energy coming out from the surface of the earth. The vortex energy is not exactly electricity or magnetism, although it does leave a slight measurable residual magnetism in the places where it is strongest.

There are four main energy vortexes in Sedona. The subtle energy that exists at these locations interacts with who a person is inside. The energy resonates with and strengthens the Inner Being of each person that comes within about a quarter to a half mile of it.

This resonance

happens because the vortex energy is very similar to the subtle energy operating in the energy centers inside each person. If you are at all a sensitive person, it is easy to feel the energy at these vortexes.

If you are planning a trip to Sedona, here is a map to help you easily locate the four main energy vortexes. On the map, a diamond indicates the location of a vortex. Although the Sedona area has many hiking trails that only a vigorous hiker can enjoy, the vortexes are all easy to get to, and no strenuous hiking is required to get to any of them.

Sedona's Energy Vortexes

The Four Vortexes

Finding the Strongest Energy.

Juniper trees respond to the vortex energy in a physical way that reveals where this energy is strongest. The stronger the energy, the more of an axial twist the Juniper trees have in their branches. Instead of going straight down the branch, the lines of growth follow a slow helical spiral along the length of the branch. This spiraling effect can sometimes even bend the branch itself.

Twisted Juniper Branch

Entrance to Boynton Canyon

57

Vortex located at small knoll

Strong vortex energy all around Bell Rock

Bell Rock

Cathedral Rock

The Vortex made me do it

Vortex on the creek next to Cathedral Rock

Airport Vortex

The vortex is located behind the saddle in the
rocks near Airport Road

Bell Rock Vortex.

Bell Rock is located on Hwy 179, just north of the Village of Oak Creek (5 miles south of the junction of Hwy 89A and 179). Its distinct shape makes it easy to spot, and parking and trails are clearly visible. You will notice that the energy is strong as soon as you get out of your car. You don't have to do any climbing to feel the energy at this vortex. Notice the twisted Juniper trees all over Bell Rock. The energy at this vortex is very powerful and strengthens all three parts: the masculine side, the feminine side, and the balance.

Boynton Canyon Vortex.

From the junction of Hwys. 179 and 89A, drive 3.2 miles west on 89A and turn right on Dry Creek Rd. Follow the signs for Boynton Canyon (this takes you along Dry Creek Road 2.9 miles to a "T" intersection where you turn left, then another 1.7 miles to another "T" where you turn right, then 0.1 mile to a parking area on the right). If you end up at the entrance to Enchantment Resort, turn around and go back 0.3 mile to the parking area. From the parking area, enter Boynton Canyon Trail. Go 250 yards, then take the left fork to stay on Boynton Canyon Trail. Go another 400 yards to the Vista Trail sign. Take the right fork and follow the Vista Trail up the hill. Follow the cairns (red rock trail markers in wire barrels) along this trail, and soon you arrive at a 30 foot high knoll. The energy is strongest around this knoll. Notice the very twisted Juniper trees all around this trail. The energy at this vortex strengthens the masculine/feminine or yin/yang balance.

The Balance between the masculine and feminine side is almost as important as growth itself. Even a less evolved person, if he is balanced, at least treats others the same way he treats himself. And that is what balance is all about. If the masculine side strongly outweighs the feminine, you are too strong for the amount of goodness you have, and you tend to do harm to others because you can be pushy and take unfair advantage of others. On the other hand, if the feminine side greatly outweighs the masculine, you have more goodness than strength, and you tend to let others push you around and take advantage of you. Emotions are a good indication of this balance. If you feel anger more easily than fear, your masculine side is stronger, and if the opposite is true, your feminine side is stronger. Having a good masculine/feminine balance also helps relationships by strengthening the things that make relationships work well, such as intimacy, commitment, honesty and openness.

Red Rock Crossing/Cathedral Rock Vortex.

The easiest access to this vortex, driving only on paved road, is to drive 4.3 miles west on 89A from the junction of Hwys 89A and 179, and turn left on Upper Red Rock Loop Rd. Then go 1.8 miles and turn left on Chavez Ranch Rd. Follow the pavement .8 mile and turn left into Crescent Moon Park ($8 fee to enter). Drive as far into the park as possible, then walk to the creek. As you walk east along the creek toward Cathedral Rock, you will feel the energy getting stronger. The strongest energy is where the creek is closest to Cathedral Rock. At this point, the spires of Cathedral Rock are hidden behind the cliffs on the other side of the creek. The energy at this vortex strengthens the feminine side.

This vortex can also be approached from the Village of Oak Creek by driving along Verde Valley School Road to the end, and then walking along the other side of Oak Creek. Also, if you enjoy hiking and climbing, there is a third route that will bring you close enough to this vortex to feel its energy: From Hwy 179, drive in Back-o-Beyond Rd .6 mile to the parking area at the base of Cathedral Rock, and then hike up the creek bed toward the center of Cathedral Rock.

The Feminine Side can be viewed as being on a scale that has goodness at the high end, and the opposite, which is badness or evil, at the low end. In contrast to the masculine side, which strengthens the ability to stand up for your own rights, the feminine side strengthens the ability to allow others their rights and not interfere with those rights. The energy at this vortex strengthens the things you normally think of as

61

feminine, such as kindness, compassion, patience, and the ability to let others need you and depend on you. And it strengthens the ability to anticipate the impact of your actions before you act, which is what considerateness is all about.

Airport Vortex.

From the junction of Hwys 179 and 89A, go 1.1 mile west on 89A and turn left on Airport Rd. Go .5 mile up Airport Rd. to the parking area on the left. Walk up the trail to the saddle between the hills, where the Juniper trees are very twisted. You may also want to walk up to the top of the small hill on the left. From this vantage point you can see most of Sedona. The energy at this vortex strengthens the masculine side.

The Masculine Side can be seen as being on a scale that has strength at the high end and weakness at the low end. People who have a strong masculine side are self-confident. They have the internal strength to take charge of their own lives, and to claim their rights in life. This make them good at standing up to people who try to take away their rights by force, intimidation or manipulation. Having a strong masculine side means being good at taking risks when appropriate, being decisive when necessary, and being able to focus or concentrate in order to get things done. It also means being good at figuring out how to get out of life what is desired; figuring out how to operate responsibly, and how to reason without distorting reality. Conversely, people who have a weak masculine side often doubt their abilities, and many things intimidate them.

A twisted juniper tree

There are several energy centers, or vortexes of subtle energy, located in the Sedona area. (In Sedona, the energy centers are referred to as vortexes rather than vortices.) The energy from these vortexes saturates the whole area in and around Sedona, and can be noticed in a subtle but general way anywhere around town. If you actually go to one of the vortex sites, which is where the energy is strongest, it can be a very uplifting experience. The energy you take in at one of these energy centers can stay with you and affect you positively for days afterwards.

The Energy of Sedona

In addition to being a beautiful and serene place, Sedona has long been known as a spiritual power center. This is because the power that emanates from the vortexes produces some of the most remarkable energy on the planet. This energy is the reason Sedona is full of people that are "on the path", that is, people who have made a commitment to grow and become as much as they can spiritually. It is also the reason Sedona area, bringing with it a variety of spiritual practices and alternative healing modalities, and it is the reason Sedona has sometimes been called a spiritual Disneyland.

We have personally found the energy centers at Sedona both exciting and growth inspiring. If you are at all sensitive to the more subtle things, the experience of standing at one of these vortexes, and letting the energy flow into you and through you, can be almost overwhelming. People come from all over the world to experience this.

If you are planning a trip to Sedona, here is a map to help you easily locate the four main energy vortexes. On the map, a diamond indicates the location of a vortex. Although the Sedona area has many hiking trails that only a vigorous hiker can enjoy, the vortexes are all easy to get to, and no strenuous hiking is required to get to any of them.

****

Diana and I have been to Sedona on several occasions and there is no question of its beauty. As to sensing or witnessing the powers of the energy Vortexes, we have not had that experience. This is not to say that we don't believe they exist, it is just our experience that we have not felt any of the effects described in either of the articles on the subject in this section of the manuscript.

We lived in Desert Hot Springs for four years and did not have Energy Vortex experiences that we were aware of there either. However, we do believe that there is something strange happening that is causing unexplainable effects on the environment and the people living there.

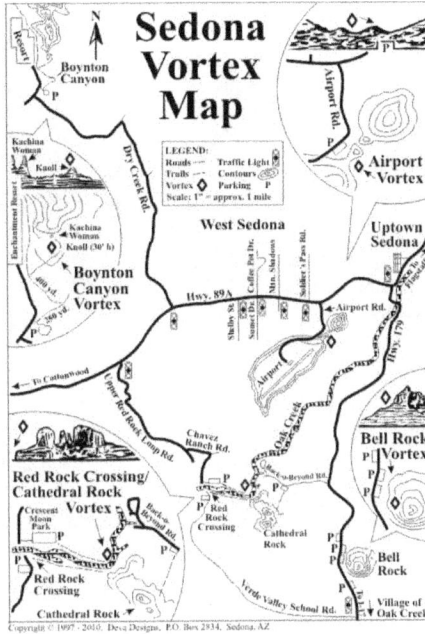

One of the secondary reasons for researching and writing this book is to ask for help in my attempt to prove or disprove the existence of the Energy Vortex and the effects, if any, it may be having on the inhabitants of Desert Hot Springs. I believe that until and unless we find the answers, the mystery will remain unsolved and the city will continue as it has for over a hundred years continually affected with what nobody can explain or really know why.

The following article written in 2008 will give you an idea of how much the locals believe in the powers of the Energy Vortex for better or for worse. Assuming there is an Energy Vortex, being able to harness that power would seem paramount to the city and its inhabitants' future.

What The Vortex Means to the City
by Dean Gray
September 2, 2008

Vor-tex [vawr-teks] – noun, plural.

1. Something regarded as drawing into its powerful current everything that surrounds it.
2. (in Cartesian philosophy) A rapid rotary movement of cosmic matter about a center, accounting for the origin or phenomena of bodies or systems of bodies in space.

Desert Hot Springs, CA - As this city attempts to redefine itself, it is the word Vortex that is not just figuratively but literally at the center of its plans. It will be attempting to draw into its downtown core a powerful current of economic activity.

While the second definition above may seem esoteric, it is actually close to the thinking of city planners that describe Desert Hot Springs plans in terms of air, water, fire and earth. The hope is to use the more esoteric to create a powerful economic current missing in the city.

As a model for its downtown redevelopment, city planners are looking to another city that successfully employed the concept of Vortex as it business base, Sedona , Arizona .

Sedona advertising promotes the city's vortex as "swirling centers of subtle energy coming out from the surface of the earth. The subtle energy that exists at these locations interacts with people. This energizing centers inside each person.

That city's hook is proclaiming the vortex as an uplifting experience. People come from all over the world to experience the positive effects. The thinking goes, the vortex descriptor also defines Desert

Hot Springs, which is rich in similar qualities, just misunderstood and under marketed.

A recent trip by city planners to Sedona gave them a better look.

Sedona encompasses a cottage industry of vortex tours run by local notables like Angel Lightfeather, Mary Morning Star, Phaedra and others. Psychic Ravenne De Lumiere is offering personal tours along with "psychic readings and breath-work with meditation complete with self-activation and heart opening realignment within."

De Lumiere welcomes children and dogs to tour "Nature's Amusement Park" in Sedona's vortexes filled with different types of psychic "Energy Rides."

In atmospheric physics, a mesavortex is on the scale of a few miles (smaller than a hurricane but larger than a tornado). Desert Hot Springs ' vortex planner are thinking along similar lines, taking a successful brand and uniquely modifying it.

It is not certain if Desert Hot Springs planners envision Sedona's mix as metaphysical healing center with a rich and diverse esoteric tradition and its thriving commerce in the eclectic mix of merchants selling prayer candles, meditation incense, and dream-catchers.

It is uncertain if Desert Hot Springs will draw the galleries of arts and crafts showcasing creative local talents and bringing in revenue to artists, craftsman and shopkeepers as Sedona does. But like Sedona, guests from all over the world already visit Desert Hot Springs for expensive retreats and big-buck accommodations at exclusive small spas to experience healing in a thriving conflagration of "health-nuts" and "psych-biz" generating serious revenue to city coffers for a small community off the beaten path.

City planners are working to increase tourism and spa visitors by increased marketing and a more effective visitor center.

Creating the many modalities of healing for Desert Hot Springs is still all on paper. To date the city has committed over $700,000 to plans developed by The Planning Center of Newport Beach to help in the vortex creation.

****

On with the History

Very soon after homesteading began on the north side of the valley, the area situated south of the new community on the floor of the valley, and home to the Agua Caliente Tribe of Indians began to develop and grow as properties were leased from the Indians and subsequently developed with vacation homes for the rich and famous.

During the late 1920's the area now known as Palm Springs, caught the fancy of Hollywood movie stars as a getaway from the hustle bustle of Los Angeles and was formally incorporated on April 1st 1938. Meanwhile, homesteading continued to expand north of the main highway (now Highway 10) to the foothills of the Joshua Tree National Forest.

. Then, in 1932, L.W. Coffee was encouraged by Yerxa to move into the area, develop the land and sell lots. Later Coffee laid claim to being the originator, founder, and developer of Desert Hot Springs, giving the community its name on July 12, 1941 as he promoted his properties and then built one of the community's first spas.

The original town site of one square mile was centered at the current intersection of Palm Drive and Pierson Boulevard. Many of the celebrities visiting and owning properties in Palm Springs would venture up the hill to

Coffee's spa to enjoy the hot non-sulfur smelling mineral water.

While the climate of the two growing communities north and south of Highway I-10 is relatively the same, there is a distinct difference between them, that being elevation, geology and wind.

Higher in elevation from the desert floor and Palm Springs, of between 500 to 1,500 feet, Desert Hot Springs can be as much as 10 degrees cooler in the height of summer. However, Palm Springs on the south side of I-10 is sheltered from the constant high velocity desert winds and shaded in the late afternoons by the towering Mount San Jacinto, rising to an elevation at the summit of 10,834 feet above sea level, and is the second highest mountain range in Southern California.

Desert Hot Springs is not as fortunate, as it is lying directly in the path of those unforgiving desert winds, quite often reaching 45 to 55 miles per hour and more, lifting and carrying the fine desert sands with it. Therein lays one of the most definitive geographical reasons for the comparatively slow and hap-hazard growth of Desert Hot Springs. Visitors have said "the wind will peel the paint from your walls and car". This may be an exaggeration, but it comes close to reality when you are trying to maneuver your vehicle or stand up against the blowing sand.

The following was taken from the Desert Hot Springs Historical Society web site posting dated October 18, 2005:

1933: Coffee organizes a trust whose beneficiaries were the various owners in the area that would become Desert Hot Springs. He began to drill for water, leasing a small drilling rig and hiring Earl Howard, "a real well driller." Drilling proceeded from early May to late June, when they had "about 65 feet of water in the well at a temperature of 140°. The weather was warm; I was not accoustomed [sic] to it, so all activities ceased until November of the same year." Eventually the well was extended to a depth of 333 feet.

Before 1938, Coffee had sold 14 1-acre lots. "The corner of Palm Drive and Eighth Street was purchased by J.W. Vivian of Santa Barbara [who] contracted for the first home to be built at Desert Hot Springs, a beautiful three-bedroom stucco with tile roof."

Coffee had built his first bath house at Palm and Pierson. "We then installed an electric light plant, operated with an old Studebaker engine, which supplied lights for the bath house and the adobe. This plant furnished us about twelve lights, which was hardly enough..." Coffee added a butane gas range and began serving meals. He applied for a beer and wine license "which was not hard to get at that time." Weekend crowds often slept in their cars because there were no rooms.

During 1941: Coffee built and opened the first commercial bath house, which was 120 feet long, with separate men's and women's sections. More than 2000 people showed up for the grand opening on July 12 and partied until 2:30 AM. At the time Desert Hot Springs consisted of only 1 1 and less than a score of homes.

Several years before the city incorporated, Coffee created a large square grid-patterned subdivision within the boundaries of the new area establishing lots with north, south, east and west, street patterns. Had Coffee planned the streets to follow the direction of the Energy Vortex in those early days, as Roger Sunpath suggests, maybe things would be

different. The Energy Vortex would be working more
favorably. We can only speculate.

After six years of operation, The Coffee Bath House
burned to the ground in 1947 and a new bath house was
constructed. Was the Energy Vortex exhibiting its power? A
water company was formed in 1948 and Coffee publicly
predicted that Desert Hot Springs would have a population of
30,000 by 1960. That prediction proved to be way off the
mark in timing, with population approximately 27,000 in
2011, fifty-one years later than Coffee's prediction, gaining
approximately 12,000 in the last ten-years.

By virtue of what I have been able to find in my
research, I have reached the conclusion that there was a time
in the early history of Desert Hot Springs when the chances
for it becoming a successful, viable and vibrant community
seemed close at hand. Certainly the more formal dress of the
participants in the following pictures of the Desert Hot Springs
Rotary Club, indicate an outwardly exhibit of prosperity in the
city's inhabitants. However, from the mid 1980's to the
present, the city steadily declined, while the rest of Coachella
Valley cities prospered.

———

The following excerpts from the posting of the Desert
Hot Springs Rotary Club's History page, chronicles its birth and
growth from 1946 to 1990. Logically, tracking the Rotary's
growth should be an indicator of the growth of the
community at large and it seems to be for those early years in
the city's history. The Club boasted having 48 members in
1963. When I joined the local Rotary in 2004, it barely had
enough members to sustain itself, many of them Snowbirds
(cold-country, part time residents) thereby tracking with the
city's decline.

THE TOSS OF A COIN

Early in 1946 a Realtor from Downey California, Samuel M. Dudlext, came to Desert Hot Springs. He _allow the drug store building located on the west side of Palm Drive just south of Pierson Blvd. Sam had been a Rotarian and Past President of the Downey Club. While on the desert he made up at the Palm Springs Club.

About that same time a Frank P. Kibbey from Laguna Beach came to Desert Hot Springs. Frank had been in the restaurant business in Laguna and a member of the Lion's Club. Frank bought the Idle Hour I on the west side of Palm Drive just north of Pierson Blvd. Frank was a Past President of the Lion's Club.

Sam and Frank felt the need for a service club in Desert Hot Springs and with the flip of a coin it became Rotary. The Palm Springs Club sponsored the new club.

Charter night was held December 5, 1947 in the patio of the Idle Hour I. Charter members were:

Charter night was held December 5, 1947 in the patio of the Idle Hour I. Charter members were:

Samuel M. Dudlext, President
Frank P. Kibbey, Vice-president
Ralph E.K. Jones, Secretary/treasurer
Howard R. Claxton, Director
Lawrence W. Coffee, Director
John L. Haidet, Director
Richard E. Launer, Director
Richard A. Maher, Director

Bill Effinger

Paul A. Price, Sergeant at arms

Joseph H. Bailer
Glen Backhart
Albert A. Burrow
Clarence C. Covey
Lane W. Crossley
Paris P. Dills

George Ellis
Albert M. Elton
Frank P. Gautiello
Donald F. Hinkley
Albert F. Todd

Rotary International President: S. Kendrick Guernsey

(Jacksonville, Florida)

1948/1949 CLUB PRESIDENT:
GEORGE ELLIS

1949/50

CLUB PRESIDENT, HERBERT A. ECCLESTONE

Herb Ecclestone, the third president of the Club was a married man, if he had children, they would have been adults by then. Herb was in some sort of investments. Seemed very successful but had lots of time to devote to civic affairs. In the Valley and thru out Riverside County he was known as "MR. DESERT HOT SPRINGS." Kept the people in Riverside aware that Desert Hot Springs existed. Most instrumental in getting a library for the community. A President of the Water Board. Very dignified man who quietly went about getting things done. AL HORTON 10-24-96

1950/51

CLUB PRESIDENT, LLOYD G. GIBBS

Lloyd Gibbs was a very young minister of the Baptist Church. Married with a young family. Very admired man in the community. Active in youth projects. Far too soon the Church I him to Ontario.

Lloyd died at a very young age. He had continued his work with the church in Ontario and youth activities. His funeral, in a large church still required outside public address system for many could not get into church. Overflow crowd of your people, Boy Scouts, etc. AL HORTON 10-24-96

1951/52

CLUB PRESIDENT, FRANK P. KIBBEY, SR.

Frank Kibbey, the loser of the coin throw, was very active in the community. He worked hard to get the water company into a water district. The "Cabin Sites" area of Desert Hot Springs consisted of property north of Pierson, West of Palm, East of West and South of 8th Street. This area was all dirt streets. Frank formed a committee to get the property owners to _alloween_y pay their share to have the streets in this part of town black topped. It worked! Later he did much the same thing for the area South of Pierson to Hacienda, between Palm and West. These streets had a very thin worn out black top that was replaced with a street more up to code. The Kibbey's had three boys. One left the area after high school, Frank stayed in town, worked for the Water District and later served on its board. Ed stayed in Valley and at this time a Rotarian in La Quinta. AL HORTON 10-27-96

1952/53

CLUB PRESIDENT, JOSEPH R. KANYA

Joe Kanya was first principal of the Desert Hot Springs Elementary School. When school was condemned and re-located to West Drive and Second Joe was still there. He is now retired, living with his wife of many years, Minna, in Palm Springs. AL HORTON, 10-27-96

1953/1954 CLUB PRESIDENT: JOHN W. KEAN

A Tourist Destination:

Desert Hot Springs became a tourist destination in the mid 1950s due to the number of small spa hotels and boutique hotels, topping out at 40-plus where the number remains today, although some are not in the best of condition.

The city's relative seclusion appealed to urban "escapees" and a few Hollywood notables. Soon Realtors® arrived to speculate, as thousands of lots and streets were laid out over a six square mile area and many homes were built and purchased by retirees as the area grew. However, due to the exceptionally rapid development and growth of Palm Springs, the state highway separating the two communities, and constant high winds, Desert Hot Springs was taking on the reputation of being "on the wrong side of the tracks." Commercial and residential developers shunned the city. Nor does it seem, were commercial developers encouraged to bring businesses into the city.

The Ariel photo below is a view of what existed of Desert Hot Springs in 1954, before Coffee began his 600 lot sale development.

Bill Effinger

9 - 13 - 54

1954/1955 DESERT HOT SPRINGS ROTARY CLUB PICTURE

1954/1955 CLUB OFFICERS: (left to right) Gib Halloway, Howard Carr, District Governor Walter Hepner (?), Walter Klocke, Charles Meadows, George George, Charles Sakin.

The Vortex made me do it

DATE FESTIVAL PARADE, INDIO, FEBRUARY 1955
ROTARY FLOAT — FIRST PRIZE

1955/1956 GROUNDBREAKING FOR NEW LIBRARY

Bill Effinger

1955/1956 DESERT HOT SPRINGS ROTARY CLUB PICTURE

1955/1956 NEW LIBRARY 66350 PIERSON BLVD
LEROY E. STEWART'S PRESIDENT'S PROJECT

ROSTER 1958/59

President: Alan Horton,
Vice-president: Pete Elliott,
Secretary: Bert Langlois
International: Chuck Starr
Community: Skip Wright
Vocational: Harry Chester
Club: Bud Booth

R.I. President: Cliff Randall
#534 District Governor: Robert Y. Hollingsworth

Membership (48)

Al Horton	Bud Booth	Harry Chester
Red Kean	Skip Wright	Cliff Babin
Herb Seales	Chuck Starr	Gib Holloway
Don Hulbert	Ted Spellaza	Ted Leonard
John Mack	Joe Kanya	Walter Klocke
Jack Carlton	Ray Lushy	Herb Ecclestone
Charles Harwood	Mark Green	Dewey Carson
Jim Jackson	Lloyd Brison	Al Johnson
Carlin Knight	Rudy Ludwig	Cy Covey
Earl Perkins	Jack Green	Sam Benton
Dick Roderick	Howard Carr	Bob Newman
Jack Yon	Judge King	Jack Furman
Frank Kibbey	Elmer Rebiger	Bob Norris
Pete Elliott	Tom Winsburrow	Aaron Eaton
Bert Langlois	Charles Sakin	Sam Dudlext
Don Hinkley	Doc Stewart	Charles Elliott

Meeting Places

THE DESERT SENTINEL   Thursday, December 21, 1961

ROTARY CLUB of Desert Hot Springs at a dinner recently given at the Highlander Restaurant, special tribute was paid to the organization's past presidents. Pictured here, Rotary presidents receive plaques honoring their service to the club and to the community. Front row, left to right: President Ted Spellaza with past presidents, Harry Chester, Cliff Babin, District Governor Ron Ellis, Herb Ecclestone. Standing: Herb Seales, Gib Holloway, Red Kean, Frank Kibbey, Dr. LeRoy Stewart and Al Horton. (Shaw Photo).

Joe Kanya between Kean - Kibbey

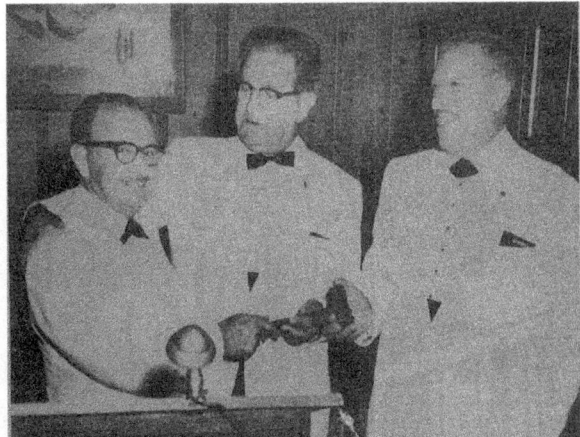

EYES SWIVELED toward the camera, Charles A. Eliot accepts the gavel as incoming president of the Desert Hot Springs Rotary Club from outgoing president Ted Spellaza, as District Governor Ron Ellis performs installation chores.

1962/1963 CLUB PRESIDENT: CHARLES A. ELLIOT
(General Contractor)

The town was officially incorporated on September 17, 1963 with a vote of its approximate 1000 residents. By that time, the new city had taken on a somewhat mixed personality, with scattered trailer parks, a few commercial buildings, spas and cafes scattered among several conventionally constructed houses. Unfortunately, the income level of the new city inhabitants was well below the Southern California average, as many residents were retirees, which set the stage for what followed. But the Rotary Club seemed to roll right along.

1963/64

CLUB PRESIDENT, JACK W. MOREY

Morey did so many things for Desert Hot Springs that I can't begin to name them. Most of the time no one was aware of what he was doing. He gave of his time and money. A Cement Contractor, he poured many slabs, etc. for different charities. The Turkey Shoots which were held several days a year were at his Ranch. He participated in the shoots and was most generous with his help. AL HORTON 10-27-96

GROUNDBREAKING— Scout building Ground-breaking at Wardman Park launched the construction of a beautiful new building by members of the local Rotary Club. Sponsoring this new project, Rotary members will donate material and time in building the new structure for Boy and Girl Scouts, Cubs and Brownies. Photo shows group of Rotary members with Charles Miner, mayor of City of Desert Hot Springs, Jack Morey, Rotary president and John "Red" Kean of the local Park District board of directors, digging in preparation for pouring a cement foundation. (Shaw photo).

Bill Effinger

1963/1964 NEW SCOUT HOUSE

ROTARIANS ALL—Installation of new officers of Desert Hot Springs Rotary Club at the Highlander Restaurant Saturday night was a highlight of the club year. Here Jack Morey, third from left, congratulates incoming president Don Hulbert, second from right. Between them is LeRoy Steward, installing officer from Indio Rotary Club. At left is John Mack, vice president, while Bill Carey, sergeant-at-arms, is second from left. At far right is Mayor Charles Miner, new club secretary. (Blumenthal photo).

1964/1965 CLUB PRESIDENT: DON HULBERT

Don and Enola had a wonderful party house. They had Rotary parties there and hosted parties in other locations, Whitewater, etc. They attended many International Conventions. Don was a TV technician and other electronics, intercoms, etc. He and Enola were also major partners in the Highlands Corp. They build a house in Baja and moved there some years ago. They finally moved to Lakeside in San Diego County. Both died in 1993, first Enola and Don a few days later. AL HORTON 10-27-96

Two: Two decades of irrational thinking

Assessing what can be discerned from the preceding historical photos and attached notes and then attempting to piece together where Desert Hot Springs was situated in the economic spectrum at the time, one could conclude that it was growing, but only growing with homes. Other than the spas and a few convenience stores, nothing sizable enough to develop revenue that would sustain the city's operations came into being, during those formative years.

From my experience in city government as a former mayor, incorporating a city might sound like a good idea at the time, but without a sound and balanced plan, the idea can be a bad one, and that may be where the problems for the fledgling city on the hill began.

Commercial development in Desert Hot Springs is geographically challenged. Boxed in to the West by the White River Hills, the north by the Joshua Tree National Forest, the east by endless desert and the south by Highway I-10, the only draw for retail sales businesses is the residents of Desert Hot Springs itself. Not exactly a demographic that appeals to sophisticated numbers crunchers looking for likely places to open new business ventures.

Desert Hot Springs never got off-track; it really never had a track to get off of in the first place. The adage "two wrongs don't make a right" looks like it was in play here: Deciding to incorporate while not having a well thought out plan to run the city, or the geography to recruit and support businesses became its future—always playing catch-up trying to cover yesterdays' mistakes, rather than developing and implementing a sound plan.

Given the above, the city's destiny may have been cast in concrete from its formal beginning when all subsequent efforts to make it something it could be, became futile because it was not believed possible. Prosperity requires belief and desire of the parties hoping to acquire it to make it a reality. Without desire and belief, nothing will happen.

Other than the occasional movie-star visitor coming to soak in a few of the hot mineral water spas in relative seclusion, there was very little commercial activity in the early years. One of the earliest and still operating restaurants situated in the center of town close to city hall, is the "Sidewinder" originally opened by the Erickson family as "Erickson's" which became the regular meeting place of the community's "movers and shakers" and has continued to be regularly frequented by newcomers and old-timers alike. The restaurant's walls display several historical photographs of the area along with autographed pictures of famous movie stars of yesteryear on its walls.

The following excerpt from an article contained in the Historical Society pages, sets the stage for those times and the people living there:

Jerry Skuse (July 17, 1937 to November 23, 2006)
by Maggie Abbott

If you visit Jerry at home, propped up horizontally in his cushioned recliner, or see him sipping his one daily cup of coffee early in the morning at The Sidewinder, that's if it's one of his good days, you might be fooled into thinking this is some old guy. Then he starts to talk in his rich dark humorous voice, telling laconic yarns about the city he loves, and you can't mistake the young mischievous spirit that's buoyed him along all his life.

His curiosity and involvement with the romance of Desert Hot Springs took Jerry to become a photographer first, historian and archivist eventually. We wouldn't be aware of the wealth of our city's history without him. As well as the pictures he took himself, he collected up all those fascinating photos on the walls at The Sidewinder, and knows every moment of the ups and downs that continue to be the story of DHS. Neither does he spare his edge when he pounces on the bad mistakes and wrong turns which have brought the city down when it could have continued to be a world renowned center for healing and the enhancement of life. He gruffly condemns the guilty but is still a believer.

Jerry talks affectionately about the town in those days, "From 46 to 62, it was a darn good place, everybody helped everybody, it was a different world then, but the minute it became a city, forget it. When his family arrived here all the streets were paved and the land subdivided, water and electric in, one square mile, all done by L.W.Coffee, whose development was from 8th Street to 8th Avenue, and Gus Wardman, 8th Street to Mission Lakes Boulevard, and over to West Drive. They had a vision.

"It was all about the hot mineral water during those years. Cabot Yerxa and Coffee advertised all over the world, sending out postcards acclaiming the healing benefits of the spas for arthritis and many other physical ailments. Coffee called it "A Wealth of Health."

He remembers a girl called Jackie, who was brought here on a stretcher in 1949, so crippled with arthritis she couldn't do anything except lay in bed. Jerry told her he went in the pool every day, so they took her down, put her in the hot mineral water on the stretcher, and six months later she was running around. There are many stories like this, and witnesses to it in the spas every day. That was the time when lots of people came and put in little hotels and it was a spa city.

****

From some indications, Desert Hot Springs was on a reasonable path to becoming a city with a future, experiencing periods of growth in the 1980s and very early 1990s, but there is no evidence that leaders were pursuing economic development, even at this late date in the city's existence. One could almost assume that this was the intent of the city's leadership. If so, that position proved to be misguided.

During the early 90's it appears things began to happen (or not happen as it were) within the community that set the stage for the city's decline.

The devastating and costly impact of the city being dragged into an eleven-year law suit by the developer of the Silver Sage mobile home park over the city council's ridiculous action of discriminating against affordable housing, which the city ultimately lost, began the city's decline. Also, the rapid growth and expansion of neighboring cities and development throughout Coachella Valley, created Vacationer competition for the Spa businesses in Desert Hot Springs, with many down valley resorts offering spas and gambling.

The city, now a full-fledged bedroom community with only its Spas to generate commercial revenues, was finding out much too late that it could not sustain itself. The infrastructure began to deteriorate, crime was on the rise and businesses were closing, unable to survive the downturn of the city's past fortunes.

In 1993, a 3-star hotel, Mirage Springs Hotel Resort opened, but despite good reviews, the spa-hotel closed its doors in 1998. Today, the re-opened and operating Miracle

Springs Resort and Spa, occupies the site, successfully brought back to life by its current owner, Michael Bickford.

Active members of the Desert Hot Springs Community clearly wanted change, as there was a plethora of candidates running for council seats in 1996. A list of candidates and their campaign statements are contained in a booklet titled "Whetstone" published by Joseph Cowles, some of which is reproduced below.

Michael Bickford, owner/operator of two of the most successful and TOT revenue generating businesses in the community, makes a statement to the community in the book, as do other community leaders. Most of them seem to know what needs to be done, as the highlighted paragraphs show, but unfortunately it has never seemed to get to the implementation stage, no matter what the stated challenges have been, or who the council members and mayor happen to be at the time.

———

Ten and Ten in Ten

Starting with 1997 and continuing to 2007 there had been ten city managers and ten police chiefs, one of which was a convicted felon and as result, not allowed to carry a gun. Not exactly what one would call a stable environment.

The Desert Hot Springs community at large, the voters, or presumably in this instance, the non-voters have consistently allowed the city to drift into obscurity. They seem to care enough to complain, but not enough to show their strength of purpose when it comes time to select their leaders. In short, it would seem that nobody wants to put forth the effort to undertake the required changes, thus allowing the status quo to continue, which in turn becomes the classic example of "the more things change the more they stay the same". Put a different way, there has been consistent inconsistency.

Certainly the multiple management and police chief turnovers have been major contributors to the problem, but my belief is that the problems run deeper, many of which remain today. However, things do seem to be improving somewhat.

Change in Desert Hot Springs has been an anathema to its residents. They want change, but until very recently haven't acted to make change other than to elect new council members each election, which in turn hire and fire new managers and police chiefs. The Negative Energy Vortex is surely at work here. How else can one explain the situation?

You might think I'm joking. Not so. Too much sun and wind does strange things to people. When the temperature reaches 120 degrees Fahrenheit and remains there for days on end, it's depressing—ask my wife Diana, she'll tell you. And then, there's the Energy Vortex.

The community contained twenty-five churches in 1996 of various denominations and one synagogue at a time when there was less than 10,000 people living there. That's one church for every 140 families and a whole lot of praying going on with very little results if they were all praying to make the city a better place to live, which they certainly should have been. The Church Roster below was prepared and distributed by former council member Gary Bosworth, who had an untimely death during his third term in office.

Houses of Worship
in Desert Hot Springs

Saint Anthony's Episcopal Church
Reverend John M. "Jack" Wehrs, Sr.
19990 Mountain View Road
329-2799

St. Elizabeth Church
Reverend Father Edward McGuinnes
66700 Pierson Boulevard
329-8794

Community United Methodist Church
Dr. Vernon Story
66735 Pierson Boulevard
329-3928

Temple N'Vey Shalom
Rabbi Barbara Sachs Speyer
66665 Pierson Boulevard

Kingdom Hall of Jehovah's Witnesses
65201 Two Beach Palms Trail
329-4425

Seventh Day Adventist Church
Pastor Gary Ford
11711 Palm Drive
251-9992

Christian Center of Desert Hot Springs
Pastor Timothy Heath
66511 Eighth Street
329-5076

Desert Hot Springs Baptist Church
Doctor Steve A. Mesarch
11911 Little Morongo Road

Reorganized Church of Jesus Christ of Latter Day Saints
66850 Two Bunch Trail
329-1000

St. Benedict's Orthodox Catholic Church
13057 Tram View Road
329-3294

Gateway Christian Fellowship
66854 Acoma Avenue

Seventh Day Adventist Philippine-American Church
13570 Ocotillo Road
251-2112

New Vision Church

329-5168

Calvary Southern Baptist Church
Pastor Jack L. Miller
14200 Mountain View Road
329-3645

Christ Lutheran Church
Pastor Paul E. Miller
66290 Estrella Avenue
329-9292

United Pentecostal Church
Pastor Paul D. Walker
65241 San Jacinto Road
329-0692

First Baptist Church
Reverend Max Want
66272 First Street
329-5355

329-9524

Sky Valley Ministries
Pastor Jim Hubbard
71760 Dillon Road
251-3439

West Valley Chapel Church
Reverend Dan Duncan
11625 Palm Drive
329-6382

Church of Jesus Christ of Latter Day Saints
Bishop Perry Bang
66067 Santa Rosa Road
251-7039

Grace Church
Pastor Joseph P. Lombardi
17400 Bubbling Wells Road
251-2413

66086 Pierson Boulevard

Victory Outreach Ministries
12191 West Drive
251-1081

Water of Life Chapel
Pastor Joyce Okert
66970 Hacienda Boulevard
251-1870

Church of Christ of Latter Day Saints
12100 Verbena Drive
251-7360

Church of God in Christ
61595 Garnet Avenue

Fountain of Living Water Christian Church
11625 Palm Drive
347-0054

Published as a Community Service by Councilmember Gary Bosworth

The almost unbelievable tale of the Jewish Temple who's former Rabbi/Pastor Steven Mesarch a Christian Pastor before changing his name and religion to Rabbi Alon Barak, is told later in Part Eight.

Reverend Paul Miller of Grace Church is, and has been an active participant in local politics and well regarded by his parishioners and members of the community. He is front and center during many council and planning commission meetings, speaking on behalf of the community on issues of crime, code enforcement and community outreach.

––––––

The Political Landscape of the irrational years:

Please excuse the quality of the following reproductions. The booklet and Church flyer we found was water-stained and quite paper-aged, but still readable. The Publication titled "Whetstone" A journal of public opinion was printed in October 1996. The use of the word Whetstone, is probably a play on the word which is a stone used to sharpen knives—perhaps imparting the notion for people to get more sharp in their thinking. Good idea but it didn't seem to work

The publication contains campaign statements from eight candidates vying for three seats on the council (two for council and one mayoral. Greg Rupert; Paul Allen; Gary Bosworth; Gary Shearer and Kathy Smith were running for the two open council positions, Mike Sergrist; Patricia Shwartz and Jerry Pisha were running for mayor. There are also articles concerning issues of the day, and some endorsements for candidates from Michael Bickford; Howard La mere;

Pastor Ralph Joseph, of the Harvester Christian Center, in Riverside and Thomas P. Moen, Jr.

The common theme running through all of the candidate statements and community member comment papers as one would expect, are the issues uppermost in everyone's mind for the betterment of the city. These issues were:

- High Crime & influx of parolees
- Poor Road & street conditions
- Lack of retail & industrial businesses (No jobs for locals)
-
- Need for incentives to bring businesses to the city

These issues could be found in almost any city in any part of the state, or even the entire nation, with the possible exception of the constant influx of paroled felons into Desert Hot Springs. Should a survey have been taken, and people asked what there complaints were, the parade of parolees would top the list, I am sure. The Parolee situation remains a constant, with little let up, even with pleas from city officials to Sacramento, adding to frustrate outsiders from looking to build new businesses in Desert Hot Springs.

The individual Desert Hot Springs issues were not the main problem, but when taken as a whole, and realizing the same issues had remained for nearly twenty years, virtually ignored by sequential administrations while the rest of Coachella Valley cities were developing exponentially, one can see how discouraging and self defeating this became. Then when adding to these issues, the total absence of any meaningful commercial or industrial development to boost needed tax revenues, the situation takes on a hopeless appearance.

The arrival of Rick Daniels in 2007 changed all of that. But I am getting ahead of myself.

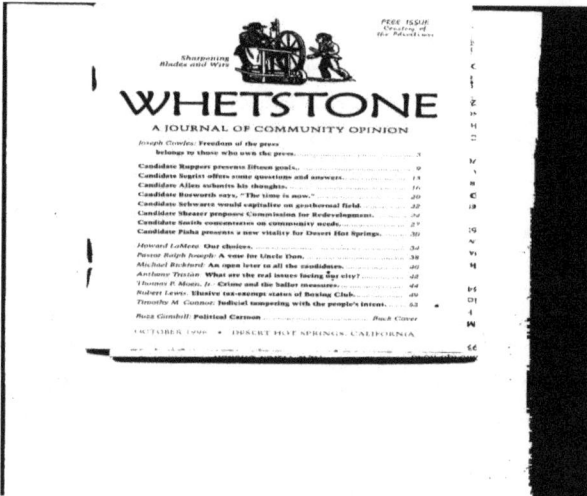

The only way to predict the future
is to have power to shape the future."

Eric Hoffer
The Passionate State of Mind (1954)

What are the real issues facing our city?

RECENTLY THE FUTURE OF THIS TOWN has been looking dim. Businesses have been closing, jobs are declining, violent crimes are rising, more houses are being boarded up, and we are struggling to obtain "our own" police department.

Why, all of a sudden, are we struggling to remain an organized, self-sufficient community? Why must we look to surrounding cities for help in our own city?

These are some of the questions that have me and many others concerned for the future of this city. I've been a resident since 1979 and I've never seen this city faced with such problems, of this degree!

What are the causes and solutions of these problems? First of all, we as a community need to recognize the problems, search for their causes, and resolve them with direct actions.

Elections are coming up and the people of this town are searching for the right person as our Mayor. We need to ask ourselves what are the priorities of each of the candidates, their long-term goals, their past contributions to our town, how they plan to achieve their goals, and what experiences they possess which will convince us that what they promise is realistic.

I would like to hear some of these major problems addressed by the candidates. What are the real issues? Let us deal with the problems, situations and other facts that make Desert Hot Springs a depressing place to live!

Let's be realistic: one of the main reasons most of the citizens of this town live here is because rent is cheap—not because this city has jobs to offer, or because it has many beautiful recreational facilities for the large number of youths and young adults in this town, or because there are major shopping centers with movie theaters. None of these characteristics, which are crucial to the existence of an efficient city, exists.

Other cities in the Valley are expanding in population and business at the same time, but we remain a residential city. We've had opportunities to increase employment, such as the maximum security prison. But it was turned down. By whom was it turned down and why, is the question.

Just recently, in the past six months, the city has made an effort to provide the youth with some type of public recreational activity that will keep them occupied in a positive, healthy manner, and may also deter them from drugs and gangs—thanks to a concerned man by the name of Steve Quiñones, Sr. I am a witness to the fact that some of the youth have involved themselves with the Desert Hot Springs gym and boxing facility which is leading them away from the streets and gangs. I am familiar with these young adults due to my three years' experience working for the Palm Springs School District as an instructional Aide in the elementary and junior high levels. Now there is a possibility that the gym may be closing due to certain city officials who have their own plans and intentions in mind. There is also a possibility that the youth under eighteen who do not currently pay monthly fees may have to start paying. Initially, the whole objective of the gym was to provide a free program for the youth, which primarily consists of low-income families; but as usual, money is favored over the well being of people—especially in government affiliated/funded programs.

What is to become of a city that seems to ignore the needs of its citizens? Will the city officials, businesses and citizens

Candidate Bosworth says, "The time is now."

WORKING TOWARDS A NEW DESERT HOT SPRINGS: As we move forward to the future we must build a foundation for a rebirth of Desert Hot Springs. The past two years have seen the beginnings of that foundation.

We on City Council have worked hard to clean up crime in our streets. With the passage of either of the tax measures on the November ballot, we will be able to quadruple the number of police officers on the street through comprehensive community based policing.

Desert Hot Springs has rejoined the Palm Springs Desert Resorts Convention & Visitors Bureau. This has already far increased revenues to the city more than the cost of rejoining.

The widening of Palm Drive, after a eight year delay from prior city councils, is finally back on track with ground-breaking next year. This fabulous gateway to our city, combined with the opening of the new Desert Hot Springs High School, will foster a new interest in our community.

With the completion of Mission Springs Park, together with the Mission Springs Water District, we have just finished a project that has increased the park land of our city by about a third.

There has been an increased interest in Code Enforcement throughout the city with the tripling of our code enforcement staff.

Long overdue maintenance of our streets is finally

receiving the attention it deserves. Earlier this year Hacienda between Palm Drive and West Drive was widened, while the resurfacing of Hacienda east of Palm Drive is almost ready to go out for bids. This is just a start of the infrastructure improvements planned for the future.

The TIME IS NOW for us to build on this foundation.

We must finish the work we have started. The passage of either of the tax measures will not only allow us to quadruple the law enforcement on street, but it will finally allow us to restructure the budget of the city.

As I outlined in the March Newsletter sent out by Kathy Smith and myself, we will be able to double the money being spent actually repairing our streets. This will be possible by paying the $200,000 annual salaries for the street crews out of the general fund where it should be in the first place—NOT the Gas Tax Fund for street repairs.

We will be able to do the same with the Redevelopment Agency. By no longer charging an eleven percent service charge to RDA, an additional $200,000 per year will be available for many worthwhile RDA projects. This includes such things as residential and commercial rehab projects, and sorely needed sewer hookups to protect our groundwater.

I propose we go a step further. I propose a thirty percent across the board cut in planning and development fees. This will be a major incentive to builders and developers to bring positive projects to the city. It will be a true shot-in-the-arm to increase the tax base in Desert Hot Springs.

I also propose that the city investigates the possibility of doing zero-based contracting for Animal Control services. This way Animal Control Services could be provided to the city at no charge in return for the assignment of the Animal Control Fees. This has the potential of providing a much higher level of service at absolutely zero cost to the city. The money saved could easily provide the needed funds for a long overdue Director of Recreation Services in Desert Hot Springs.

20

21

96

An open letter
to all the candidates.

DEAR CANDIDATES:

As a resident, property owner, businessperson, hotelier, and parent, I have a personal stake in all areas of what happens in Desert Hot Springs. I have lived here a long time and will continue to live here. My interests do not go away and will still be here long after City Councils have come and gone. Almost anything that happens or exists in Desert Hot Springs will affect my business or my family such as: law enforcement, public schools, youth recreation, roads, advertising, public safety, libraries, tourism, other businesses, community groups, and other areas too many to mention.

Each and every year, my business brings at least 70,000 visitors to Desert Hot Springs. It contributes a minimum of $50,000 in property taxes, $62,000 in Sales Taxes, and $80,000 in Transient Occupancy Taxes. I also support a local payroll of over $500,000 and I spend more than $100,000 each year in advertising—which promotes Desert Hot Springs along with the Spa Hotel.

Naturally, I have a personal stake in how our city appears to these visitors. When they come to my hotel, I want them to have a wonderful, healthful and memorable experience. This includes not only the hotel, but the surrounding area. Some of these people, because they came to my hotel, have stayed on to purchase homes and sometimes bring their businesses here.

I desire to be, and will be, an integral part of this community. Because of this, I want to share with you the benefit of my knowledge and experiences on the issues we face. We are on the same team and that is the way it should be. You make up your own mind, as you should, but it never hurts to get all the facts that you can, to make a judgment.

My involvement in Desert Hot Springs has put me in a position to understand a great deal of the history of the city, its citizens and community leaders. Because of this involvement with many people in various service organizations, I have a good general picture of civic interaction. I can and want to provide input on vital issues. It is extremely important to me to have a voice in those issues which will have significant impact on how my business grows (or fails), how the surrounding area looks, such as beautification (or neglect), how the crime problem is being ameliorated or eradicated (or increased), and how the future of Desert Hot Springs is being decided (or neglected).

As with many others who have been in business here for a long time, my economic investment is very important. Equally important is something known as "sweat equity," which is the accumulation of many hours put into making my business the best it can be, many hours devoted to various civic organizations, and many hours put into working for the city in other ways. This is why I want my input heard.

I believe you are rational, thoughtful, logical persons and will not easily let emotion sway you.

It is my hope, and my interest as a citizen and voter, that you consider what I have said in this letter. As I have often stated, I love Desert Hot Springs and I want to see it progress into the exceptional city it can be.

Sincerely,

MICHAEL BICKFORD
Desert Hot Springs Spa Hotel

40

41

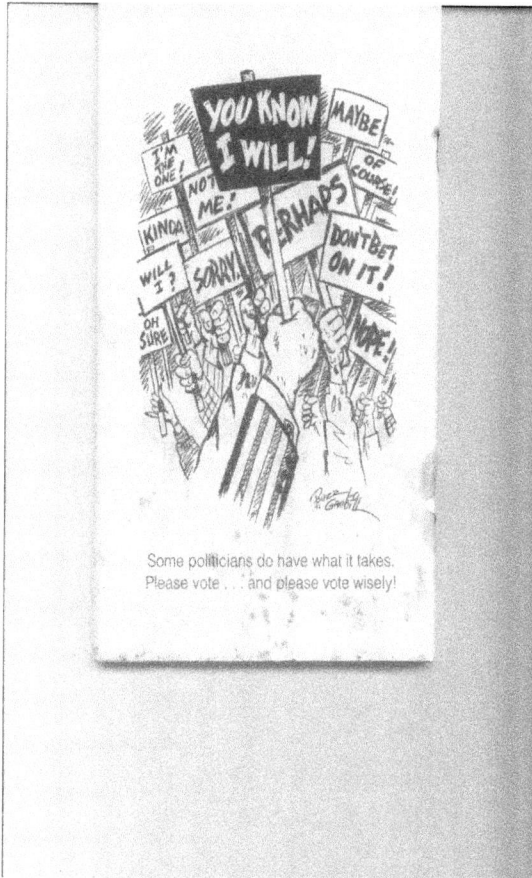

Some politicians do have what it takes.
Please vote . . . and please vote wisely!

Included in the above October 1996 issue of Whetstone, was a 3.5" x 5" confidential questionnaire mailing card entitled "Desert Hot Springs Crime Survey" further establishing that crime was a major issue at the time. Apparently the parolee situation was festering even before then.

The city's inability to stop the state from allowing the in-migration of convicted felons, sex offenders and child molesters remains a mystery to me. I do have my suspicions, but putting them here would not be wise.

The Vortex made me do it

Desert Hot Springs Crime Survey

1. Have you been the victim of a crime in the Desert Hot Springs area within the last 24 months? ☐ Yes ☐ No

2. If Yes, what type of crime? _____

3. Was the perpetrator caught? ☐ Yes ☐ No

4. If caught, has the perpetrator been tried?
   ☐ Yes ☐ No   Sentenced? ☐ Yes ☐ No

5. How safe do you feel in the Desert Hot Springs area?
   ☐ Very safe ☐ About average ☐ Not safe

6. Compared to other Coachella Valley communities,
   do you feel Desert Hot Springs is ☐ More safe ☐ About the same ☐ Less safe

7. Compared to major metropolitan areas (such as Orange County or Los Angeles),
   do you feel Desert Hot Springs is: ☐ More safe ☐ About the same ☐ Less safe

8. Do you own a handgun for personal protection? ☐ Yes ☐ No

9. If Yes, have you ever carried your handgun in town? ☐ Yes ☐ No

10. Whether or not you are presently a gun owner, would you be willing
    to participate in a community-sponsored handgun safety course? ☐ Yes ☐ No

Confidential Questionnaire—DO NOT Provide Name & Address

Sharpening Blades and Wits

Postcard Rate

The November issue of WHETSTONE will focus on Crime in the Desert Hot Springs area. Your confidential response to our Crime Survey will be very much appreciated. Thank you very much!

WHETSTONE
Event Horizon Press
Post Office Box 867
Desert Hot Springs, CA 92240

One would believe that if/when crime can be controlled and the city managed properly, promoting, Desert Hot Springs, much like Palm Springs could become a haven for the affluent. But it will take planning and exceptional execution to overcome the years of neglect and mismanagement.

There is every reason to believe that given half a chance, the Positive Energy Vortex powers that some claim exist, could seize the upper hand in Desert Hot Springs, releasing its residents from the apparent strangle hold the Negative Energy Vortex has had on the community. You can believe this or not, but something unusual has been holding the city back. For a community to have as many active volunteers involved in trying to make things better, and things always going wrong, there has to be an explanation.

Consider the strong points of the city:

- Fifteen-hundred feet above the valley floor, it is the highest in elevation of all the cities in Coachella valley and as a result, cooler in the heat of summer.
- Natural mineral hot springs containing documented therapeutic qualities, without any sulfur smell. Most other hot springs in the valley and elsewhere have the sulfur odor.
- Some of the finest, award-winning natural drinking water in America.
- A history of being the first settlement in the entire valley, containing the very first home to be built, now a museum receiving thousand of visitors a year.

These positive elements are a marketing professional's dream. The city's story properly told and promoted, along with stable leadership and management could become the "shining city on the hill" some love to declare. Good leadership will only come to Desert Hot Springs when the citizens themselves take charge and demand more from their representatives. When that happens, those who believe in the Energy Vortex can truthfully say: "The Vortex made me do it!"

Pictures and descriptions on the following pages were taken from the Desert Hot Springs Historical Society web site.

Cabot's Pueblo Museum

A top attraction in the Palm Springs area, Cabot's Pueblo Museum is a Hopi inspired Pueblo that is a unique treasure to the Coachella Valley, located in the heart of Desert Hot Springs.

The Museum is nearby to Joshua Tree, Rancho Mirage, Palm Desert and Palm Springs. This Southern California landmark is within 10 minutes of the Palm Drive exit from the 10 Freeway.

Built by Cabot Yerxa (b. 1883) on property he homesteaded in 1913, he worked on the property until his death in 1965. Cabot journeyed through the desert; gathering reclaimed materials from as far east as the Salton Sea, north to Morongo Valley, south to Palm Springs and west to White Water.

The structure is hand-made, created from reclaimed and found objects. The Pueblo is four-stories, 5,000 square feet and includes 35 rooms, 150 windows and 65 doors. Visitors will notice many unique features: including windows and doors collected and reassembled from abandoned homesteads, old telephone poles, buck board wagon parts and many other materials used creatively.

On the guided tour, visitors journey through the life of Cabot Yerxa and his family including artifacts collected from their adventures dating back over 100 years. Hear his story from the Dakota Territory to Mexico, Cuba, Alaska, France, throughout California and the Southwest, including the founding of Desert Hot Springs, California.

The museum is open year-round for single tours, and scheduled group tours and hosts special events.

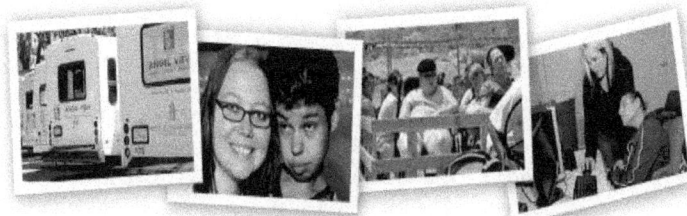

Serving the Valley for More Than 55 Years

In 1954, Angel View Crippled Children's Foundation was founded on a natural hot mineral water spring in Desert Hot Springs, CA by a group of parents whose children suffered from polio. The therapeutic waters, considered among the highest quality in the world, soothed the children's aches and pains and helped in their rehabilitation.

The children's visionary parents named the new charitable foundation Angel View after a naturally occurring rock formation at the base of Mt. San Jacinto. With dedication of purpose and the generosity of supporters throughout the desert, a 52-bed rehabilitation facility was constructed on donated land high up on Miracle Hill Road in Desert Hot Springs. Originally, clients were cared for at this facility which now serves as the organization's administrative center.

When polio was eradicated, Angel View expanded its treatment program to care for children and young adults with orthopedic disorders, many of whom were also developmentally disabled. We now care for clients with a full spectrum of orthopedic and neuromuscular disorders.

Today, Angel View operates 18 group homes for the developmentally disabled. Our newest home, which opened in 2008, marked an important expansion of our services. The Marion Ashley House was built to provide 24-hour nursing care to disabled infants and toddlers who have been removed from their homes by the court system. Also in 2008, we launched a Day Program for developmentally disabled adults from throughout the Coachella Valley.

Looking forward, we anticipate our 19th home opening soon. It will expand our ability to provide care to developmentally disabled individuals whose conditions are medically fragile.

As we have since 1954, we will continue to monitor the needs of the community and provide the intensive services needed to care for the developmentally disabled.

****

Two Bunch Palms

Throughout the years, many celebrities have come to Two Bunch Palms Resort & Spa to shed the trappings of their fame while donning the simple life in the legendary Two Bunch robe. Enticed by the magical allure of mineral waters, natural beauty and therapeutic relaxation, many have come to make their spiritual mark on Two Bunch Palms Resort & Spa. While we continue to welcome any number of well-known guests, none are as notorious as the original "Scarface" himself, Al Capone.

(As Copied from the Two Bunch Web 2011–03–01)

With each change of the city's administration since incorporation in 1963, came declarations and promises to 'clean up the trash"; "fix the roads and streets"; 'recruit businesses" and "reduce crime". Unfortunately, promises made were not promises kept, and so it has been and remains, much to the dissatisfaction of the residents.

All new cities experience growing pains. Volunteers with different backgrounds step forward to become the city's leaders through the democratic process of running for office, and when elected do their best to act on behalf of their constituents. However, inexperience in accepting the important role of governing can often lead to negative consequences such as what happened to Desert Hot Springs at the most inopportune time in its relatively young life.

The next chapter explains how a bad city council decision became worse by a subsequent bad decision of the mayor, resulting in a mistake of astronomical proportions, for which the city will be paying for a long time.

Three: A near fatal blow

With the city growing in population and new homes
being constructed to house them, there continued to be no
apparent effort to develop a revenue base that would sustain
the growth. As said before, economic viability of any
community demands a balance of commercial enterprises
that will not only serve the needs of the residents, but will
generate income to augment property taxes. Precious little
income remains in a community for its economic survival as it
is. The Lion's share goes to the state.

Meanwhile, the valley began expanding eastward.,
slowly in the 50's, at first: Cathedral City; then Palm Desert;
Indian Wells; Bermuda Dunes; La Quinta, and Indio, each
developing high-end second homes, and some more modest
for the worker-bees. But the expansion was always on the
south side of Highway I-10, the main east/west route for
trucking, paralleling the single rail freight railroad line from
Los Angeles to all points east.

Increased home development in the valley brought
commercial, industrial and retail centers along the south
corridor, fueling the economy of the neighboring cities of
Desert Hot Springs, that "shining city on a hill". Unfortunately,
commerce continued to elude Desert Hot Springs, nor
apparently did its leaders seek to bring business into the city
with any great effort.

Department stores big and small, grocery and drug
store chains, hardware stores and all types of commerce
began to fill in the commercialy designated properties south
of I-10, where Desert Hot Springs residents would (and still

107

do) treck to buy their staples, clothing, furniture and other home-making needs. Naturally, sales tax revenues from those purchases stayed in the neighboring cities, helping them to expand even more, as Desert Hot Springs continued its role of being a bedroom community on the road to municipal poverty.

Then in the early 90's, located on a large plot of land adjacent to, but not within the city boundaries of Desert Hot Springs, the development of the private Mission Lakes Country Club and Golf Course came to being, along with several hundred for sale lots, where over the years hundreds of beautiful custom homes were built and occupied.

Residents and members of the Country Club living in Mission Lakes have staunchly opposed any moves of annexation into Desert Hot Springs, claiming an immediate drop in home values if they should acquiesce to the many attempts by the city. Desert Hot Springs could use the Assessed valuation, and tax income it would produce, but as yet, it is not to be. Some positive strokes from the Energy Vortex could probably help here.

Compounding the revenue vs. expenditure problem, was the Desert Hot Springs city council's decision to have their own Municipal Police Force rather than contracting with the county. Research shows there was a strong sentiment amongst the city's constituents that the County Sheriff's protection was inadequate, blaming the high crime rate as a direct result. In retrospect it appears that conclusion was erroneous, as the high crime rate continued almost unabated until very recently, due in most part to the steady influx of parolees from state facilities and the city not being able to afford to hire enough police to control them.

With little to virtually no income from commerce other than Transient Occupancy Taxes (TOT), Two grocery chain markets and one medium-sized department store, the city was losing ground and running in the red by the late 1990's. Then a near fatal blow was dealt to the financially ailing city through a series of missteps by the city council and mayor, resulting in a costly judgment being levied against the city. The community's citizens will be paying off that debt for many years to come.

As stated earlier, Desert Hot Springs had experienced two recalls; ten hired and fired city managers and ten police chiefs in a little over ten-years, until the current manager Rick Daniels was hired. The city is still emerging from a major bankruptcy brought on by the settlement of an ill-conceived lawsuit with a developer a few years ago. Who wants to argue that this isn't strong evidence of the Negative Energy Vortex at work? Read on--these are facts, not fiction:

The Silver Sage Lawsuit:

Rather than settle the lawsuit when they had the chance, the city leaders chose to appeal, then losing and becoming sadddled with a six-million dollar debt afterexpending thousands of dallars attempting to defend their position. That ultimately forced the city into Bankruptcy. official elements of the sordid tale follow:

Damages for Lost Profits Not Too Speculative

May 31, 2001 | Bulletin No. 060101

In Silver Sage Partners, Ltd. v. City of Desert Hot Springs, 2001 WL 585539, the Ninth Circuit Court of Appeals determined that a developer had adequately proved the damages that it suffered as a result of opposition by the City of Desert Hot Springs to one of the developer's projects.

Facts

Developer, Silver Sage Partners, Ltd., was organized to purchase and develop low-income housing at a mobile home park in the City of Desert Hot Springs, California. Developer ultimately received a commitment for a 55-year mortgage in the amount of $4,233,265 from the California Housing Department under its Rental Housing Construction Program. However, under Cal. Const. Art. XXXIV, § 1, before the transaction could go through, the low-rent housing project had to be approved by local voters. City's council voted to deny approval of the project.

Developer sued City under the Fair Housing Act. A jury returned a verdict in favor of Developer in the amount of $3,040,439. The jury verdict was ultimately reduced after the district court found that it was "grossly excessive." Therefore, Developer appealed to the Ninth Circuit Court of Appeals.

The Court of Appeal's Decision

The Court of Appeals rejected the district court's finding that damages regarding lost profits were "too speculative." The district court based its finding on evidence allegedly showing (1) that the projected income stream would not have been sufficient to pay much if any of the principal or interest on the loan and (2) that the partnership could not have received a profit until after it had paid off the loan (which it would not have been able to do).

According to the Court of Appeals' interpretation of the evidence, however, Developer had specifically

projected payments of interest for the first fifteen years and payments of principal thereafter. Furthermore, the Court of Appeals determined that there was no evidence showing that Developer could have made a profit only after the entire loan was repaid. Rather, there was expert evidence that Developer would have received some profits in any year where operating income would exceed payment on the loan.

Date: 06-01-2001

Case Style: Silver Sage Partners, Ltd. v. City of Desert Hot Springs

Case Number: 99-56917

Judge: Judge B. Fletcher

Court: United States Court of Appeals for the Ninth Circuit

Plaintiff's Attorney: William J. Davis, Min Chang and Won Chang of Davis & Company, P.C., Los Angeles, California

Defendant's Attorney: Kevin Patrick McVerry of Graves, Roberson & Bourassa, Thousand Oaks, California

Description: Silver Sage Partnership, Ltd. is a partnership organized to purchase and develop low-income housing at a mobile home park in the City of Desert Hot Springs, California. Paul Saben and Richard Earlix were the partnership's principals. In 1990, the partnership entered into an agreement with Huntington Savings and Loan to purchase the Silver Sage Mobile Home Park, which was located in the city. The partnership initially sought to finance the project with bonds to be issued by Riverside County. Although the county approved a bond resolution for approve or disapprove low-rent housing projects under article XXXIV is reserved for the voters in the community and cannot be delegated to the city council." However, the partnership could not take advantage of the ruling by seeking a referendum on its project because by the time the court of appeals ruled, the RHCP program had exhausted its funds. 3 In addition to the city, plaintiffs also sued the City Council for the City of Desert Hot Springs as well as many persons in their official and individual capacity. By the time of trial, the district court had either dismissed or summarily adjudicated all claims against the individual defendants. Plaintiffs do not appeal from those decisions. Plaintiffs also brought various state law claims and a claim under 42 U.S.C.� 1983. The district court either dismissed or summarily adjudicated these claims. Plaintiffs do not appeal those decisions.

After trial, the jury found for plaintiffs by general verdict and awarded them damages in the amount of $3,040,439. The city filed a motion for judgment as a matter of law or, in the alternative, a new trial. The district court denied the motion for a judgment as a matter of law and denied the motion for a new trial as to liability. However, because

It found the jury's verdict "grossly excessive," the district court denied the city's motion for a new trial on the issue of damages conditional on plaintiffs' acceptance of a remittitur to $388,146.20.

Plaintiffs rejected the remittitur and a second trial on damages was held. After trial, the second jury awarded nominal damages for plaintiffs. After entry of judgment, plaintiffs filed a motion seeking to have the district court "amend" the second jury's damage award or, in the alternative, for a new trial as to damages. Plaintiffs also sought an injunction ordering the city to cease violating the Fair Housing Act. The district court denied both motions. However, the district court did grant plaintiffs' motion to reconsider its previous denial of attorney's fees. The district court decided that since plaintiffs had established the city's liability but had only obtained nominal damages from the jury, it would award plaintiffs $57,000 in attorney's fees.

Outcome: Because the district court abused its discretion and committed legal error in imposing a choice on plaintiffs to accept a remittitur or face a new trial on damages, we reverse the district court's order and remand with instructions to reinstate the first jury's verdict. Because the district court improperly shifted the burden to the plaintiffs to demonstrate irreparable injury, we vacate the district court's order denying plaintiffs' motion for an injunction and remand for reconsideration. **REVERSED AND REMANDED WITH INSTRUCTIONS.**

****

Strapped for cash and unable to satisfy the judgment, the city took the unprecedented step of filing for bankruptcy protection rather than dis-incorparate, which the county did not want them to do, as they (the county) would then be faced with having to serve the community with its required services. That was a non-starter for the Supervisors, Vortex or not.

Resort City Files for Bankruptcy

Finances: Desert Hot Springs acts after a judge rules its assets can be seized. Civic operations will continue unabated.

December 21, 2001 | SCOTT GOLD | TIMES STAFF WRITER

Desert Hot Springs, part of the cluster of communities that comprise the ritzy, anything-goes oasis of Palm Springs, has filed for bankruptcy protection, crippled by a legal judgment handed down this week, officials said Thursday.

The city filed for protection under Chapter 9 of the federal bankruptcy code, an emergency measure that protects its assets and property and eventually will allow the city to adjust its debt, estimated at $8 million.

113

"We had to do it . . . to protect the city, to protect the citizens," Mayor Matt Weyuker said.

A federal judge declined Tuesday to block a development group that has long sought damages from the city for seizing its assets. The city, which could not cover the about $6-million costs of the case, feared that its only other option was to unincorporate[sic] and instead filed for bankruptcy Wednesday after an emergency council meeting.

Desert Hot Springs is believed to be the first government in California to file for bankruptcy since Orange County sought protection in 1994, after losing more than $1.5 billion on its investments, said Megan Taylor, director of communications for the League of California Cities in Sacramento.

Tuesday's ruling was the latest twist in a long-standing dispute over a 1990 City Council decision.

Eleven years ago, the council threw out Silver Sage Partners Ltd.'s plan to build a mobile home park. The company, which could not be reached for comment Thursday, filed a lawsuit claiming that the city had violated the Fair Housing Act by, in effect, discriminating against low-income families.

A jury awarded Silver Sage $3 million. The city fought the judgment, and the case has been lumbering through the court system ever since. At one point a jury reduced the judgment to $1.

But in July, the U.S. 9th Circuit Court of Appeals reinstated the $3-million judgment and added nearly $3 million in interest and legal fees. Tuesday's ruling allowed Silver Sage to proceed.

"They had no idea this was coming as quickly as it did," said Gary Sherwin, vice president of market development for the Palm Springs Desert Resorts Convention and Visitors Authority. "The city had no choice but to file [for bankruptcy], given the situation they were in."

Although residents and business leaders are understandably alarmed, said Sherwin, "the community is going to continue to function. . . .

****

The unfortunate misjudgment of Desert Hot Springs leadership at this very critical period in time began a downward spiral for the city that subsequent administrations have never really been able to overcome. When bad politics get mixed in with bad decisions nothing good will come out of it.

However misguided, there has never seemed to be a lack of puffery and overblown optimism among the power structure of the city's politicos and business leaders, leaving the city's citizens with false hope, as the following article demonstrates;

Local business leaders share bright outlook

By Apfelbaum, Sharon
Publication: The Public Record
Date: Friday, January 4 2002

We asked some of our favorite in-the-know business folks to make predictions about the economy in the year 2002 What surprised us was the general mood of optimism in the local business and development community.

Diane Matzner, who owns three retail shops in downtown Palm Springs, says, "We had our second highest sales day at Mosaic on the 24th of December. In November two of our three stores (Mosaic, Mariposa and Aristokatz) hit their sales goal of a 30 percent increase over last year.

Palm Springs Tourism's change in advertising direction helped a lot. Following the September 11 terrorist attacks, the agency consciously redirected its advertising dollars toward one group: the Southern California 'drive' market. It worked. Billboards and radio ads on the coast have paid off. Our business has been filled with the drive market which more than made up for what we lost in international visitors," revealed Matzner.

Bryant Francis, an- service development coordinator for the Palm Springs International Airport, was equally upbeat. "I predict the airport will experience a banner year in 2002. Our ongoing discussions with current air carriers and with potential new ones lead me to say that, even if we're only moderately successful, we'll still break records adding new services."

> Restaurateur Ric Service, owner with wife Patty of the popular Las Casuelas Terraza, uses similar words: "I'm expecting Palm Springs to have a banner year in 2002, and the hospitality industry will lead the way. People will need lots of rest. They will travel to the desert, not to Hawaii."

Convention and Visitors Authority executive director Mike Fife added, "The economy had already felt a pinch and things were slower than anticipated prior to September 11 . October and November proved to be two of the Coachella Valley's worst months in about the last ten years. Hoteliers were predicting a twelve percent decline overall.

"Now things look different. We have started to see more future bookings and what seems like a genuine turnaround. Based on the improved December numbers, hospitality folks are predicting that twelve percent is a worst-case scenario. And when the direction changes, we're ready," concluded Fife.

Realtor Lois Carter agrees. "I think we'll have a good season. The Baby Boomers are still coming on-stream. People will vacation where they can drive, which means the desert. The general feeling in our Classic Homes office is optimistic."

City Manager Patrick Pratt says Rancho Mirage is basking in its surfeit of new development. A city with three resort hotels - Westin Mission Hills, The Lodge (formerly the Ritz Carlton) and Marriott's Rancho Las Palmas - Rancho Mirage now boasts 39 restaurants, with another half dozen on the drawing board. The River, a newly opened mixed use development, represents a $50 million investment by the Snyder Company.

> "Financially, it looks like a stronger quarter coming up," says Pratt. Slowing is not the long term trend. There won't be any prolonged down cycle here."

Wearing both his hats, rancher-realtor Paul Ames predicts, "Agriculture: mixed. It will be a fine year for lemons, tangerines and Valencia oranges. Real estate: great. I've never had as much fun as I'm having today in real estate in the green end of the Coachella Valley. There are good projects, good sellers and good buyers."

Dick Oliphant shares his optimism. "2002 will be another good year. I see a recovery in the hospitality industry. Housing will maintain its steady pace, driven by low interest rates.

"Our Coachella Valley market is so diverse now, with a full range of employment opportunities and myriad housing, with a population over 300,000 and growing, we stand a good chance of missing the downturn bullet now piercing the rest of California," predicted the longtime local developer.

A slightly less positive Robert Brock, longtime CPA with Lund & Guttry, wears no rose-colored glasses. "Although we see the commercial and residential real estate boom on every comer, most of these projects were launched at least 12 months ago. Not much of any significance is getting underway today.

"Historically, the desert has been the last place to feel economic downturns, and the current national recession is no exception. What helps salve any slowdown here is our affluent and economically active senior/retirement population, along with visitors spending their leisure dollars here," concluded Brock.

The city of Desert Hot Springs, unable to come up with the enormous payment required by a decade-old lawsuit involving the Silver Sage mobile home development, declared bankruptcy earlier this month.

Mayor Matt Weyuker makes this prediction: "Our declaration of bankruptcy will help lift the Silver Sage lawsuit cloud that has been hanging over our heads for the last decade. In spite of what may appear to be, greater things are ahead for the city of Desert Hot Springs. The next year will bring a whole new wave of growth and prosperity that our city has never before experienced, surmises the hard working mayor.

Finally, former Desert Water Agency executive director and dedicated domino player Jack Oberle forecasts with a metaphor: "Dominoes 2002 is the only way you can't lose. Economic recovery is eminent in 2002."

And that surely articulates what local financial leaders are thinking.

****

How wrong those Weyuker predictions were, which we are sure was due in no small part to the "revolving door" in city management, police chiefs and planning personnel that ensued following the bankruptcy. There is no question that there were mixed signals coming from almost every corner of the community with very few of the participants in agreement as to what the problems were or how they could be corrected even if they could have agreed.

About then, Mayor Weyuker was distracted by his own problems when he was forced to file for personal Bankruptcy:

Desert Hot Springs mayor files bankruptcy a year after city

By The Associated Press

DESERT HOT SPRINGS —

By The Associated Press

Desert Hot Springs mayor files bankruptcy a year after city

DESERT HOT SPRINGS — Nearly a year after the city became California's first government entity to file for bankruptcy in seven years, Mayor Matt Weyuker said he's declaring bankruptcy, too.

Financially crippled by a legal dispute involving a former employer, Weyuker confirmed in a letter to residents this week that he has filed for Chapter 7 bankruptcy protection.

In the letter, Weyuker, 69, said he was wrongly fired from his position at a university and a subsequent lawsuit coupled with a weakened stock market have sapped him and his wife of their savings.

"We are, of course, deeply embarrassed by this turn of events," wrote Weyuker, who has been mayor since 1999. "We simply ran out of money and other assets ...." Last year, the city filed for protection under Chapter 9 of the federal bankruptcy code. The emergency measure allows the city to protect its assets and property while adjusting its debt — estimated at $8 million.

The filing followed a federal judge's ruling that upheld an award against the city in a decade-old dispute with a mobile home developer. The company claimed the city violated the Fair Housing Act and discriminated against low-income families. The developer won a $3 million judgment. After attorneys fees, interest and penalties, the award totaled more than $6 million.

The bankruptcy filing last December was the first by a government entity in California since Orange County filed for protection in 1994, after losing more than $1.5 billion on its investments, according to the League of California Cities.

Weyuker, who said he has no plans to resign as mayor, worked at Western University of Health Sciences, based in Pomona, for 21 years and was serving as director of government relations when he was elected mayor in November 1999. After being fired in July 2000, he filed a wrongful termination lawsuit, alleging age bias. The case is set for trial in 2003.

An early morning call to a Western University spokeswoman was not immediately returned.

By The Associated Press

****

Meanwhile, the entire Coachella Valley was in a raging building boom, with developers scampering for more land to build homes on. Thousands of acres of land were being gobbled up at obscene prices, but always south of I-10.

Once it appeared there was no where else to go for raw land, builders and developers turned their eyes north of I-10 and made a mad dash for the shinning city on the hill. They came in droves. This would have been a good time for the negative Energy Vortex to come into play. Come to think of it, maybe that's what happened but in the wrong way. Instead of stopping the home builder/developers, the Vortex forced the city to make the wrong decisions in the land rush. You've got to watch that Vortex, it will get you when you're least expecting it.

———

Planning for Desert Hot Springs future:

My attendance at the first public "Visioning Meeting" in September of 2003 was to participate in the structure of a new General Plan. The old one never worked apparently. I was very impressed at the large turnout of community residents and business people, and returning home, I mentioned to Diana how refreshing to see such interest among the city's Citizens in wanting to help develop a new plan. The leadership in 2003 seemed to recognized that enthusiasm also. However, it is now 2011 and a concise, complete General Plan has yet to be adopted after thousands of hours of consultants, community members, city staff, planning commission and council members' time, and hundreds of thousands of dollars being expended.

The city has recently developed the "Vortex Plan" for the central part of the city at Pierson and Palm Drive, and some re-facing of several commercial buildings is taking place as I write. But it will take a great deal more than a superficial face lift to help gain required momentum in commercial development, particularly in the current and unpredictable economic climate we find ourselves in today.

When the land rush came to Desert Hot Springs, city leaders, rather than taking the long view and parlaying this new found wealth of hungry developers into a long range plan for carefully managed growth, took the short view. The new General Plan seemed to get pushed aside to make way for the onslaught of developers laying siege on the Planning Department pushing new subdivisions for approval. The city leaders were so desperate for money they were approving residential subdivisions at breakneck speeds, counting on what I will term here as "fools gold": the planning and permit fees for the short term benefit of their depleted General Fund.

Within three short years, Desert Hot Springs staff, planning and council had approved more than 15,000 new residential lots, and not one commercial, residential or industrial project was in the final planning stage. This was a recipe for disaster in my view.

About this time, I was frantically trying to get the attention of anyone who would listen, through my newspaper articles and appearances in council and planning meetings, pleading that unless there was a concerted effort to reach out and bring commerce to the city it would be consumed by itself, unable to meet the costs of serving the new inhabitants with basic domestic services, such as police; fire; road maintenance; sewer; water and trash pick up. Then the mayor gave his "state of the City address:

Desert Hot Springs mayor declares turnaround year

By Kleinschmidt, Janice
Publication: The Public Record
Date: Tuesday, February 8 2005

Mayors love their cities - and sometimes their cities love them back. Desert Hot Springs Mayor Matt Weyuker falls into that category.

The city's mayor since 1999, Weyuker received no less than two standing ovations at his Jan. 26 state-of-the-city address. The first came before he began speaking and was an acknowledgment from the full house of his perseverance, not only through the city's financial struggles, but also for his grace through an undiagnosed neurological condition that has left him in a wheelchair and slowed and slurred his speech.

His sense of humor, however, remains intact. Upon calling for the "slide show" (PowerPoint) operator, the mayor began, "This is what I did on my summer vacation."

Getting down to business, the mayor said 2004 "was a transition year for our city, yet it was a metamorphic time for us.

"Major strides" he continued, "were taken to assure the residents of our great little city with the big heart a future."

First and foremost, the city emerged from bankruptcy in 2004 not a small task given the $9 million debt it faced after losing a lawsuit filed by a developer. The mayor lauded city staff and the city council for hard work and creativity, but singled out Vice Mayor Mary Stephens for "unswerving perseverance."

123

Alluding to his slow speech, the mayor then explained that he asked Stephens to assist him in reading his state-of-the-city address so the luncheon audience would not be there until dinner.

Stephens began specifics with community safety, which has a 2004-2005 budget of $4,577,608, including police, fire, code enforcement and animal control expenses. In October, the city council approved a $490,854 increase to the police department budget of $2.7 million for additional staffing, equipment and operational costs. In January, the council approved a further increase of $17,244. The additions pay for three more officers (for a total of 27 sworn officers), additional overtime and replacement of a police car.

Also in January, the council approved a $183,624 bump in its contract with Riverside County to increase staffing from two to three firefighters. 'This increase has been long overdue for one of the busiest, unsung departments in all of Riverside County," Weyuker said.

Code enforcement was budgeted at $305,467. Animal control expenditures were budgeted at $260,343. "We've gone from having one of the worst shelters in the county and euthanasia rates to one of the best in Southern California," the mayor said.

Nearly $4 million has been budgeted for "long back-burnered capital improvement projects," Stephens said, enumerating street repairs and repaving, sewer pavement rehabilitation, recycling, replacement of city vehicles (possibly CNG models) and new Desert Hot Springs Civic/Community Center. Completed projects include street rehabilitation, traffic signals, a BMX park under construction north of Hacienda Avenue between East and West Arroyo drives, a Veterans Memorial Park just south of Mission Lakes Boulevard and west of Palm Drive, the comprehensive master plan update

124

that started in September and land acquisition for the new civic center.

Several 2004 capital projects were completed under budget (by $10 to $28,000), including traffic signal, drainage, road and sidewalk improvements. The comprehensive master plan update is budgeted at $350,000.

Congressman Jerry Lewis was credited with helping the city secure $1.2 million in federal funds to design, engineer and begin construction on the new civic center. "But we'll need about $12 million more to bring the project to completion by 2008," Stephens added. The City Hall/Civic Center Project comprises new facilities for City Hall departments, a park, amphitheater, Olympic-size pool, 20,000-square-foot Boys & Girls Club and 20,000-square-foot community center.

In the 2004-2005 budget, the city council approved creation of a reserve of more than $1.9 million. "Much of this figure is due in part to all of the new growth, although much of it is spoken for," Weyuker said. More than $200,000 has been set aside to repair damage to streets caused by January rains. Other reserves are earmarked for vehicle replacement ($75,000), bankruptcy bond payments ($495,000), emergency medical services ($75,000), and increased employee benefits ($500,000), as well as $225,000 for unknown liability claims, $250,000 for economic uncertainty and $260,000 for future programs.

Desert Hot Springs set a record in 2004 with $171 million in building permits issued, including 1,086 single-family residences valued at $146.4 million. The city has approved 16 housing developments, totaling more than 10,000 additional singlefamily homes. "Some of these large projects include golf courses and other amenities," Stephens said. Stone Ridge comprises 2,200 homes, and Highland Falls comprises 3,500 homes, two golf courses, a clubhouse and restaurant.

125

Additionally, there are several commercial projects in the works: (1) Guardian Self Storage, a 96,000-square-foot storage facility consisting of 13 buildings on 10 acres east of Little Morongo Road, north of Two Bunch Palms Road; (2) an office/light industrial development on 15 acres in the same area; (3) light industrial facilities on 9 acres east of Little Morongo Road, south of Avenue 15; (4) an office/retail/restaurant center with 67,760 square feet on 6.6 acres at Mission Lakes; (5) an office/retail center with 13,920 square feet on .9 acres at 13125 Palm Drive; and (6) a 6,452square-foot Starbucks at Two Bunch Palms and Palm drives.

"The city is investigating alternative energy sources to integrate into new development projects whenever possible," Weyuker noted. "This will also mean tapping into emerging, new technology." In January, the city adopted a water-efficient landscape ordinance.

"One of the things that the recent rains showed us is that when the roadways become flooded that Desert Hot Springs becomes cut off from vital emergency medical care. We must find ways of assisting the newly formed Desert Hot Springs Medical Center [coalition] to obtain the funding necessary for it to become a reality," Stephens said.

The annual state-of-the-city address was the mayor's last. He has chosen not to run again after his term expires in December. "My health condition has diminished the amount of time I can spend on your behalf being your mayor," he said. "But we're still accomplishing a great many things that you were promised by me and the rest of the city council. Thank you for your patience with your city leaders. It hasn't been easy on any of us while the city council, city staff and other civic leaders have been attempting to dig our city out of the mess that someone got us into. This is but a beginning for our city," he concluded. "The best is yet to come."

And with that, the mayor received his second standing ovation.

****

Ah yes! Tell them what they want to hear and they will love you---but will they love you in the morning?

The following article is indicative of the potential popularity of the "Spa City' during this time. Unfortunately this exposure and other articles before and since have never created enough interest in the general public to help the city grow into what it would like to become: an international destination city.

Cohesive and sustained planning is required to develop national attention for such a goal which has never been developed by the city. It takes more than adopting a new logo and slogan "Spa City".

Constant change in city management had caused a "shoot yourself in the foot" operational dysfunction which changed direction every few years. Articles such as this have never been capitalized on by the city or its spa owners to the extent needed for broad international recognition. Meanwhile, Palm Springs drowns in publicity, virtually smothering Desert Hot Springs.

Everyone knows of Palm Springs, but most people when asked about Desert Hot Springs rarely have ever heard of it and commonly ask: "Where is that"? Below is a great article written in 1988 for the Orange County Register, but unfortunately, the title has a double entendre:

Get Soaked in Desert Hot Springs

Trip of the Week

June 05, 1988 | MICHELE GRIMM and TOM GRIMM | *The Grimms of Laguna Beach are authors of "Away for the Weekend," a travel guide to Southern California.*

DESERT HOT SPRINGS — It's the water that brings visitors to this quiet town at the western end of the Coachella Valley. They come to swim and soak in the steaming mineral water that bubbles from the earth into dozens of pools and spas.

To drum up business in its early days, Desert Hot Springs' promoters touted their water as a natural elixir with healing properties for arthritis, rheumatism, neuralgia and gout. Even today there's a spa/hotel especially for arthritic patients.

Many visitors, however, head to mineral pools at the bargain-rate mom-and-pop motels. Others soak away their aches at one of the valley's most exclusive resorts, Two Bunch Palms.

Also popular is the Desert Hot Springs Hotel and Spa that boasts eight mineral pools of various sizes and temperatures. There's even a new three-room bed and breakfast, the Travelers Repose, with its own pool and spa.

In the past five years Desert Hot Springs added several modern accommodations, starting with the small but full-service Sunset Inn, the town's first new hotel in a decade.

It was followed by the largest hostelry, Royal Fox Inn, with 113 rooms and an RV park. Latest to open is the Desert Palms Spa Motel. In all, this town of 10,400 offers more than 60 lodgings with mineral pools.

Cooler Than Palm Springs

Desert Hot Springs is spread across the gentle foothills of the Little San Bernardino Mountains at an altitude of more than

1,000 feet. That means summer temperatures are several degrees cooler than in Palm Springs and other neighboring resorts.

En route to Desert Hot Springs there's an out-of-the-way place for family entertainment, the Rainbow Rancho trout farm along the Whitewater River.

To get there from Los Angeles, drive east on Interstate 10 past the junction to Palm Springs and exit at Whitewater. Turn left to cross the freeway and join Whitewater Canyon Road that winds five miles up to the Rainbow Rancho Whitewater Trout Co.

Look for huge cottonwood trees that surround freshwater ponds filled with rainbow trout of all sizes. The hatchery has been operating for about half a century and supplies thousands of pounds of fish to public and private lakes in the Southland.

Best of all, two ponds have lots of fat trout that are ready to bite. Anglers of all ages are practically guaranteed fresh trout. And they can cook their catch on a grill in the picnic area or take it home.

You pay $2 for rod and reel, bait, bucket and towel (up to three people can use the equipment). The trout caught are weighed. You pay $2.35 a pound, including cleaning of the fish upon request.

The fishing ponds at Rainbow Rancho trout farm are open every day except Monday from 9 a.m. to 5 p.m. Call (619) 325-5570 for more information.

****

As to the mayor every body loved, and his statement that *"The city is investigating alternative energy sources to integrate into new development projects whenever possible,"*

129

he spent his entire time in office declaring that the prolific fields of wind turbines in the valley generating alternative energy for thousands of homes in the power grid should be outlawed because they were unsightly and killed birds.

Compounding the inept leadership at the time and convinced that promoting the city as an "International Health and Wellness Center, was going to increase commercial activity, the city council adopted three ordinances in 2003, thereby permanently establishing a large portion of potentially commercial properties to be required to develop only spa-oriented businesses, virtually freezing out anything that would not be devoted to hot water activities.

The multiple ordinances (V-S; V-S-V & V-S-C) effectively disenfranchised several hundred property owners from the use of their property as originally intended, causing a firestorm of protests and demand letters.

In 2003 I was asked to pursue alternative uses by one of my clients, as he owns 2.3 acres in the V-S-C zone, which was originally subdivided into eleven single family lots. But by virtue of the zoning,   potential development has been effectively eliminated for many years to come, if ever. As a result of my efforts, I have a massive file of documents & letters obtained from city records which one day may serve a useful purpose, but as yet we have been unable to get the city to allow any development to take place on the site. In the meantime, I have shared the documents with appraisers and attorneys who are seeking remedies from the city for their respective clients.

If nothing else, the VSC Ordinance which was hotly contested at the time virtually sealed the fate of any hope the city might have had in bringing traditional commercial businesses into some core areas of the city. My opinion is that the entire VSC Ordinance should be changed to better adapt to the realities of commercial development to rectify this.

Topping this, Mayor Weyuker's legacy to his shining city on a hill was his ten-year battle against the valley's MSHCP initiative, one of the largest environmental undertakings in the United States, and a monument to conservation as well as energy generation. Calling supporters "Lizard Lovers" and "Tree Huggers" Weyuker created the enmity of all the other cities in the valley and the Coachella Valley Association of Governments, (CVAG) thereby costing the city more than a million dollars in fines and fees to get into the conservancy, once a new mayor and city manager took charge.

The official document below details the negative machinations caused by the city's misguided leadership referring to Desert Hot Springs as "the problem child" in the valley. Not a good thing for a community seeking recognition as and international anything. (*See: Issues controversies PP 103*)

Coachella Valley Multiple Species Habitat Conservation Plan

Scott Ibaraki

May 29, 2007 ... Desert Hot Springs is the problem child in the mix for the Coachella Valley *MSHCP.*

The Coachella Valley Multiple Species Habitat Conservation Plan (CVMSHCP) is a large-scale plan attempting to cater to both sides of the policy coin. With the large amount of growth in the Riverside County area of California estimated for the coming years, the Coachella Valley Association of

Governments(CVAG) is working as the lead agency to protect and conserve over 240,00 acres of land and 27 plant and animal species while also encouraging a balanced growth initiative to promote "opportunities for recreation, tourism, and job growth. The idea is to issue take permits for approved areas for developers to save them time and money in environmental considerations. The take permit cost will measure at about $5,300 per acre in exchange for streamlined permission to build. The money would be used to buy property in conserved areas to complete the reserve system planned for conservation. Not yet finalized, the public comment period has recently concluded and the outcome of the plan is looking favorable.

Chronology:

1940s and 1950s – Coachella Valley experiences rapid growth – construction of residential country clubs and recreational resorts

1970s – average growth rate of Plan Area Growth Forecast according to Southern California Association of Governments Regional Transportation Plan: a little over 4.1%

1980s - average growth rate of Plan Area: a little over 5.8%

1990s - average growth rate of Plan Area: a little over 3.4%

1994 - Coachella Valley Mountains Conservancy (CVMC) preparing scoping study recommending a Multiple Species Habitat Conservation Plan.

Late 1995, Early 1996 – CVAG, affected cities (Cathedral City, Coachella, La Quinta, Palm Springs, etc), County of Riverside, USFWS, CDFG, BLM, USFS, and NPS sign planning agreement to initiate planning effort

Late 1996, Early 1997 – Participating parties of the panning agreement approve amendment claiming plan will meet

132

requirements of Natural Community Conservation Planning Act, California ESA, and the Federal ESA. Agree to prepare a Natural Community Conservation Plan (Plan).

1998 – Public Forums held with PAG

1999 - Public Forums held with PAG

2000 - Public Forums held with PAG

June 19, 2000 – CEQA Notice of Preparation

June 28, 2000 – Notice of Intent published by USFWS in Federal Registrar – identified participants, gave detailed summary of proposed actions and planned species protections

2000s estimated growth rate of Plan Area: 145,000 new people between 2000-2020, (more than total population of Plan Area in 1980) doubling population by 2020 to make about 460,000 residents. 2030 to 2040 estimated million more new people.

November 5, 2004-March 7, 2005 – Original Public Comment Period (90 day)

February 2006 – Final EIR/EIS prepared

Early 2006 – The CVMSHCP and Final EIR/EIS released for local jurisdiction approval.

June 2006 – City of Desert Hot Springs rejects Plan. Subsequently, CVAG Executive Committee removes Desert Hot Springs as a Permittee of the Plan and revises Plan

May 29, 2007 –Public Comment Period for recirculated Draft CVMSHCP closes

Introduction:

The CVMSHCP is a regional conservation plan comprising of close to 1.14 million acres. There are a number of Permittees taking part in the plan including eight cities, Riverside County, CVAG, and various water and public land control agencies. The local Permittees joined forces to created the Coachella Valley Conservation Commission to work to implement the plan. The BLM, NPS, and USFS who control a significant portion of public land in the Plan area would participate through Cooperative Agreements. The Plan focuses on balanced growth with three main points: (1) Conserve the specified 240,000+ acres of open space, (2) Protect the 27 plant and animal species in the area which include many state and federally threatened and endangered species, and (3) advance various transportation and infrastructure improvement projects to improve the region's quality of life all the while promoting enhanced opportunities for recreation, tourism, and job growth.

Background:

Since the 1970s, the Coachella Valley and the greater Riverside County have been growing steadily and recently, it has been estimated that there will be an increase of over 600,000 in the next 13 years. This, along with the wealth of endangered, threatened, rare, and sensitive species in the area called for a comprehensive plan to make sure the two interests of development and conservation could presumably go hand in hand. As the once extensive Southern California landscape shrinks, so do the habitats an environments in which species called their homes. With the development pressure increasing, conflicts between landowning interests and State and Federal regulatory agencies for environmental protection have increased as well. The Plan has garnered considerable attention and many local, state, and national entities have their put their chips on the table.

Project Description:

Similar to many other projects, the CVMSHCP is a thorough, multi jurisdictional plan focusing on meeting Federal and

State laws for endangered and threatened species as well as protecting rare and sensitive species in the area. Overall, the ultimate achievement would be to integrate sustained ecological diversity while at the same time symbiotically cooperating with the rapidly urbanizing Coachella Valley. The MSHCP and the Implementation Agreement with it allows Permittees in the Plan to manage land use following the guidelines of "Plan Conservation Goals and Objectives," all the while upholding a sustainable and dynamic environment for economic development in the region of interest.

Proposed Action:

For full implementation of the Plan, the proposed amount of time for the Monitoring Program, the Management Program, Adaptive Management, and ongoing administration is estimated at 75 years in all. To acquire all the Permittee obligated land, the projection of time is at about 30 years. The Plan would create a MSHCP Reserve System and a thorough and detailed adaptive implementation program. By having an integrated approach to planning for the specified species, the Plan would also streamline development review processes to create predictable mitigation requirements making for more certainty for developers and saving everyone money with the larger scale process. Also, the joint EIR/EIS were prepared to comply with CEQA, NEPA, and the Federal and State Environmental Species Acts providing the potential environmental impacts that could result from MSHCP implementation.

Scoping:

Since 1994, a semblance of a planning effort for the MSHCP has been occurring. A scoping study was prepared by CVAG and CVMC to be publicly considered following by a preparation of a Memorandum of Understanding (MOU) which was considered at many public hearings of CVAG and the CVAG Executive Committee. It was fully executed in early 1996 and amended in 1997 to prepare for an NCCP.

After the MOU, a Project Advisory Group (PAG) was created employing a diverse range of contributors including the CVWD, University of California, Sierra Club, Building Industry Association, Nature Conservancy, and many others. Meetings for the PAG are always open to the public and encourage the public to come and comment on matters. In 2000, there were three important scoping meetings with the public. The first two were broadly focused on the scope and content of the EIR/EIS. The third though focused exclusively on the issue of hiking and biking trails and the affects the Plan will have on them.

Environmental Impacts:

There are 15 main categories where environmental impacts can occur. They include: (1) Land Use Compatibility, (2) Transportation, Traffic, and Circulation, (3) Soils and Geology, (4) Mineral, Energy, and Timber Resources, (5) Agricultural Lands and Activities, (6) Hydrology and Water Quality, (7) Biological Resources, (8) Cultural Resources and Native American Concerns, (10) Park Trails and Recreation, (11) Air Quality, (12) Noise, Visual / Scenic Resources, (13) Utilities / Public Services and Facilities, (14) Socio-Economic Resources: Population, Housing & Employment, (15) Environmental Justice and Children. Under the Environmental Summary Matrix in the EIR/EIS, for the Proposed Action or preferred alternative specification, every single area of impact is listed as "Less than Significant." In the extra ecological protection specifications, there are "Potentially Significant" impacts listed for Land Use Compatibility, Transportation, Traffic, and Circulation, and Agricultural Lands and Activities, but never do impacts grow worse than "Potentially Significant," a good omen and sign for the success of the CVMSHCP.

Issues/ Controversies:

Desert Hot Springs is the problem child in the mix for the Coachella Valley MSHCP. They were the only city oppose the plan the first time the EIR/EIS was circulated primarily because they possess two areas that the Plan wants to annex for conservation. Instead of conservation on mind, the city of Desert Hot Springs has money on its with the aspirations of building a massive golf resort on the annex land in question. If they had participated with the plan, they could have potentially earned the right for take permits for building projects in some habitats, a special feature of the CVMSHCP to help outline where builders could work without costly environmental delays, yet they didn't want a part in it.

After Desert Hot Springs wasted the CVMSHCP's time and money by asking to be removed from the Permittee list during the approval period, the CVMSHCP was forced to revise its Plan and EIR/EIS and just recently finished its now second public comment period. Desert Hot Springs debacle with its proposed Palmwood project is a whole other story which is still not solved, yet the Center for Biological Diversity and the Sierra Club both filed suit to challenge the approval by the Riverside LAFCO for annexation of the lands for the resort claiming a violation of CEQA in the annexation of the land and that the project would "really throw(s) the regional planning and the habitat planning in the Coachella Valley into a tailspin.

Other controversies included hikers' concerns for their beloved trails. They were scared that the development and conservation together might close out a number of their favorite trails. After much scoping and public comment, the CVMSHCP concluded through its EIR/EIS that for park trails and recreation, in proposed actions or alternatives, "Less than Significant" impacts would occur, bringing peace of mind to the recreationally minded.

Alternatives:
For the category of alternatives, there are five alternatives for the CVMSHCP to work with. First off, there is the Proposed Action/Preferred Alternative A which would establish a Reserve System, create conservation areas, and do everything the Plan hopes to do once approved. The second alternative is the Public Lands Alternative where there would be no new land acquisition making for a difficult task in conserving whole

landscapes. A third alternative is the Core Habitat with Ecological Processes

Alternative which would stress core habitat areas to conserve. The fourth alternative is the Enhanced Conservation Alternative. This would essentially be the same as the proposed action alternative, but result in less take making it slightly more difficult for developers and agriculturalists. The fifth and final alternative is No Action/No Project alternative which would result in no Plan and no permits issued. All developing projects would entail their own authorizations and the processes would still protect the species yet cost everyone more money due to the long periods of consideration and vast amounts of paper and time wasted on the same issues.

Important Scientific Data/ Use of science:
A Scientific Advisory Committee (SAC) provided the scientific data needed to substantiate the biological issues in the EIR/EIS and the Plan. The SAC consisted of biologist from the BLM, NPS, USFS, and the University of California, among a few others. For GIS services, staff from the BLM, CVAG, CVMC and the County took and processed much information for the project.
The SAC, working with many other experts in conservation biology, examined a large amount of species and created an ecosystem-based conservation program for the necessary species and habitats to be included in the Plan. Collecting the best available baseline data and information to work with took great precedence with scrupulous remote sensing and surveying of the habitats through GIS. Best available science was used to make all conclusions and estimates in the EIR/EIS.

Documents:

EIR, IA, and relevant information can be found at:
http://www.cvmshcp.org/index.htm

Geographic Area:

An extensive low elevation valley situated in a northwest-southeast direction, the Coachella Valley borders the western area of the Sonoran Desert. Approximately 100 miles inland from Los Angeles, The Valley is located on the eastern portion of the gargantuan Riverside County. The Plan area attempts to maximize the incorporation of the Coachella Valley watershed, but cuts some out due to its spread outside of the CVAG boundaries. These decisions were made to avoid extra complexities of jurisdiction. The entire area contains close to 1.2 million acres where 69,000 of the acres belong to Indian reservations not included in the Plan.

****

That fight caused the city and its inhabitants no end of civic embarrassment as well as a sizeable debt yet to be paid to CVAG. But the mayor's constituents loved him. There goes that Vortex again.

Following are some of my many articles (more than 300) which were published in the local papers at the time. I was on a different page than the mayor, but I was upbeat and hopeful for the future:

A 2005 review of DHS from a newcomer's perspective...

And prognostications for our future

January, 2006

Well here we are on the threshold of a new year. What will it bring for our community?

DHS can overcome the negatives of the past once it believes in itself by shedding its low self esteem by assuming the mantle of a vibrant, growing community ready to address the many challenges with intelligence and resolve. To do this, we must work together with our leaders, new and old to form a real plan for the future.

Will our newly formed city council work together to attain goals reflected by the electorate in the recent election? Will the recall effort succeed or fail? Will the political dust settle, even as the dust and sand blows across our fair city in violation of PM10?

Will a new, **competent** city manager be engaged to lead the administration out of its current moribund state of floating without a leader at the helm? Will the backlog of lawsuits be settled or fought in the courts, either way impacting our limited treasury? Will any of our leaders "wake up stupid" thereby creating more than our share of negative press? Will our city council continue to bow and scrape to home builders while ignoring the need for developing real sales tax revenue for the city?

Will a medical health center become a reality rather than a dream? Will Palm Drive renovation, become a priority of the new council? Will the proposed building of a new civic center be shelved until all of our streets are repaired, rebuilt and lined with sidewalks? Will the Valley Breeze Editor/Publisher become a bit less biased against our new Mayor Bias and a little more even-handed in his presentation of local news?

The questions elucidated above of course, constitute the community sensitive issues I have observed since arriving on the scene in early January of 2005 and immersing myself in the community. Not all of the issues are here, but those of significant importance to me and many of us believers in the future of Desert Hot Springs are.

Having just returned from three weeks of touring the countries of Holland, Germany and Austria, saturating myself in the history and architectural and building marvels dating

140

back to the year 300 BC, helps to put things in perspective as to where we are in DHS in the grand scheme of things and where we might go if we put our minds to the task.

As an example, it took a little over 600 years to build the Church of Saint Stephens in Vienna which is still used every day by local worshipers. That's almost three times as long as the USA has been in existence and ten times as long since Cabot Yerxa settled here. As young as the community of Desert HoT Springs is, it's entitled to a few mistakes. Not repeating them is the key.

The current assets of Desert Hot Springs far outweigh its liabilities in my view, that's one of the reasons my wife and I decided to make our home here. One can look at the proverbial "half empty" or "half full glass" when calculating what the future holds for DHS. I choose to view the future from the half full point of view.

Just before leaving on our trip, I had the good fortune of attending three extremely informative Symposia on the subject of growth and planning for the future of Coachella Valley, sponsored by CVAG. The issues covered were transportation, more effective community planning to attain balanced growth, and the need for encouraging economic development for the entire valley.

Desert Hot Springs is on the cusp of these issues and it is in the best place geographically to address them, in the view of the panelists and moderators of these three sessions. I agree.

The details of the how, what and why, are too numerous to incorporate in this article. However, the premise is what I hope to impart here.

A good way to start, and in keeping with the season of making New Year resolutions, would be for every citizen to resolve to attend Planning Commission and City Council meetings as often and consistent as possible. Make your wishes known, and volunteer for committee assignments in which you have interest and or expertise.

The future of Desert Hot springs is in our hands. Let's make it a good one.

Happy New Year!

Yours for better government

Bill Effinger

****

Building boom or land rush?

March, 2006

Beginning in mid 2003 and continuing, Desert Hot Springs has approved 24 subdivisions, representing 11,160 new homes. During the same time frame, several of the approved subdivisions have been resold to other developers and construction of homes has yet to commence on any of these projects. Some of these approved developments currently lack an adequate water supply.

Each time an approved subdivision is sold to a new builder, the cost of the homes planned to be built in the project will increase incrementally in proportion to the rise in the base land cost. When this happens, the housing affordability gap widens for buyers, resulting in a slower build-out/sell-out and the production of the needed "rooftops" which commercial/retail developers require to bring commerce and revenue to the city.

There are also 23 additional subdivisions in some stage of the city's approval process representing approximately another 2,372 homes and five courses projected to be constructed at some time in the future.

With everything in our economy pointing to a slow down in housing, it would seem that what is really going to happen in DHS is continued land speculation with very little in the way of new housing being built in proportion to the number of homes already approved.

Large tracts of land that have been mass-graded and remain sitting dormant of construction activity are a challenge to the environment and public safety, adding costs to the city without compensating revenues.

Why then should the city council and planning commission continue to approve more housing projects than what can be delivered in the near future? Assuming the last two years are an example of the absorption rate for new housing in DHS, (about 1500) there is more than a 15-year supply of approved lots. Taking the assumption further, there will not be sufficient "rooftops" to support any meaningful retail development and companion revenue for between five and ten years.

What then will the city do to fund required community services and public safety for the new homes built and occupied but not   yet enough to spur retail, commercial and industrial development revenue?

These important issues should be at the top of our new City Manager's agenda as she takes stock of the city's assets and liabilities while assuming control, and none too soon.

Yours for better government

Bill Effinger

****

DHS Economic Chaos

June, 2006 Desert Sun

Desert Hot Springs' poor planning has resulted in economic chaos for the continuously struggling 43-year old community. But a loosing proposition for DHS could be a boon to Palm Springs, now wrestling with growth issues and proposed high rise developments in its core village. A merger of these two cities could save both of their problems.

The Desert Hot Springs city council majority beginning with former Mayor Weyuker and continuing with the current group have consistently voiced their mantra of "We need roof tops" whenever the issue of the need for sustaining sales tax revenue sources to balance fiscal needs of the community is raised.

The myopic policy of focusing almost solely on home builder impact fees for revenue while ignoring the need to develop commercial and industrial projects has created a financial crises for DHS which will be extremely difficult if not impossible to overcome. One result is more than 20 management and recently hired city staff are loosing their jobs along with some police mid-management personnel. Contract services will be the rule of the day for code enforcement, engineering and planning functions due to lack of funds.

Worse, based on new home sales for the past four years, there is by any measure a fifteen year supply of graded lots within approved subdivisions and the myriad infill lots in central Desert Hot Springs. Most of the impact fees have dried up to a slow crawl, down by almost 50 percent at this writing according to city staff.

City records indicate there are 14,334 lots either fully approved or in the process, not counting the proposed Palmwood project. That would add an additional 1,268 lots, extending the projected annual absorption to a 16-year supply. The past three years' annual gross residential sales is 815 homes in Desert Hot springs. As of this month, that rate is questionable, as sales in DHS are off sixty percent for the year according to Stewart Title Company records. Add to this number another 3,000-plus infill lots in central DHS and there is a 20-year supply—truly a marketing nightmare for home builders and the city at large.

The issue of fully graded subdivisions with no building activity raises other concerns, such as blowing dust. There are 3,830 fully graded lots in western DHS contributing to blowing dust quite often exceeding AQMD PM-10 standards prompting several citizens to complain to staff and council members frequently. As new graded lots are added to the existing projects, the problem will be exacerbated.

Blinded by false hope of city coffers being filled with never ending impact fees from overzealous developers, the city council and staff fell into the trap, basically giving away the farm with unrealistic development agreements. The Highlands project development (not one stick raised as yet) is not required to

provide a fire station until the 1000th home is completed can you imagine how long that will be? The much ballyhooed Skyborne project (where councilmember Hohenstein "forgot" he owned acreage adjacent, and former City Manager Hanson had the road paved to accommodate his property that he also "forgot" to mention when it came time to vote on the project

) was originally scheduled to build a fire house, but not until the 250th home is moved into. Sound familiar?

Now that DHS has rooftops planned twenty years into the future, half of them graded but not built on and new people moving into the homes that are completed, where will the money come from to pay for the police, fire, library and myriad other services required to maintain the community, improve parks and streets and take care of the senior population? Impact fees alone won't carry the burden, that's already been proven.

Sooner or later the new citizens of Desert Hot Springs will realize the more seasoned DHS residents have allowed the inmates to run the asylum. When that occurs, and it will, a new culture of leadership will emerge and rescue the city from itself. Then the idea of merging with our neighbor to the south might take hold.

A Palm Springs more than double its geographic size with an estimated 135,000 citizens, a College of the Desert, three new golf courses and thousands of acres of developable commercial and industrial land would be quite an entrance to Coachella Valley, not to mention residential land 1400 feet above the valley floor with spectacular views to offer the affluent residents. Several multi-million dollar homes already rest on DHS hilltops, with room for many more. The hot mineral water aquifers that traverse the upper reaches of the DHS landscape would add immeasurably to the tourists' appeal of an expanded Palm Springs.

Such a joining could bolster the resulting city economy, reduce the pressures for building high rises in central Palm Springs and improve police and fire protection for the combined cities, creating a synergy where one plus one would equal three in terms of administrative cost savings and improved services for both communities.

146

Desert Hot Springs schools are under the wing of the Palm Springs Unified School District, why not place the entire city under one umbrella? Or does that make too much sense?

****

Next are some responses to the above article published in the Desert Sun. I must have struck a cord with some of our readers, and I felt quite good about it. My son Kirk writes a regular opinion column for the North County Times, a San Diego newspaper covering North San Diego County and South Riverside County. His articles are always well done, but responses are rare, and we attribute that to the fact that people are pleased with what is happening locally.

When numerous well written responses are received on a given subject which is close to the hearts of the readers, the writer knows he/she is in the right zone of interest. Such seemed to be the case with the article: We agree with your article whole Hartley{sic}. We own two houses here in Desert Hot Springs and just moved into our new home on Skyline Drive. What are the next steps in getting rid of these bums in the city council? or what would be the procedure to start the process of dis incorporating the city?

Gary and Jeanne Gortz

Right on Bill. That was the smartest comments I have ever heard from anyone coming out of DHS in your article in the Desert Sun. It looks like DHS is headed for another bankruptcy. Is there any way you see to avoid it? Is the Multiple Species Plan dead in DHS or is there any chance or opportunity for DHS to still approve it???

Alan from Palm Springs

we are new people in DHS living in Paradise Springs and I have attended several city meetings where I know you have spoken...frankly I want to know if you would consider filling Bosworth seat or have you previously serve the city of DHS ? Our summer address is up in Big Bear and we read the local Desert Sun every once in a while via the internet....

Janet Cescato

In reading your article in this mornings paper I surely agree with your thoughts on Desert Hot Springs. I think the whole City Council should be fired and get some people in office that know what they are doing instead of fighting and back stabbing.

I also think they should disincorporate although I hate they would lose their on police dept. I do believe it has done a good job in slowing down crime in the area.

I own a small home in DHS that my son has been living in for the last 3 years and I want to see the area improve.

Thank you,

Rita Stuessel

Palm Desert,Ca.

Hi Bill, my name is Yolanda and I appreciate your opinions on Desert Hot Springs. I am considering moving out that way but not sure as to whether to buy a home in Desert Hot Springs or Palm Springs. The job will be in Palm Springs but I know the home prices are lower in Desert Hot Springs. From reading all the articles on how Desert Hot Springs is run, I am not impressed. In your opinion, which location would be better? How long have you lived in Desert Hot Springs?

Thanks

-Yolanda Dillinger

Dear Mr. Effinger:

I am so glad to know there is at least one person who thinks like I do here in DHS. Your article was thrilling to read as you presented many options that would help this poor city recover from years of abuse and stupidity. Wouldn't it be grand to fire the city council! Wouldn't it be wonderful to have a real governing body (the county Board of Supervisors)! And last but most preferable of all: wouldn't it be fabulous to get ourselves incorporated into Palm Springs!

I realize we are battling extremely low rate politicians and it won't be easy to make any changes for years to come, but please know I would love to help in any campaign that would result in any of the above. I too was sad to see Mr. Bosworth go as he was the only council member who actually replied to my constant queries about the poor decision making and like you stated he seemed to be the only one who had a logical mind. Knowing that complaining isn't the answer, I wish to state that I would love to be a part of city government and have tried to speak at council meetings but was met with blank stares and an insult from then council member Will Pieper. I have a low tolerance for uninformed, self-important fools and I feel I would cause considerable infighting in a council that needs no more problems.

That being said, this is what I mean: I live around the corner from our mayor and it is going to be very hard for me not to ask him face-to-face why he consistently pays his long overdue debts at the last minute. What a waste of everybody's time. Is he running one of those deals where he has the $$ but is too cheap to part with it until he has to, or is he really the idiot he seems to be? I would like to know where this last minute $$ comes from and why he doesn't take care of his responsibilities. So you see I would end up asking too

149

many rude questions and be very unpopular with people I don't want to spend any time with anyway.....

Thank you for listening. Once again, any help you need for great changes in this city, do sign me up.

Sincerely,

Alandra Welch; 12500 Highland Avenue

****

The people were listening but the leadership wasn't. They of course, knew better than the people who elected them, on what was good for their city. Continuing to try and get the attention of leadership, I published the following summary analysis for everyone to see, hoping when the numbers were put in front of them this way, it would sink in that the city was going to be in trouble if they didn't recruit commercial development:

Summary Forecast Analysis of DHS Planning & Development

08/11/06

50 Residential projects projects	12 commercial/industrial
Total acreage = 4,733	Total Acreage = 149
Total # of Lots = 14,334	Industrial lots = 187= Graded = 0
Smallest = 4 Homes = 0	Commercial Projects = 8 Graded
Largest = 3,700 Homes	

Graded = 3,830 lots

Grading underway = 2783

Total Graded and underway = 6,613

Number of existing approved residential in-fill lots (Est.) 3,000

Total number graded/underway and in-fill lots = 9313

Historical Rate of DHS Absorption all SF (last four years) = (03-573)

(04-939) (05-931) (Yr to date-275)

(Projected for all of 06-550)

Projected yrs graded lot supply = 10 year supply @ 900 p/yr

Projected yrs lot supply including pending = 15 year supply @ 900 p/yr

****

I appeared before the council in open session, presenting these figures. But the only thing the council and management could see was dollar signs next to permit fees. They didn't seem to want to know or think about the economic future or orderly development of the city.

The mayor wanted to put those dollars in the bank so they could point to it in the coming election and tell the constituents what a good job they were doing. They didn't want to know what this all meant. I think it's called "burying your head in the sand?" and while doing so being sucked into the sink hole of unintended consequences. To that end, the best (or worst as it may be) was yet to come.

A fateful choice

We were about to become citizens of Desert Hot Springs through a series of decisions we made, while wanting to change our lifestyle, and Diana's desire to change her place of employment, ending her long and tedious every-day drive to and from Torrey Pines in San Diego; a one-hour drive each way.

My initial research into the potential of Desert Hot Springs and the related building boom underway was enticing to me and I felt there was opportunity for me in my field of land acquisition and pre-planning of commercial development. That, coupled with the urging of Diana's good friend Cheryl, who had just purchased a home there and was touting the growth opportunities was enough to point us in that direction for our next adventure.

We both love new adventures and new places and with the building boom going on in the Imperial Valley, the move at the time seemed like it would be a good one. The adventure didn't quite work out the way we planned it, but I have no regrets. Well, maybe a couple.

Four: Our introduction to Desert Hot Springs

Diana and I had placed a deposit on a home being built in Desert Hot Springs in September, 2003 as an investment for our future. Diana's friend Cheryl had purchased a home and was living there at the time and it looked like there was opportunity for me. Working with developers and cities, buying land and processing the plans through departments to obtain project approvals and entitlements as a consultant, is what I have been doing since leaving the active role of running a major subsidiary of a publicly held development company.

Soon after Diana gave notice she was leaving the Torrey Pines based Institute of Immunology, I was visiting the planning department in DHS, and noticed a job posting for an Administrative Assistant/Grant Writer to work with the Assistant City Manager. Following my norm of, "When opportunity knocks you should be listening," I grabbed an application and brought it home for Diana to view.

Diana wanted some down time before going to a new job, which was understandable. The house we had a deposit on in Desert Hot Springs was delayed because of some property-line problems the developer was having with the Mission Lakes Country Club HOA, adjacent to the new subdivision. So even if Diana were to get the position, we didn't have a place to live. But, being the responsible person she is, she filled out the application and mailed it in anyway.

A few weeks later, Diana was called for an interview. After the interview, she talked to Cheryl, and on the chance that the job was offered, Cheryl said we could stay in her home during the week, as she was only there on weekends, still working in San Diego. Diana was offered the job. So now it was decision time. Doing what I do, I can work anywhere, but I did see opportunity in the entire Coachella Valley and all neighboring cities of Desert Hot Springs where I could apply my talents.

Always up for a new adventure, Diana decided to take the job, so we decided to rent out our home in San Marcos when the new home was finished, then move to Desert Hot Springs. Meanwhile, we accepted Cheryl's hospitality to live in her house during the week and return to San Marcos on weekends until our home was finished.

Diana was hired by the city to be Administrative Assistant to the Deputy City Manager, John Soulliere in March of 2005, and several months before our home was scheduled to be finished.

At the same time, I was writing my regular column for the local paper, *The Valley Breeze*, to get my name out there for my consulting business, which added to our getting socially involved in the community.

Being publicly critical of how a city is being run when your wife is working for that city as an assistant to one of the people managing the city is a good way to cause problems. I was happy, Diana was not; politics is anathema to her. I was inconsiderate of her feelings in the matter and blinded by my zealous pursuits, for which I have since apologized, but remain ashamed for my actions.

———

Plunging into the brewing political cauldron of Desert Hot Springs:

Almost two-years before moving to the city, I found myself involved in nearly every organization in town. Buzz Gamble, publisher of *The Valley Breeze* sponsored me in the Rotary Club. Councilman Hank Hohentstein invited me into his "inner circle" of his supporters, most all of them developers with projects in the city. Walt Luce of Meyer/Luce Development Corporation was the quasi "leader" of that group. An old guard group of "King makers" headed by Richard Cromwell, III invited me to take part in their weekly behind closed-doors political group meetings in the miracle Springs Resort Hotel, as they chose and groomed potential candidates for the city council. I had become an "insider" while living outside. I made some lasting friendships in that group, and a few enemies. Such is politics.

My first visit to the Desert Hot Springs Planning Department revealed 41 approved or pipeline residential projects, containing a combined total of more than 15,000 residential lots, which was staggering by any measurement. I was stunned. Then I was told there was a scheduled "visioning meeting" to discuss the creation of a new General Plan. I attended all of those evening meetings, commuting from my home in North San Diego County to Desert Hot Springs, a round trip of some 250 miles.

Sometime during this period, Mayor Matt Weyuker took ill with a debilitating illness that left him severely speech impaired, requiring everyone to strain in an effort to understand him. None the less, he insisted on running the meetings (regular and workshops) which was painful to watch and participate in, making the already too long meetings all that much longer. There was no question of his dedication, stamina and desire to serve, but making everyone suffer because of it was, I felt, a little over the top, and quite difficult to conduct council business.

———

We found Desert Hot Springs to be a very friendly place:

155

We made friends quickly, even as we were commuting home to San Marcos on weekends, staying in our friend Cheryl's home until ours was finished and we could move there permanently.

Cheryl's sister Stephanie and her husband Jim were living in the Mission Lakes Country Club area and they introduced us to Lee and Chrissy, both were professors, one retired and the other teaching at the College Of the Desert (COD) as its known. Chrissy is an outstanding cook and a whirlwind in everything she does. I'm sure she's an outstanding teacher as well. Lee is a car buff, a great host, and between them, they introduced us to many fine people in the Valley.

We continued to be surprised at the openness of our neighbors and new friends as we began to insert ourselves into the community. Reading an article by a very famous writer, such as what follows, also helped give us a good feeling about our new neighbors and friends.

Paul Krassner, like his friend Gorge Carlin, and unlike many of us, doesn't take life too seriously, a lesson I could do well to emulate. Quite often I am shocked to find that the world will actually go right on spinning, no matter what I may be doing to help it along at the time. Krassner's description of Desert Hot Springs is a different and less critical look at the city, quite unlike much of what is contained on the preceding or following pages. Krassner's article does give us a possible clue to the dilemma facing those who like me, would like Desert Hot Springs to enter the 21st Century. That clue resides in two words in the opening statement: "splendid isolation".

Quite possibly, the number of transplants from the "big cities" who want the city to remain arcane; rough hewn; quaint and isolated, far outnumber those of us with the opposite view. This has been Diana's take since we immersed ourselves into the community. (I may have just had an epiphany).

It's not hip, but it's heaven

DESERT COOL | Where I Live by Paul Krassner

Desert Hot Springs provides something Venice never did: splendid isolation along with its quirky, small-town vibe.

February 10, 2005 | Paul Krassner

During THE FOUR YEARS and 10 weeks that my wife, Nancy, and I have lived in Desert Hot Springs, we've observed the evolution of a small town into a burgeoning city.

One of the early signs was the opening of a Thai restaurant. So many customers showed up on the first night that it ran out of food. The latest sign is that the rumor of a Starbucks being on the way has turned out to be true.

In our neighborhood, the city has just put in a sewer system and paved the roads. On the main street, Palm Drive, traffic lights have replaced the honor system at a couple of intersections. A UPS branch recently opened. A medical center is on the cusp of pure fantasy and planning stage. And, to quote the front-page headline in the current issue of a gung-ho conservative biweekly tabloid, the Valley Breeze, "Desert Hot Springs Police Add New Taser X-26 Weapon to its Arsenol [sic]."

The population was 7,000 when Nancy first visited here in 1978. Now it's 20,000. There are 40 hotels and spas that

157

pump the odorless, healing mineral water out of the ground at 120 to 180 degrees. And last year, the cold water, which is filtered through sand several hundred feet below the hot water aquifer, won the Gold Medal for Best Tasting Municipal Water at the Berkeley Springs International Water Tasting competition. We no longer buy bottled water.

Our move from Venice Beach to Desert Hot Springs -- from the motion of the ocean to the magnificence of the mountains -- was prompted by the fact that the rent in Venice kept going up exponentially, a 7% increase every year for 16 years. Then we discovered that in Desert Hot Springs, anybody could get a mortgage if they had a pulse. We had never owned a house before. Now we were ecstatic, owning our own home and garage-- even the car had its own room -- yet we were simultaneously aware of the preposterousness of "owning" land.

We'd been coming here occasionally on weekends since 1985, so we knew about the intense heat, but we've learned to appreciate air-conditioning. We loved the isolation -- nobody drives to Desert Hot Springs by accident -- and the sparse traffic.

There was only one movie theater here, and that building is now a church, but there are art houses as well as cineplexes in the more ostentatious cities, Palm Springs and Palm Desert, and on the way we pass streets named after such celebrities as Frank Sinatra, Dinah Shore, Bob Hope, Gerald Ford and, most recently, Kirk Douglas. "You don't have to be dead to have a street named after you," Nancy said, "but it helps."

We made the move shortly after I published the final issue of the Realist, a satirical countercultural journal I launched in 1958. (Although when People magazine called me "father of the underground press," I immediately demanded a paternity test.)

I still write columns and articles, but my main obsession these days is working on a long-awaited (by me) first novel. Writing fiction enables one to have imaginary friends without being considered crazy.

We were fortunate to have real friends who had already moved here. We met Lane and Carol Sarasohn in 1987, when Lane, Carol and I were writers, and Nancy shot mini-documentaries for a short-lived series on Fox, the "Wilton North Report."

A few years later, Lane and I were writers on the syndicated "Ron Reagan Show." Now, with his two co-editors in Los Angeles, he produces "Ironic Times," a weekly online satirical publication, from his home in the desert.

One afternoon, Lane suddenly felt guilty about not having a regular job. He went for an interview with the owner of the Desert Hot Springs Spa Hotel and the Miracle Springs Hotel, Mike Bickford, known by his employees as Mr. B. Within a few months, Lane became his chief assistant and troubleshooter.

Every month, I go with him to the Mayor's Breakfast. After reciting the Pledge of Allegiance, everybody stands up and, one by one, introduces themselves. Here a chiropractor, there a Realtor. My favorite is an undertaker who says the same thing each time: "I'll be the last one in town to let you down."

Lane later became general manager of Miracle Springs and served two terms as president of the Chamber of Commerce, but before all that he gave my first comedy album, "We Have Ways of Making You Laugh," to the hotel's event organizer, and she arranged for me to perform at the Desert Hot Springs Chamber of Commerce officers and board of directors installation dinner.

According to the alternative paper the Desert Post Weekly,
"In the extraordinary case of Desert Hot Springs, there is a
convergence of five energy vortexes meeting in one place. In
general, people are drawn to energy vortexes and power
spots in search of enlightenment and inner peace; they are
attracted by the invisible force and its therapeutic effects."

The paradox of my own peculiar spiritual path is that I'm
an unbeliever who engages in constant dialogue with the
deity I don't believe in. As a stand-up comic, I always say,
"Please, God, help me do a good show," and then I
always hear the voice of God boom out, "Shut up, you
superstitious fool!"

Desert Hot Springs had changed its official slogan from
"People, Pride and Progress" -- no, it wasn't a multiple-
choice question -- to "Clearly Above the Rest," and so it
came to pass that the theme of this particular dinner
would be Heaven. Th waiters and waitresses would be
dressed as angels. The stage would be overlain with a
cottony white cloud, enhanced by a fog machine. There
would be a blond angel playing the harp.

At 7 p.m., the salad would be served. At precisely 7:15, a
clatter of pots and pans would be heard, and then I would be
thrown out of the kitchen, directly into that heavenly scene.
Oh, yes, and I would be dressed as the devil, who had been
kicked out of heaven.

I had never played a character before, but I rented a devil's
costume -- black shirt, red pants, bow tie, jacket, cape, tail
and horns, a silver three-prong pitchfork -- which I donned in
a restroom for the staffers behind the banquet hall at Miracle
Springs. I looked in the mirror, pulled my hair into a point on
my forehead and said -- to the image of Satan -- "Please, God,
help me do a good show." I may have been the
personification of evil, but for an instant it felt like God and

the devil were in perfect harmony, until I heard the voice of God boom out, "You must be kidding!"

I proceeded to conduct a one-devil roast of various local leaders in the audience whose eternal souls I had previously purchased, revealing how I had kept my part of each deal. I admitted my role in getting the president of the chamber of commerce reelected and confessed that I had secured a green card for the police chief's undocumented Mexican nanny.

A court decision had required the city to pay $3 million plus legal fees to real estate developers who unsuccessfully attempted a low-income housing project, but I disclosed that, in order to raise the money, I had set up a meth lab for the mayor.

Actually, in order to keep from going broke by paying the judgment, the city would later declare bankruptcy. However, the new slogan would not be changed to "Clearly Above the Credit Limit."

I exited heaven through the kitchen. In the corridor near the restroom, I overheard a woman say to her companion, "Right now, I would sell my soul for a massage." I surrendered to the impulse, walked behind her, tapped her on the shoulder and said, "Just sign right here." This was a unique moment, to be preserved in amber for posterity.

Nancy had advised me not to mention in this essay that I missed living in Venice, but in the very process of writing about Desert Hot Springs, I realize how much I've become attached to living here.

Paul Krassner is the author of "Murder at the Conspiracy Convention and Other American Absurdities," with an introduction by George Carlin, which can be found at paulkrassner.com.

Bill Effinger

****

Attitude can go a long way when we are assessing our lives and life styles. Newbies and adventurers that we were, we believed we wanted to be part of this new community and the life it promised. Opting to keep the original house we had made the deposit on as an investment and rent it, we purchased a custom home high up in the north-east quadrant of the city. Diana finally had a home that wasn't a "tract home" located on a great corner lot that looked out over the entire valley below, on a cul de sac named "La Paloma" my favorite Mexican song—what could be better? And like Paul Krassner, we felt like we were in heaven.

We were so impressed the day we moved in; our neighbor across the street brought us a bowl of fruit, two others came to introduce themselves and offer us plants from their garden. They made us feel at home almost before we had a home.

Three months later, August of 2005, found us hosting about 75 people in our new home to celebrate our anniversary and my birthday, which are both on the same day. Our guest list was a combination of friends from San Marcos and Desert Hot Springs, our neighbors and our family. Bruce Barrett, one of our neighbors and a well known sommelier in a posh Palm Springs eatery, brought some great wine as a housewarming gift.

Buzz Gamble, publisher of the local "Valley Breeze" and his wife (both have since passed away) attended, taking several pictures for the paper and we all had a great time. We purposely had not invited any of the people in political circles, wanting to keep the party light and friendly.

———

Getting politically connected

Council member Hank Hohenstein had sought me out shortly after I began writing for the Valley Breeze, and we became friendly. When I joined the Desert Hot Springs Rotary Club, several members invited us into their social circle, and Diana made some friends at the city through her work there. The Local Chamber of Commerce mixers expanded our social network, and soon we were quite busy socially.

Around this time, I volunteered to host a group of Hank Hohenstein's friends from Kyrgyzstan, where he and his wife had been making annual trips to teach English. The event was delightful and quite humorous as it turned out.

Hank and his wife arrived with their eight guests, among them two students who acted as their interpreters. When they arrived, the leader of the group presented me with a Felt, Tribal Chieftain's Hat, and a miniature Felt replica of a Yurt, which is a tent-like home used as the Nomadic herders travel. The Kyrgyzstan's by nature, are Tribal Nomads, traveling from place to place, carrying their Yurt-home with them on their camels. Our guests were city dwellers and business people, but they wanted to give a gift reminiscent of their heritage, and it was greatly appreciated.

A brief description of Kyrgyzstan and its people follows which was taken from a Google posting:

Kyrgyzstan

Kyrgyzstan is a real paradise for people who want to have a rest from civilization. The diversity of the landlocked, mountainous country is the essence of Kyrgyzstan and gives the country its unique identity. Along with its attractiveness as one of Asia's main tourist destination, it is best known for its mountains, nomads, horses, felt carpets and fermented milk.

Kyrgyzstan takes up an area of 198,500 square kilometers and is home to 5.2 million people. More than 93 percent of the country is mountainous and a quarter of it is covered with forests. Our country boasts breathtaking mountains, picturesque lakes and charming cities and towns that are full of culture and history. Kyrgyzstan is landlocked and situated on the crossroads of the Great Silk Road. Kyrgyzstan has 7 regions:

With over 80 species of mammals, 330 species of birds, 50 species of fish and about 30 of reptiles and amphibians, Kyrgyzstan has a rich and diverse wildlife.

Examples include: snow leopards, mountain goats, badgers, bears, camels, eagles, foxes, gophers, gulls, hawks, horses, lynxes, marmots, martens, porcupines, raven, sheep, Turkmen rats, wolves, woodpeckers, yaks.

Our people are famous for their great hospitality. Kyrgyz say, that all guest are sent from God.

That is way they are so kind with foreigners. They are always interested in your family, country and places where you have been. When you come even to a remote yurt in the mountains they will always treat you with food and drinks. Also Kyrgyz saved all their traditions and their unique nomadic culture.

There is a lot of virgin nature and in general people are careful with it with many efforts being undertaken to protecting the environment. As a result, you will enjoy our nature that is as untouched as many centuries ago.

The capital of Kyrgyzstan is Bishkek. Bishkek city became capital in 1978 year. Although Bishkek is just 130 years old - it is one of the greenest cities in Central Asia. Kyrgyzstan got its independence on August 31, 1991.

****

We had planned a Barbeque as Hank had suggested. I love spices and Barbequed anything, so we purchased twelve of the thickest pork chops we could find, and I marinated them the day before, adding the final touch of spices as I placed them on the grill

When Hank stepped up to help as I was placing the chops on the grill, he asked "what kind of meat is that?" My answer of course was "Pork".

"Why", I asked.

"Because they don't eat pork—it's against their religion—don't say anything, if they ask, it's steak".

"OK"

As we were well into the meal, two of the guests, who spoke reasonable English, remarked that they were so surprised and pleased at how good the meat tasted, and that it was the first meal since being in our country that was spiced as they like to do in their country.

Hank looked over at me with a sly grin and slightly red face, as I thanked our guests for the complement and moved on to another topic. Long after they left, Diana and I had a great laugh. So much for our understanding international culture.

————

Immersing myself into the community:

I became a member of the Coachella Valley Economic Partnership, (CVEP) sitting on five committees,

165

thereby expanding my network of business associates throughout the valley and ultimately becoming the city's representative for the Partnership. That is when I first met Rick Daniels who was Executive Director of CVEP at the time. My newspaper column was winning followers and glowing responses from readers.

The subject of many of my articles was the city's lack of retail, commercial and industrial properties and the need to promote that type of development to allow the city to sustain itself. Unfortunately, when the building boom began in the early 2000's, developers leaped into Desert Hot Springs with its relatively cheap land prices compared to the rest of Coachella Valley, buying up hundreds of acres. The city council in their apparent naivety, approved residential project after project, creating what some experts claimed would be a fifteen-year supply.

The Slippery Slope

From 1997 to 2007, there were ten city managers hired, fired or quit (Count them) Joe Guzzetta; Jerry Hanson: Corky Larson; Ann Marie Gallant; John Hensley; John Soulliere & Rick Daniels, the city manager as of the writing of this manuscript. During that same time period, there had been ten Police Chiefs, four Planning Directors and three City Attorneys.

With that kind of turnover in top management positions, it is no wonder the city suffered as it did. The Vortex was at work here, for sure.

Mayor Weyuker then tried to pull a fast one, and got caught up in a political firestorm in the process, stirring so much angst, that a recall petition was circulated to oust him from his job as mayor.

Broke Town's Mayor, Facing Furor, Bows to It

By CHARLIE LeDUFF
Published: July 05, 2003

DESERT HOT SPRINGS, Calif., July 1 — The mayor of this bankrupt hamlet high in the low desert insists that he is a misunderstood man.

He was not attempting a coup, he says, when he proposed extending his term for a year without a public vote. Contrary to what his detractors maintain, he was not trying to milk out an extra year of work because he is himself financially bankrupt, otherwise unemployed and generally unpopular.

The mayor, Matt Weyuker, says his motivation for trying to prolong his term and those of two allies on the City Council was to benefit democracy.

After a loud public outcry, however, Mr. Weyuker has backed down, telling a hostile crowd assembled at a Council meeting tonight that he will no longer pursue the matter, "as a result of the apparent misunderstanding of those in the community who tend to be distrustful of the motives of those of us who see the wisdom" in changing the law.

167

Desert Hot Springs is a poor town of some 15,000 people, just north of Palm Springs, that filed for bankruptcy protection a year and a half ago, in the wake of a multimillion-dollar court judgment favoring housing developers and the accumulation of some $4 million in unrelated debt. It then came to light that the mayor himself had filed for bankruptcy, after being dismissed from his administrative job at a local university and losing his nest egg in the market.

Just last year, an electorate grown disenchanted with what many see as the mayor's autocratic style of leadership rejected a ballot measure, proposed by Weyuker supporters, that would have changed the mayoral term to four years from two.

But a few weeks ago, Mr. Weyuker and the Council's two other Republicans joined to push through, on a 3-to-2 vote, legislation to add a year to their terms, due to lapse at the end of 2003.

The mayor said his motivation was to save the town some money by consolidating elections in an even-numbered year, a move that would have the salutary side effect, he said, of increasing voter turnout in local elections.

The citizenry revolted.

A recall campaign was undertaken by Mayor Weyuker's fellow Republicans. Even many of his former supporters said they believed that his true motive was personal finance: by prolonging his term, the mayor would keep his $1,200-a-month job and his health benefits, and qualify for a state pension.

"The mayor's desire for power has impaired his ability to count," said Alex W. Bias, chairman of the town's Economic Development Commission and a former member of the mayor's re-election committee. "The people told him no last year, and he tries to usurp their will."

As for saving the town money, a call to the office of the
Riverside County registrar found that not only would Desert
Hot Springs not save anything by consolidating its elections, it
would be charged about $2,500 to notify voters of the
change.

Yielding to the furor, the mayor tonight tabled a vote on the
term-extension bill, which had required passage a second
time for final adoption.

The recall campaign, meanwhile, has been dropped. And Mr.
Weyuker contemplates a run for re-election this November.

Crime was and remains the biggest problem in the city.

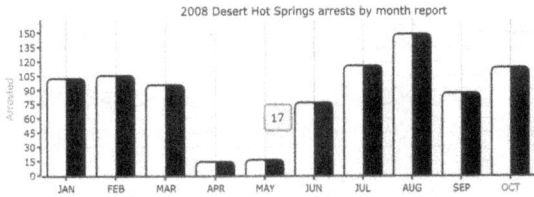

2008 Desert Hot Springs arrests by month report

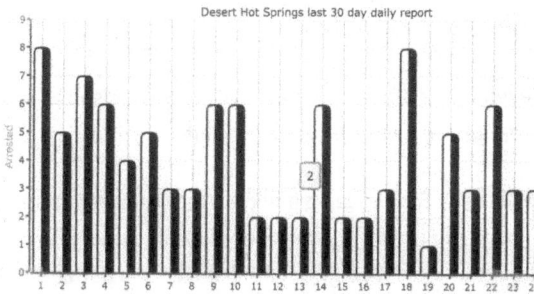

Desert Hot Springs last 30 day daily report

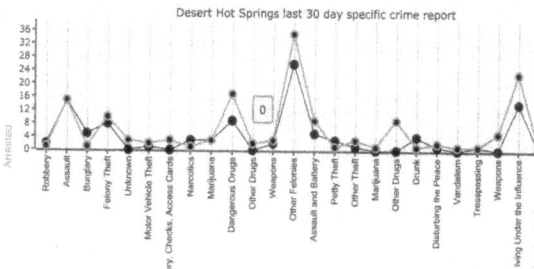

Desert Hot Springs last 30 day specific crime report

Unfortunately for the city, by the year 2009 crime and violence was on the increase as the article below shows:

411 parolees called DHS home before Friday's raid

12:01 AM, Mar. 28, 2009 |

Parolees have flocked to this city of more than 26,000 residents in recent decades due to an undersized police force, coupled with an inexpensive cost of living and wealthier communities nearby that can be targeted, officials said. Prior to Operation Falling Sun on Friday, there were 411 parolees in the ZIP code that includes Desert Hot Springs, City Manager Rick Daniels said.

Desert Hot Springs Police Chief Patrick Williams estimated more than 320 within city limits as of three months ago.

"We can't find any other community in the state that comes close to that," Daniels said.

Seven out of 10 parolees wind up back in prison as repeat offenders in California, Williams said.

Desert Hot Springs lacks any case-management programs that would help reduce the number of local repeat offenders, though the city's ad-hoc committee on the parolee crisis has recommended a multi-service facility that would offer those programs, and the idea has been adopted by the City Council.

The parolee influx "makes it miserable" for the city's residents, Daniels said.

As the nearby cities of Indio and Coachella have "locked down" recently on gangs there, many gang members have relocated to Desert Hot Springs, Daniels said.

170

Desert Hot Springs has up to seven separate gangs in the city and prior to Friday's events about 200 active members, Williams said.

The problem causes many Desert Hot Springs residents to live in fear, Daniels said.

"It's worse than intimidation. It's domestic terrorism," he said. He recounted a recent gang-related attack in which a house was hit by about 35 bullets — and nobody called 911 to alert local police.

Prior to Williams' arrival in 2006, the west Coachella Valley city boasted the highest rate per capita of major crimes — including rape, robbery, assault and theft — among all cities with less than 100,000 residents in San Bernardino and Riverside counties.

A history of violence

March 12, 2009
A man was fatally shot outside his home in the 68-200 block of Calle Las Tiendas. The victim was identified as Desert Hot Springs resident Edward Lopez, 28

Feb. 23, 2009
Desert Hot Springs resident Samuel Raye Cotton was killed at his home in the 68-100 block of Calle Azteca. Police say three people entered his home and he was shot in his the chest.

Feb. 4, 2009
Juan Pablo Munoz-Tovar, 33, a clerk at the Super One Food Store, was shot and killed at work. Desert Hot Springs resident Neil Agustus Edmund, 29, was arrested on suspicion of killing murder.

171

Oct. 10, 2008

A sheriff's deputy shot and killed Mario Mejia, 23, of Cathedral City, a car-jacking and attempted murder suspect, outside the Save A Pet animal shelter on 18th Avenue. Investigators were responding to a disturbance in the 67-400 block of Dillon Road shortly before the shooting. They found a the Mejia nearby at Grace Church on Bubbling Wells Road and chased him to the animal shelter, where he hid in a cat enclosure. He did not obey police orders and was shot.

Aug. 29, 2008

A Riverside County sheriff's deputy was shot in his face in an area south of Desert Hot Springs. Resident Javier Trani, 22, was arrested in the 15-000 block of Avenida Ramada on suspicion of shooting the deputy.

May 30, 2008

Standoff involving Anthony Paez and a second suspect. It began that evening after shots were exchanged between the occupants of a reportedly stolen car and pursuing police officers from multiple agencies, including California Highway Patrol officers. One suspect was killed during the pursuit. The standoff occurred in a house in the 16-200 block of Via El Rancho in unincorporated Riverside County just south of Desert Hot Springs.

May 28, 2008

Desert Hot Springs resident Francisco "Poncho" Salcido, 28, was arrested in the 66-200 block of First Street. Two days earlier, he was involved in a shoot-out with police, officials said. This led to a six-hour standoff outside an empty home. In an earlier search for Salcido, police went to his cousin's house in the 66-200 block of First Street in Desert Hot Springs, not far from the vacant house Salcido allegedly fled to after the shooting.

May 23, 2008
Two California Highway Patrol officers chasing a possibly stolen car were fired on by one of the fleeing car's occupants. The shooter, authorities believe, was Anthony Paez, a suspected member of a Desert Hot Springs-based gang.

****

With the above statistics, it is easy to see why Desert Hot Springs has a sullied name in Coachella Valley. Added to these figures is the perplexing history of strife within the police force itself and its multiple changes in leadership.

Prostitution is an ongoing problem in Desert Hot Springs, as in most cities, but a bit more open at times. "Ladies of the Night" walk the streets during the day trolling, we suspect for the transient parolee in need of the ladies' "services". Fights or worse, occasionally break out in a few of the less desirable Spas, or in the parking lot of a bar or convenience store. While we were living there, a prostitute was murdered in an RV, parked in one of the Hotel-spa's parking lots.

Crystal Methamphetamine is the local drug of choice, we are told, and the "overdose wagon's" siren can be heard often during the day and evening, costing the city several thousand dollars for each run, as the Ambulance must be accompanied by a fire truck according to the rules.

There currently is no medical facility in the city, so all medical emergencies must be transported to Palm Springs, 12-miles south of the city. If there was ever an example of what it costs the U.S. Taxpayer for people not having medical health insurance, Desert Hot Springs is the poster child.

The good news is that finally, 48-years after incorporation, a joint-funded medical facility is planned to be built in the center of town, and a county facility is on the drawing boards for Palm Drive, south of Vons Market, which will save the city thousands of dollars every year.

As of this writing, the new Police Chief Pat Williams, who has been in office a little over two-years, seems to have been able to reorganize the staff and is slowly getting things under control. There is hope among the residents that crime will begin to slow due to the Chief's efforts. When it does, and that news can be telegraphed to the outside world, the fortunes of Desert Hot Springs could change for the better. This is where the city needs a lot of Positive Energy Vortex flowing in the right direction.

Shortly after we moved to the city in June of 2005, the first of several ensuing scandals surfaced. Jerry Hanson, the City Manager was exposed as having been feathering his own nest at the expense of the tax payers with a gross salary that exceed $350,000 annually and a fat-cat retirement plan. The following article explains some of the issues:

City may be on the hook for $195,000 a year

State Rejects Picking Up The Tab On Hanson Retirement

The Desert Sun (September 3, 2005)

Former City Manager Jerry Hanson's controversial final contract — drafted by Hanson himself — puts city taxpayers on the hook for $195,000 a year in retirement benefits that the state says it won't cover and an additional $15,019 a month ($180,228 a year) for pay as a consultant even though he's not actually performing work, according to the contract and public documents obtained Friday by The Desert Sun. *If Hanson, 59, lives to the white male life expectancy of 75.4 years, that's $3.19 million in retirement alone that Desert Hot Springs will pay.*

But there's a possibility that the contract, which includes a provision stating that the city will pay any retirement benefits the state denies, wasn't passed properly and may be voided. "Should the council adopt it, the cost of the June 7, 2005 Employment Agreement, is huge," wrote interim City Manager Corky Larson in a staff report to the council.

Larson, who assumed the interim city manager post after Hanson's July 31 retirement, has put the contract on the council's agenda for Wednesday night — and the council will have a chance to vote on it again because of a technicality in California's open meetings law.

DHS News Poll
Do You Favor A Recall of DHS City Council?

Hot Topics: DHS City Manager Jerry Hanson

The Desert Hot Springs City Council decided to contact the Riverside County grand jury and request an investigation of land holdings by City Manager Jerry Hanson and another member of the council to determine whether there was a conflict of interest with recent development projects. Hanson has denied any wrongdoing.

DESERT HOT SPRINGS
What happened? Desert Hot Springs City Manager Jerry Hanson recommended the City Council approve a housing project, provided the developer pay for $600,000 worth of street improvements to Pierson Boulevard. Hanson bought land along Pierson Boulevard about seven months before the vote.

What does it mean? Officials with the California Fair Political Practices Commission say such a scenario could be against state law, carrying with it a fine of up to $5,000. An ethics advisor for a city manager association says such a situation has the appearance of conflict of interest.

TIMELINETimeline of recent events leading up to the council voting to contact the Riverside County Grand Jury to investigate land dealings.

March 18: City Manager Jerry Hanson fires Police Chief Roy Hill.

March 23: A City Hall leak shows Hanson earned $322,809 in 2004, well over his $125,000 salary.

March 25: Hanson hires an outside investigation firm to discover who stole his private W2 form from City Hall and leaked it to the press.

April 8: Roy Hill's attorney went on record saying Hill was let go because he was a whistle-blower. The attorney said Hill sent information about "salary manipulation" and improper land deals to the grand jury and the FBI. City Attorney Corky Larson said she had no knowledge of any ongoing grand jury investigations.

April 16: The Desert Sun publishes a story showing Hanson bought property that could benefit from StoneRidge, a project he was working on as city manager at the time of purchase. Councilman Hank Hohenstein also has property nearby and is apparently free of conflict.

April 19: The City Council, with Mayor Matt Weyuker absent due to illness, voted unanimously in closed session to contact the grand jury to investigate any wrongdoing by Hanson or any City Council members when participating in land development agreements since Nov. 1.

Trio files lawsuit vs. Hanson
The former Desert Hot Springs police chief and two other former city employees have filed a wrongful termination lawsuit against the city...

****

The above list of headlines and stories were written and posted on the local news web site in early to mid 2004, continuing through 2005 and into early 2006. Attempts to bring them up on the Desert Sun Web Site have proven futile. Evidently the paper and/or Google did not archive them after a period of time.

Shortly after the Jerry Hanson issues emerged, council member Gary Bosworth, one of the committee members with oversight on the city manager's salary and benefits, took ill. Bosworth, a three-term member of the council, had been one of the members on the oversight sub-committee responsible for negotiating and approving the City manager's contracts.

Councilman hospitalized because of pneumonia

DESERT HOT SPRINGS: Gary Bosworth appears ill at City Hall before he is admitted for treatment.

11:06 PM PDT on Friday, May 27, 2005

By WES WOODS II / The Press-Enterprise

Desert Hot Springs Councilman Gary Bosworth was taken to the hospital Thursday night for treatment of a severe case of pneumonia, friends and colleagues said Friday.

Cathedral City Mayor Pro Tem Greg Pettis, a friend of Bosworth, said in a telephone interview that Bosworth was at City Hall on Thursday and a police sergeant noticed the councilman appeared ill. The officer "made a determination he needed to be in the hospital."

Desert Hot Springs police officials took him to Desert Regional Medical Center that evening, he said.

Eva Saltonstall, a hospital spokeswoman, said Friday the hospital could not release Bosworth's condition, at the request of his family.

Bosworth has suffered from a rare form of arthritis since age 13, Desert Hot Springs Vice Mayor Mary Stephens said in a telephone interview Friday.

Stephens said when she saw Bosworth on Friday morning, he was on a ventilator and transferred from the emergency room to the intensive-care unit.

"We are a council, but we are like a family," she said. "We may fight like brothers and sisters but we still love each other."

She said he didn't recognize her when she went in his room Friday. Bosworth had also pneumonia six weeks ago but Stephens said she didn't know if it was related to his condition Friday.

Bosworth is vice chairman of the 80th Assembly District for the Riverside County Democratic Central Committee.

Pettis said he had known Bosworth 12 years.

"He's one of the most brilliant political statisticians the valley has. He brings a significant voice to Desert Hot Springs in the disabled community and the lower-income community who don't have a voice," Pettis said. "Gary has that voice for them."

Bosworth has been a Desert Hot Springs councilman since January 1995. He ran for mayor in 1999 and 2003, Desert Hot Springs Mayor Matt Weyuker said.

Bill Effinger

Bosworth has been instrumental in getting ramps put in on Palm Drive's sidewalks for people in wheelchairs, and is a defender of the city's hot-water zone for spas, Weyuker said.

Added Desert Hot Springs Councilman Will Pieper: "He's my friend and I'm praying for a swift recovery."

Reach Wes Woods II at (760) 837-4405 or wwoods@pe.com

****

Walt Luce, President of Mayer/Luce, a Desert Hot Springs based development company, while this negativity for the city was playing out was agitating for a concerted effort by all of the vested developers in the city to campaign for faster approvals and lower fees. To that end, he was calling for support and commitments from other developers to join him in his pressure campaign. Council member Hank Hohenstein was being actively supported by Luce to run for mayor in the next election. Luce also asked all of the developers in the group to join in the initiative of Republican Assemblyman John Benoit:

Developers mount effort to build more homes

08:12 AM PDT on Thursday, August 18, 2005

By SANDRA BALTAZAR MARTÍNEZ / The Press-Enterprise

Campaign information

For more information on the "Campaign for California Homeownership," visit: www.cahomeownership.com

DESERT HOT SPRINGS - A statewide campaign that aims to make it easier for developers to build new homes will ultimately make housing more affordable, especially for first-time home buyers, campaign supporters say.

The "Campaign for California Homeownership" was outlined Wednesday during a press a conference in Desert Hot Springs where participants emphasized the importance of providing affordable housing for California families, including those in the Coachella Valley.

The campaign, backed by the California Building Industry Association, proposes to "balance" housing supply and demand by making sure enough land is available to builders for housing, eliminating regulatory and legal blocks that cause construction delays and shortening the permitting process for new development, according to an association news release.

"My goal is to remove red tape wherever I can," said Assemblyman John Benoit, R-Palm Desert, standing in front of a new $400,000 home on Overlook Drive in Desert Hot Springs. The campaign also encourages Californians to sign a declaration calling for new housing. The declaration will be presented to the Legislature and Gov. Schwarzenegger's office.

On Wednesday, a black and white poster hung from the podium, depicting a family of three with enlarged print that read "Missing," alluding to the missing first time home buyers.

****

This proposed action set off my internal alarm. The concept as I saw it, while advantageous to residential developers, could destroy the city of Desert Hot Springs if allowed to continue. My experience of being involved in development within other cities and as a former mayor was

181

clear to me: Allowed to continue, this initiative would hurt and possibly destroy the city.

Trying to get the attention of the city's citizens and leaders, I wrote an Op-Ed piece suggesting the city was headed in the wrong direction if it wanted to grow and develop into a balanced and sustaining community, which was published in the Desert Sun in mid-August following the above article after it appeared in the Riverside Press Enterprise:

Between 2003 and 2009, I wrote over 300 articles for the three Valley papers. Subsequently, I wrote and published a small book titled "I Told You So" which contains most of my *Valley Breeze*, *Desert Local News* and *Desert Sun* published articles and opinion pieces. I then handed them to friends and colleagues during the council campaigns. This made some people happy and some unhappy. Contents of a few of those articles are in this manuscript and identified as such. One follows:

A call for common sense

There is an unprecedented homebuilding boom in Coachella Valley, not seen since the building surge following WWII when cities were literally being constructed overnight along California's Southern seaboard cities.

No place is the current boom more evident than what is underway in the once dormant and languishing community of Desert Hot Springs. More than thirty individual home building projects ranging from 14 homes to over 3000 houses totaling a projected 12,000-plus single family and condominium homes are in some form of process or construction. This begs the question, is the seemingly unchecked growth in new housing good or bad for the DHS community?

There is a fundamental fact, that every new home built will be a financial debit to California cities. In other words, homes do not, have not nor ever will pay their own way. The cost of services required by residences far outweighs the property taxes derived from them. Revenues to sustain a growing city must come from sales taxes.

One-time developer fees commonly referred to as Impact Fees provide a quick deposit into city funds, which most often is used to improve roads, put in street lights and other sundry infrastructure needs to accommodate new housing, but when those funds are used, the required services such as police, fire, libraries, street maintenance and their costs remain forever.

As a new resident of DHS and member of the development community for over 50 years, I have grave concerns about the pace of building and the lack of visible sources of sales tax revenues to sustain the growth of Desert Hot Springs.

Homebuilders (and I have built many) are driven by market demand and like all businesses must make a profit to be successful. I have often said that if there were two bankers and one builder on an island, there would be an overbuilt condition. Builders go where the market is and where they can get the money to build their product. The chase for buyers and the money to feed the supply of homes rarely takes into consideration, the basic needs of the communities in which the homes are being built.

The often stated "build the homes and the commercial/retail will come" does not always hold true. Some communities in California and elsewhere have learned this the hard way. The result is skewed traffic patterns and retail businesses locating near, but not necessarily in the city needing the revenue to sustain the services required by residents. Therein lies a serious conundrum.

Big-box retailers and commercial chains are demographic and formula driven marketers, using driving times, major highway visibility and community income levels, as their guide to placement of their operation. A case in point is the Home Depot now being built directly across from Lowes in Palm Springs at Ramon road and Gene Autry Trail. Why there and not Desert Hot Springs? I suggest the reason is because they have done their homework and they know that those of us in DHS that require what they have for sale will drive the fifteen minutes it takes to get there. Also, there is a huge market for home improvement supplies in the Palm Springs area, and very little need in DHS for quite some time.

Will Big-box retailers come to DHS? Of course they will. But that is not the question. The real question is will enough big retailers come to the city soon enough to develop sustaining revenues for the required services before the city runs out of sufficient funds.

I suggest that before it's too late, DHS leaders need to address the issue head-on with the building community and seek their help by adopting a quid-pro-quo ordinance that will allow only a given number of new home permits issued for a given number of commercial and retail businesses established in the city.

Yes, the home builders will cry foul. However, once they find that working with the community and their peers in commercial development will bring much needed sales tax revenues to the city, everyone will benefit.

Allowed to continue building homes unchecked by anything other than demand, Desert Hot Springs could be doomed to being a bedroom community unable to maintain adequate police, fire and all other service necessities for operating a balanced community. This seems like common sense to me, how about you?

184

Bill Effinger is a Marketing, Management and Forward
Planning Consultant and can be reached at 760.736.3073 or
bill@billeffinger.com

Unfortunately, the message fell on deaf ears. As a matter of
fact, Deputy City Manager John Soulliere, said: "We are a
bedroom community, and that's what the people want."
Undeterred, I continued to sound the alarm every way I could.
With the election approaching, I reached out to the voters
through one of my articles in The Valley Breeze which was
published in late August:

Accountability

Accountability! That's the action word today. We want our
school teachers to be accountable to us. We want our federal
and state government to be accountable to us. We want our
local government to be accountable to us. We object to our
neighbor's nationality being chosen to a position over ours.
But are we accountable to our leaders? Are we accountable
to ourselves?

When is the last time you attended a Planning Commission
meeting? A city council meeting? When is the last time you
participated in a Chamber of Commerce mixer? A parent-
teacher unction at the school? Did you vote in the last
election? When did you volunteer for community service at
the Senior Center, Library or Thrift shop? Have you voiced
your objections to the political status quo by writing to your
local newspaper? If not, why not?

Accountability isn't a one-way street. We get the government
we don't vote for.

We complain about our leadership, but when it comes time to
work for change, we are too busy, don't want to get involved

because it might be bad for business, or just plain don't give a damn.

How many of the current Desert Hot Springs' complainers will actually go out and work for change by walking precincts, writing letters to the editor and financially supporting their favorite candidate?

I challenge every person of voting age living in DHS to make an effort to learn the issues of importance to the future of our community. Seek out and talk to the candidates, question their motives and plans for the city. Ask how you can help them in their quest for office, assuming you agree with their positions on the issues.

Above all, go to the polls and cast your ballot. Be accountable to the future of Desert Hot Springs. You owe it to yourself and your neighbors.

Bill Effinger is a Marketing, Management and Forward Planning Consultant and can be reached at 760.736.3073 or bill@billeffinger.com

Five: From Dust To Dust

The natives were getting restless and talk of a Recall was starting to circulate, Russell Betts, a community activist was pressing the city to adhere to the Coachella Valley's PM10 ordinance requiring blowing dust management and getting little results for his efforts.

A Recall committee was formed with Betts, Gabriel King and Patrick Gillespie, owner of a local auto repair facility, to raise money for targeting Hank Hohenstein and Mary Stephens. Hank was embroiled in the controversy of his "Waking up stupid" public comment and Mary had been put on Walt Luce's payroll as a bookkeeper, creating a major issue of probable conflict of interest for her.

Mayer/Luce had nine projects underway in one form or another within the city, all requiring council action at one point. The Desert Sun wrote very critical editorials on the subject and petitions were circulated. After a prolonged and energetic campaign, the required signatures fell slightly short of qualifying for a recall. But a head of steam had been built up to oppose both of them in the coming election.

On The Trail Of Dust...

By Russell Betts (April 10, 2005)

Following yesterday's severe dust event coming from Skyborne and Mission Springs Water District project along Pierson Blvd. , I spent the morning contacting some of the parties responsible for the dust violations.

Those conditions in case you did not take a drive out Pierson towards Route 62 or did not look to the west to see the dust

clouds on Sunday afternoon, amounted to a literal whiteout condition for those driving Pierson and dust that inundated homes directly west of Skyborne.

At one point along Pierson visibility was so poor a car came to a skidding stop just inches from a car in front of it that was forced to slow down by the blowing dust and poor visibility.

At the intersection of Indian and Pierson, several cars came to a stop and could not proceed through the intersection until a dust cleared. One women out for a Sunday drive in a convertible and stopped at the intersection could do nothing more than bury her face in her hands and wait for the dust to pass and the cars in front of her to start moving again..

187

The dust was coming from two sources. One was from the pipeline projects being installed along Pierson by Desert Pipeline for Mission Springs Water District. The other was from the 100 plus acre Skyborne housing development.

Both MSWD and Skyborne are this morning pointing fingers at each other as the cause of the dust. City officials are meeting with Skyborne and presumably will have talks with MSWD as well.

For the record, both MSWD and Skyborne were gross dust violators on Sunday.

Coming from the MSWD pipeline installation were blinding, rolling clouds of dust that were the cause of the near accident and inability of traffic to proceed. From the Skyborne project were clouds of dust inundating homes downwind and sending dust blowing across the downtown.

This morning I contacted MSWD to advise them of the problem and spoke to Executive Assistant Barb Carr. She confirmed the grading along Pierson is work being done by MSWD to install a sewer line. Carr said a water line is also being installed but that the water line was a Desert Hot Springs City project and not an MSWD project.

Desert Pipeline is the company doing the actual sewage line installation work on Pierson. In a call to them this morning, they advise that a water truck was out on the project earlier in the morning but could not confirm if they were watering more than once a day on weekends and on Sunday.

Desert Pipeline was asked if there are plans to seal the finished grade once the installation work is complete. A common practice to control dust after grading is complete is to apply a polymer binder or a vegetation enhancing binder to control dust.

Desert Pipeline said they would talk to MSWD about applying a binder to the finished graded areas but that it is not contracted to apply the binder. They estimated the cost to seal the finished grade to be about $35,000, something the company said it can not absorb and that MSWD will have to pay for.

A call has been placed to MSWD to see if they have contracted with another company to apply a binder of if the water district plans to leave the finished grade unsealed. Without a binder, every time the wind blows, conditions on Pierson will be as they were on Sunday afternoon until vegetation naturally takes over, a process that can take up to two years.

If a previous sewage installation project along Mission Lakes Blvd. and completed nearly a year ago is any indication, it seems the common practice is to leave the grade unsealed. The Mission Lakes Blvd. sewage line has been the source of high amounts of dust.

Gary Brockman, MSWD Director of Operations & Maintenance said the Mission Lakes Blvd. line is not and MSWD project but rather was done by Century Vintage for its Mountain View project. Brockman said that control of the Mission Lakes Blvd. sewage line will be turned over to MSWD but that that had not yet occurred.

Brockman did not know if MSWD would require Century Vintage to seal the finished grade prior to MSWD accepted control over it.

On the dust coming from the Skyborne project, reports of dust were first called into Desert Hot Springs PM10 inspectors about 2 p.m. At that time, City PM10 inspectors were already on the scene and had called Skyborne about the dust. Well after dust had started blowing, no water trucks were operating on the Skyborne site.

Skyborne is saying this morning that their trucks were watering all the way up to 7 p.m. last night. But, at sunset, well after 7 p.m., large clouds of dust could be seen rolling off the Skyborne project. If the trucks were watering, they were not getting a handle on the problem. And, they had not been on site prior to city code enforcement calling them.

Immediately downwind of the Skyborne project are houses located on West drive. Those houses took the brunt of the dust from Skyborne and at times the visibility of the homes was significantly impaired by the dust.

Today winds are expected to be over 25 mph in the area.

****

Following my own advice, the best way to help make change, is to get active in the political arena and try to help elect the people that best align with your views. So that's what I set out to do.

Alex Bias is African American and had been involved in Desert Hot Springs politics for many years, often taking on the establishment. He had served on several city commissions and committees, was active in the Chamber of Commerce, presented himself well, always dressed to the nines, and wanted to be mayor. A negative to that desire, was that he had developed a large number of detractors for what many said were his questionable business practices and financial dealings with locals. But he had also been very effective in many ways within the community and had some strong financial supporters, the most prominent being Fred Noble, owner of Wintec, the largest windmill owner/operator in the valley. And Alex vowed to work hard to become mayor.

After I researched some of the written material that had been distributed throughout the community about Alex, I concluded that he was being targeted more because he was black than any of his dealings, and Buzz Gamble, a strong vocal bigot, was part of the group of Alex Bias detractors.

Looking back, I can see how wrong I was in that assessment as Bias took charge and his two-year term was fraught with his misunderstandings of the simplest of procedures and what his roll as mayor was.

Based on my desire to understand Alex, Diana and I set up a meeting with him in the coffee shop of the Miracle Springs Resort Hotel. Diana is a very perceptive person, and my best editor and critic. I value her opinions. We had coffee with Alex and talked for over an hour, leaving with some mixed feelings.

The deciding point for me was shortly after our meeting with Alex, when an active member of the community and a Spa owner, dropped a large package of hit pieces on my front doorstep, which were directed toward Alex from years past, with all kinds of sordid accusations, racial innuendos and what I felt to be false claims. I phoned the person and said I was insulted that someone would think that I could be swayed by such discriminatory trash. We never spoke again.

The most energetic of Alex's supporters was Gabriel King, himself one of the more controversial persons in the city because of his aggressive behavior and his web site "Friends of Desert Hot Springs". Gabriel was a provocateur. We (Russell Betts, Dean Gray and I) all decided to back Alex for mayor and Gabriel led the charge with his web site. Unfortunately mistakes such as this cannot be undone they have to run their course. It soon became clear that once elected, Alex Bias would serve only one term.

We did not want Mary Stephens to win, as she had corrupted herself by working for the biggest developer in the city, and in our collective opinion was a puppet of Matt Weyuker, whom we all agreed had not been good for the city.

Disclosures also surfaced, showing city manager Hanson to have been acquiring and speculating on land parcels in the path of progress where city acquisitions of right-of-way would reward those ownerships, ultimately resulting in a Grand Jury investigation.

The disappointing details of greed and corruption in Desert Hot Springs began to seep into the news channels and once again, the city was looking like the unwanted stepchild of the valley. Long considered out of step and out of control, the city was seemingly in a self-destruct mode, unable to wrench itself from the grips of poor governance. The Vortex was surely at work here.

Russell Betts, Dean Gray and I decided we would see if we could confront Hohenstein with what we knew about some of his dealings and force him to resign. I was given the task of setting up the meeting in Hank's home, hoping that if we presented our case in front of his wife, he would agree he

192

had done wrong and resign—it was a long shot but worth the try.

We arrived at the appointed time, sat down in Hank's living room with his wife present and proceeded to tell him what we knew. The more Hank talked, the more deeply he dug the hole he was already in. He admitted he knew that Hanson was specking on properties in the path of progress and admitted that he didn't alert his fellow council members. He also attempted to defend his actions on the property he had acquired next to the project he had voted to approve, while also admitting that he had been the planning consultant on the project as well.

We were incredulous. "How could you have done these things and not think they were at the very least, pushing the envelope on conflict, if not clearly a violation?" Dean Gray asked. "I just forgot" was all he could offer. With that, we broke up the meeting and left, not sure what our next move would be, but determined to make sure Hank would never again hold an elective or appointed office in Desert Hot Springs. Then the word got out on the street. The Vortex can be sneaky at times.

The result of that meeting with Hohenstein put the fire under the move to recall Hohenstein and Stephens. For Hohenstein to openly admit to us that he was aware of Hanson's land speculation and his attempt at skirting his responsibility in "forgetting" that his property adjoined the project he voted on without mentioning it to his fellow council members or the City Attorney, was the last straw.

The Hanson affair lingered and caused a great deal of angst among members of the council, and then Councilmember Hank Hohenstein was found to be in violation of the California Fair Political Practices Commission for not

193

disclosing his land purchase contiguous to a major development that he voted on, publicly declaring in his defense that he "woke up Stupid". After a protracted investigation, Hohenstein was fined $8,000 for his infraction of the law.

Strife nags city officials

DESERT HOT SPRINGS: A recall and a call for a federal audit are among their troubles.

10:54 PM PDT on Saturday, September 10, 2005

By WES WOODS II / The Press-Enterprise

Desert Hot Springs officials, who recently heralded the city's emergence from bankruptcy, now find themselves dealing with a call for a federal audit, mounting criticism of the former city manager's last contract, and efforts to recall members of the City Council.

With elections approaching in November, what all of this means for Desert Hot Springs' future financial health is uncertain.

On Wednesday, the Desert Hot Springs City Council voted in closed session to ask the U.S. Department of Justice to audit its finances for the past five years.

Gabriel King, who runs a Desert Hot Springs Web blog, said he asked the city to request the audit, which Councilman Hank Hohenstein confirmed Thursday.

King was dismissed with the rest of the city's Planning Commission in 2004. He ran unsuccessfully for City Council in 2003.

It's unclear whether the federal government would even have a role in such an audit.

194

"I've never heard of this happening. I'm not sure what arm of the department would handle this," said Thom Morzek, spokesman for the U.S. Attorneys' Office that handles seven counties including Riverside County, in a phone interview Friday.

At the City Council meeting on Wednesday, council members Hank Hohenstein and Mary Stephens were served with recall papers. Some residents protested the city's process to find a new city manager to replace Jerry Hanson, who resigned this year.

Residents at the meeting said one candidate was favored unfairly when he met with several city officials and others at a party hosted by Dorothy "Dot" Reed.

Hohenstein called the recall effort politically motivated, adding that the Fair Political Practices

Commission is already investigating him for a potential conflict of interest in a land holding.

With 60 days until the election, he questioned the recall's timing.

Hohenstein has taken responsibility for failing to disclose the potential conflict of interest he had in a vote on the 2,000-home StoneRidge project. The councilman, who owns property near the project, has publicly apologized for voting on it without disclosing his land holding.

Desert Hot Springs businessman Patrick Gillespie helped organize the recall, but King served Hohenstein and Stephens at the meeting.

"When I submitted that, it wasn't just me and Pat, it was 30 other people," King said in a phone interview Thursday.

Toward the end of Wednesday's meeting, the final contract for Hanson, worth thousands more dollars than his 2004 contract for $323,000, was voided by the City Council. A California Public Employees'Retirement System retirement benefit of $20,000 a month had been included in the contract, interim City Manager Patricia "Corky" Larson wrote in the staff report.

After the contract was canceled at about 11 p.m., some of the few remaining audience members applauded.

Dave Huntoon, a senior fellow for the Rose Institute of State and Local Government at Claremont McKenna College who studies the Coachella Valley, said the political problems are unlikely to hurt the pace of development in Desert Hot Springs.

"There is so much positive going on, in terms of the economic situation, it shadows over," Huntoon said from Claremont, noting that he has not followed the recent political fights in the city.

Other observers had a different take.

Desert Hot Springs' image is suffering from the ongoing turmoil, said Bob Marra, owner of Wheeler's Publishing, a demographic and economic information company based in Indian Wells.

"The brand associated with it, the feel with Desert Hot Springs, is in a bad situation," he said.

Marra said commercial development is lagging behind single-family residential building in the area. "If they're not getting commercial development, especially for retail to follow ... it becomes a realproblem. Housing costs more money than it makes money for (the city)."

Reach Wes Woods II at (760) 837-4405 or wwoods@pe.com

****

Then the following article appeared, adding more fuel to the simmering firestorm rapidly approaching a point of explosion, ultimately sealing the fate of Hohenstein and Stephens.

Turmoil Threatens Newfound Prosperity
Desert Hot Springs is booming, but two city officials are suspected of benefiting illegally.

By Louis Sahagun, L.A. Times Staff Writer

DESERT HOT SPRINGS, Calif. — After languishing for decades as the low-rent alternative for service workers from nearby Palm Springs-area resorts, this desert outpost known for its relaxing thermal waters is booming.

The population of 19,400 is expected to double by 2015. Lots that sold for $8,000 a few years ago fetch 10 times that amount. City coffers are brimming with building fees.

But the town's newfound prosperity has not brought stability. As city leaders grapple with the demands of explosive growth — widening roads, increasing services, building sewers — allegations have surfaced that at least two prominent officials may have used their positions to benefit from the growing affluence. These are among the issues:

• A potential conflict of interest involves a councilman's vote to approve a major subdivision without disclosing that he had purchased land nearby. The City Council is scheduled to discuss the matter Tuesday.

• The council has requested that a county grand jury investigate a land purchase by the city manager, who later urged the council to approve a development and road upgrades near his property.

197

• The city manager fired the police chief last March, a few days after he went to the FBI and county prosecutors with what he described as "evidence of possible criminal activity within different functions of city government."

"Our greatest problems have always been naiveté and ineptitude," said Lane Sarasohn, president of the Desert Hot Springs Chamber of Commerce. "You make the best of the cards you're dealt, and this city is still playing with very few face cards."

'Old Chaos,' 'New Chaos'

The city is still stinging from the stigma of its 2003 municipal bankruptcy. Desert Hot Springs was on the losing end of a 1995 lawsuit brought by a developer after the City Council rejected his project. The city was under court order to pay $10.8 million in damages. Only last year, the city floated a bond to pay off the debt. But the protracted litigation and bankruptcy had kept developers away for nearly a decade.

Adam Sanchez, head of the local Boys and Girls Club and a member of the city's Planning Commission, has come to refer to bankruptcy as the city's "old chaos" and the controversies currently rattling City Hall as the "new chaos." Residents and developers alike are worried that political woes will hinder the growth and vitality that they have long hoped for.

City Atty. Patricia Larson said the district attorney's office has "talked to a number of people" and confirmed that an investigation has been launched. But, she said, "I haven't a clue about what they are looking at."

Ingrid Wyatt, a spokeswoman for the Riverside County district attorney's office, would neither confirm nor deny that there is an investigation.

In the meantime, skip loaders are chewing up the landscape in California's 25th fastest-growing city, which used to be little more than a hodgepodge of mom-and-pop businesses, trailer parks, modest homes with septic tanks and spas that catered to snowbirds. Today, new stucco homes with panoramic views of mountains and desert-scapes command $250,000. The first shopping centers are sprouting along the main drags and crews are repairing some of the worst roads in the desert.

Necklace of Cities

Southern California's newest boomtown is spread across alluvial plains in the northwest tip of the Coachella Valley, part of a necklace of cities that stretches 30 miles from Palm Springs to Coachella. Newcomers there are a mixed lot, and many were priced out of neighboring cities of Rancho Mirage, Palm Desertand Cathedral City.

Take mortgage broker Scott Lantman and his wife, Diah, who recently moved out of a Palm Springs condominium and into a new 1,935-square-foot house here with a spectacular view of Mt. San Jacinto. The couple paid $220,000 for the house.

"We heard so many negative things about this city, that there were bad people living here, and drugs and gangs," Diah Lantman said while watering the lawn of a frontyard decorated with palms and edged with red brick. "But we think this area is changing fast. We just love it here."

After years of being little more than a desert burg with barely enough money to pay for essentials, city organizations, including Little League teams, the Boys and Girls Club and the Fourth of July parade committee, are receiving donations and sponsorship from developers eager to win over townsfolk.

But given their significant financial stake in the community, the developers are also worried about the controversies enveloping City Hall.

In a boardroom draped in subdivision maps, Walter Luce, chief executive of Mayer-Luce Development Group, put it this way: "We have $140 million invested in this town. We are going to move this city forward, and protect our investment.

So we are demanding political stability — no, we are dictating it," Luce said. "What is needed right now is a good city hall with competent people."

The City Council is slated to discuss a controversy on Tuesday involving Councilman Hank Hohenstein.

In 2002, Hohenstein bought a 16-acre parcel within 300 feet of a major housing development, Stone Ridge. At the time the project was in its early planning stages. About three years later, in February 2005, Hohenstein voted to approve Stone Ridge but didn't tell the City Council of his land holding at the time.

Hohenstein said he believed the land was far enough away to avoid controversy. But the proximity of his land to the development raised concerns among his council colleagues when they became aware of the issue last March.

'Second Thoughts'

Generally, under the state political reform act, government officials are prohibited from participating in government decisions if they are likely to affect their personal economic interests, said Jon Matthews, a spokesman for the California Fair Political Practices Commission.

"A few days after voting in favor of the project, I had second thoughts," Hohenstein said. "I later apologized to the City Council because it brought controversy to Desert Hot Springs. But I do not regret buying the property or my vote for the project."

Larson, the city attorney, said last week that Hohenstein "should not have voted on the Stone Ridge project."

"It is critically important that the city show how this error came about," she said.

"Councilman Hohenstein will recuse himself from this matter," Larson said.

200

A month and a half ago, Desert Hot Springs launched a nationwide search for someone to replace City Manager Jerry Hanson, who plans to retire effective today.

Hanson had intended to serve as interim city manager until the council could hire a replacement. But in a June 30 letter, he said he would resign, saying that inquiries by The Times and the Desert Sun about his finances and land deals had made him a polarizing figure in the city.

Despite his retirement, Hanson will stay on the city payroll for an indefinite period as a $125-an-hour consultant, Larson said.

In June, the council unanimously voted to request a grand jury investigation of Hanson's land purchases in town.

Hanson said he bought about 10 acres in June 2004 for about $250,000. Seven months later, he issued a staff report recommending that the City Council approve the proposed Stone Ridge housing project, which is near his land. Based on Hanson's recommendations, the council on Feb. 1 approved the 2,100-unit project, contingent on the developers' paying for $600,000 in street improvements.

The issue sparked controversy when City Councilman Gary Bosworth complained that Hanson had not publicly disclosed that he owned the property. Nor did he leave the council chambers when the project was being discussed.

Bosworth filed a complaint in April with the Fair Political Practices Commission alleging that Hanson may have used his official positions as both city manager and city engineer to influence city staffers and the council to process and approve Stone Ridge.

"At the very least, that appears to be a possible conflict of interest, or unethical," Bosworth said in a recent interview.

Larson said she did not view Hanson's land deal as a conflict of interest because the property is more than 2,500 feet from the project boundary line, therefore meeting legal requirements.

Hanson said in an interview last month that he recommended that the council require the Stone Ridge developer to pay for such street improvements as curbs and sidewalks on Pierson Boulevard, a main east-weststreet, including work along a stretch of the road skirting his acreage.

"I hope my property value goes up," Hanson said in the interview. But more important, he said, is that the entire city will benefit from the street improvements.

Hanson, who has a base salary of roughly $125,000, triggered more controversy after someone leaked his W-2 form to the Desert Sun.

In an interview with The Times, Linda Kelly, the city's administrative services director, said Hanson earned at least $322,809 in 2004, including $89,269 in vacation pay, about $5,000 in health benefits and a $92,215 buyout of a severance pay clause in his city contract.

The disclosure outraged residents, including Chamber of Commerce president Sarasohn.

"It was an embarrassment for our city," Sarasohn said in an interview. "I thought it was like taking candy from a baby. Jerry used his lawyer's skills to get more money from the city than the city intended to give him."

Hanson said he believes he should be credited for the city's revival and said he is proud of his work for the city, which included demoting, transferring or firing dozens of employees he regarded as incompetent.

Among them was former Police Chief Roy Hill, who was fired in March, after he reported allegations of corruption to the FBI and the district attorney.

The FBI declined to comment on the matter.

In a prepared statement to reporters, Hill said, "Over the past months, I have obtained information ... from many different sources that appears to be evidence of possible criminal activity within different functions of city government. As chief of police,

I did not have the resources, nor the ability, to properly pursue this criminal probe, but I had an obligation to my sworn oath of office and the citizens of Desert Hot Springs to take action."

Municipal rules grant the city manager full authority over hiring and firing city employees, including the police chief. The City Council did not contest Hill's dismissal. Hanson replaced Hill with an interim chief who was convicted on one count of falsifying a police report in 1998 in Hawaiian Gardens.

"Morale in the police department has nosedived," said Paul Steier, chairman of the Desert Hot Springs Public Safety Commission. "A number of experienced officers have started trying to process out to other law enforcement agencies."

On another political front, Desert Hot Springs City Councilwoman Mary Stephens, a front runner in the city's ongoing mayoral race, recently took an accounting job with Mayer-Luce, one of the biggest developers in town.

Since taking that job, Stephens has promised to recuse herself from voting on matters involving her boss.

In the November election, voters will fill two City Council seats and elect a new mayor. Campaign issues have focused on ensuring long-term economic stability, increasing public safety for a growing population and cementing confidence in city government.

But even that may not satisfy residents who have come to believe Desert Hot Springs' transformation into a red-hot housing market was a mixed blessing. Many of the city's 48 spa owners have started buying adjacent empty lots in hopes of sustaining a semblance of "open space" around their establishments and to prevent nearby septic tanks from polluting their wells.

'I Feel Cynical'

Steve Lowe, manager of a spa remodeled to resemble a hotel in Paris frequented by avant-garde writers and artists, compared the arrival of massive housing developments to a "tsunami of red barrel tile."

"I used to be hopeful," Lowe said. "Now, I feel cynical about what appears to be just plain old suburban-style sprawl. I'm so angry about it that I don't go to City Hall meetings anymore."

That kind of talk worries mayoral candidate Stephens.

"This city needs a lot of nurturing right now. People are wound up and scared. They don't trust their politicians or developers," she said. "But now that we have a little real money, we're going to start behaving like a real city. Desert Hot Springs is not normal. But we're getting close."

****

My youngest son Brian, a U.S. Navy Retiree, but still working for the Navy as a civilian, is always interested in what his dad is up to while watching from afar; in this case, Vancouver Washington. He wrote an Opinion post for the Desert Local News, well worth reading at any time:

To understand my general opposition to recall elections, I have to share a little background on my own experience relating to 27 years of marriage to my wife, who is originally from the Philippines. Over that time we have made a substantial investment in property in the Philippines in order

204

to build a nest egg and a second home for our retirement. The Philippines is poised for what we hope will be an economic boom; but our optimism for the future is tempered by the risk we are taking in making the investment in a country that has suffered from a persistently unstable political climate.

The Philippines is comprised of 7,000 islands, 98 distinct local dialects, a Muslim insurgency in the South, a Communist insurgency in the North, and a Christian pseudo-theocracy, all held together by a fledgling constitutional republic that is rife with corruption and a revolving-door government. The unruly political apparatus changes presidents, senators, and representatives as often as you and I change shirts. There have been two impeachments of two presidents in the span of 3 years, along with countless coups attempts, political assassinations, and recalls of members of congress both at the national and provincial levels. The result of this chaotic political climate is that the Philippines, despite a very intelligent, resourceful and industrious population and a culture wholly dedicated to family, is an economic and political basket case in an area of the world where their wealth and influence should be on a par with their neighbors in the region – Taiwan, Japan, Singapore, and China, to name a few.

The roots of their unstable democracy are not peculiar to just the Philippines. They are endemic among just about every democracy, in that typically an election is not approached as an opportunity to vote FOR something, but AGAINST something. A recall election is the ultimate example of this phenomenon. By its very nature, a recall election is a negative statement that, if successful, creates a void, a vacuum, a black hole that is all-too-often filled by poor candidates with questionable qualifications who are swept into office by the cynical view that anything is better than what came before. Given Desert Hot Springs' sordid history with regard to recall elections, one has to wonder why another recall would turn out any different.

I'd like to think that one day, Desert Hot Springs will take its place in the region as a full-service community that is a draw for tourists and is envied for its economic and cultural richness, instead of the bastard child of the Coachella Valley. I'd like to see the same for the Philippines. Unfortunately, right now they both appear to be heading down the same dark alley for the same reason. There's an old saying that if you always do what you've always done, you'll always get what you've always gotten. It's always been my view that if voters aren't given something to vote FOR instead of against, the future is not likely to change for the better.

Brian Effinger

****

Much to my delight, the recall effort failed, but the relationships of everyone involved in the attempt remained intact, and ultimately became the support group for the movement to elect a new mayor. Walt Luce, along with Mayor Weyuker was endorsing and pushing the developer consortium in backing Mary Stephens to become the next mayor. We all agreed to work hard to keep that from happening.

I had opposed the recall in almost every article I wrote that year in the Desert Sun and the Valley breeze, and was proud that the recall failed to materialize, even though my friends, Russell Betts, Dean Gray and Patrick Gillespie were fighting for the Recall.

Having been a target of a recall movement many years prior by a disgruntled developer while I was mayor of the city of Buena Park, I had no interest in what I feel is vigilante government. Recalls should be used as intended: to throw out a proven crooked public servant, and for no other reason I can think of. Corruption was very evident in this case, but another recall effort in Desert Hot Springs was just more bad publicity for the suffering city. My last article on the recall took to task, its sponsors (my friends) and their volunteers, appears below

Beating a dead horse

Desert Local News

Leaving an early breakfast at La Toscana café, last Sunday I found two folded recall flyers placed under the wiper blades of my car. The parking lot for the hotel and adjoining church was packed with cars, all of which contained the same two flyers on their windshields, decrying the time-worn DHS city manager fiasco as if it just happened. That horse is dead, guys. It is time to move on.

Obviously, the recall gremlins were at work, fast spreading news of yesterday, in place of positive efforts for tomorrow. How unfortunate. I thought to myself how sad it is these well-meaning but misguided individuals can't seem to channel their efforts for positive change through the system of government which we all have access to.

Desert Hot Springs Has four public city council meetings, one Planning Commission meeting, one Public Safety Commission meeting, one Housing Commission meeting, one Community & Cultural Affairs Commission meeting, one Building Appeals/Design Review Board meeting and an Ad Hoc Annexation Committee meeting every single month, all open to the public, and every meeting has time set aside for citizens to air their views as required by law. What is wrong with using the system the way it is designed? How many of the recall gremlins have consistently appeared before these governing bodies offering their suggestions or voicing their objections on issues? I haven't missed a council meeting or Study session in a year and until the heat of the election period, none of the gremlins were seen, save one, once in a while. Why not?

Regular attendance by citizens during government meetings is the best way to keep government in line. When the public serves as its own watch dog, by being a visible participant in the process, there is no way the mistakes of the past will occur. While it is true the Hanson contract was a dumb act by our council, it's also true that it happened a long time ago, and now it is being dealt with. I might add that the matter will have two fresh minds to help resolve the issue as best as it can be. I will trust our new mayor and council member to help guide the process, but I will also be attending the council meetings as usual, that way I can watch, listen and ask questions as anyone can.

Beating the dead horse of a mistake long gone will accomplish nothing but continued and unnecessary turmoil for our city, its residents and prospective new businesses. Reticence and concern about our unstable government must be replaced with confidence that DHS is growing up. Until the Wild-West image of vigilante law in Desert Hot Springs is dispelled, our future will remain doubtful.

Yours for better government Bill Effinger

Mayor Weyuker then surprised us all by taking a firm stand on the controversy surrounding the removal of the recall committee's signs which had been ordered by city staff, no doubt directed by Hohenstein and Stephens.

DHS Mayor right in letting voters have their voice 07 10 05:

Signs urging Desert Hot Springs residents to recall Vice Mayor Mary Stephens and City Councilman Hank Hohenstein go to the heart of the First Amendment and should be allowed to stand, Mayor Matt Weyuker said Wednesday. Give the mayor a standing ovation. He has given free speech precedence over petty politics.

Weyuker said he will tell city code enforcement officers to cease and desist tearing down the signs. About 50 signs were planted at intersections along Palm Drive, the primary road leading into Desert Hot Springs. "Although I don't agree with the recall, the recall signs should be permitted in and along these medians, just as most candidates have used them in the last three or four elections," Weyuker said via an e-mail interview. "I believe that this is referred to in the U.S. Constitution as 'freedom of speech.'" Weyuker, who is not seeking re-election in the November election, says that whatever the law says, it has been "patently ignored by candidates and not enforced" - until now.

****

Once again, the Desert Local News web site posted a series of stories surrounding the Hanson affair, continuing coverage through the election, the result of which was Alex Bias became Mayor, and Yvonne Parks was elected to the council, and by rotation, Gary Bosworth became Mayor Pro-tem, but confusion reigned supreme, as the new council was extremely indecisive.

———

The election of Alex Bias ended my relationship with Buzz Gamble and my column in his bi-monthly newspaper "The Valley Breeze". Gamble, born and raised in Oklahoma, was never able to shed the bigotry of the by-gone days of the south. He was anti-Semitic; disliked Blacks and Mexicans, frequently writing or hosting and publishing articles stating as much. He, along with many who agreed with him, did not want Alex Bias to become mayor. And of course stories like this didn't help Alex's image either:

DHS mayoral hopeful facing eviction order

thedesertsun.com

A man vying to be a mayor who would bring fresh leadership to this city hit by controversy is due in court on Monday on his fourth eviction since 1999. Mayoral candidate Alex Bias has been involved with at least seven lawsuits and is currently being evicted from the space he rents to run his realty business, according to Riverside County court documents. Bias, in an interview with The Desert Sun Wednesday, confirmed he has filed suit or has been sued because he refuses to allow people to "bully" him. And most of his cases, which included three prior evictions, were settled out of court.

****

Alex's election dealt a serious blow to the power elite of Desert Hot Springs, causing them to regroup and begin a campaign to block everything and anything Alex tried to do for the full extent of his tenure as mayor. The result was to set Desert Hot Springs back further in the eyes of its neighbors, while the Valley's most read newspaper, "The Desert Sun" took delight in writing negative articles about the city "on the wrong side of the tracks."

****

DHS NEWS WIRE

DESERT SUN   NATIONAL   LOCAL BLOGS

Election among factors to slow manager hunt
The seven-month search for a city manager of Desert

Hot Springs was slowed by a number of factors, but the wait for...

Decision on Desert Hot Springs city manager tonight

Ann Marie Gallant, the city manager of King City, appeared to remain ambiguous Monday about whether she will leave her position to come to Desert Hot Springs...

DHS City manager field narrowed to 2

And then there were two. That's the number of city manager candidates remaining for the Desert Hot Springs City Council to choose from.

Council: No city manager yet

The Desert Hot Springs City Council remains at an impasse, unable to name a city manager candidate again Monday night.

Council puts off choice of manager

The Desert Hot Springs City Council emerged from a closed session Tuesday without naming a top candidate...

Endeavors to replace Hanson nearing end?

The City Council today will likely name the top choice for city manager and begin negotiating with him, a councilman said Thursday.

It's official - Gallant now city manager for DHS

Ann Marie Gallant signed a contract with the city at Tuesday's City Council meeting, making her...

Desert Hot Springs City Council's city manager: Gallant

Ann Marie Gallant will take her fourth job with a city in five

years following a decision by the Desert Hot Springs City
Council to hire her as city manager...

Hanson out of sight, but not out of mind
Jerry Hanson is out of sight, but the embattled former Desert
Hot Springs city manager remains forefront in the minds of
those investigating...

Mayor believes Pomeranian was intentionally poisoned
Mayor Alex Bias now believes his pet Pomeranian was
poisoned intentionally.

Nowak confirmed as lead City Manager applicant
The City Council on Tuesday will likely name the top choice for
city manager and begin negotiating with him, a councilman
said Thursday.

Bias hopes to have decision on city manager today
Growth, traffic and prestige were among the items Mayor Alex Bias

touched on in his first State of the City address.

Desert Hot Springs mayor seeks new players on team
Mayor Alex Bias says he wants to create a transition team -
and possibly hire an executive search firm - to help search for
a new city manager.

Desert Hot Springs close to hiring a new manager
The people of Desert Hot Springs waved bon voyage to one
captain and came closer to bringing another on board
Wednesday evening.

City in flux as the year's snags persist
With new members of its City Council in place, Desert Hot
Springs is proceeding with its search for a new city manager.
The city's taking steps toward resolving issues from a string of

controversies that started in March with the firing of the city's police chief and continue today with multiple ongoing investigations and a recall effort of two council members.

City staff can testify in Hanson litigation
Desert Hot Springs city officials and employees will be able to testify in court about privileged information in connection with a claim filed by former City Manager Jerry Hanson.

Internet can make quite a tacky vice
Depending on what you ask her and when, Desert Hot Springs Vice Mayor Mary Stephens has a different explanation that jeopardizes her credibility.

Desert Hot Springs extends city manager's contract
Interim City Manager Corky Larson will stay on at the helm of the city for an undetermined amount of time, the Desert Hot Springs City Council decided Tuesday.

City calls in FBI to help sort out its books
Desert Hot Springs will ask the FBI to look at its books for the last five years.

City manager pick delayed
After many outspoken residents asked the city to wait, the Desert Hot Springs City Council announced Tuesday it would not choose a new city manager before the November election.

****

DHS NEWS WIRE

DESERT SUN   NATIONAL   LOCAL BLOGS

The Weaning of the Candidates
Candidates "B" *and* "A"

Desert Hot Springs News and Views - September 21, 2005

It may be after the fact, but some thought regarding the council's other candidate for the city manager slot, Candidate "A", raises some questions about just how the city council went about coming up with its final two selections.

We've already seen that Candidate "B" David Lane has issues and now seems to be out of the running. Amid that controversy, which included a guided tour of the city by Vice Mayor Mary Stephens, the other candidate seems to have escaped scrutiny. At least in public.

According to the Desert Sun, Candidate A, now identified as Ann Marie Gallant. accepted her first position as a city manager in 2004. That position was in Gustine, California where she signed on under a three year contract.

According to the Desert Sun and other newspapers, Gallant left the position in Gustine after serving there less than a year, this to take a position in April 2005 as the King City, California city manager where she now is employed.

This is September 2005. And that being the case, if the council had given her the job here in Desert Hot Springs, it would have been her third job as a city manager in two years.

If you are an employer looking at a resume that contains this type of job history, you consider the person a job jumper. Yet Gallant made it through the screening process to become one of two finalist. It is very curious thinking on the part of the city council regarding Candidate "A" and not just "B".

For those interested, the Desert Sun article is linked here.

Vice mayor defends candidate's tour of town

There was nothing improper about a city manager candidate's

214

tour of Desert Hot Springs, Vice Mayor Mary Stephens said Friday.

City asks feds to look at books
Desert Hot Springs city officials officially asked the Department of Justice on Friday to audit the city's financial department, saying they have had "several reports alleging suspicious activity."

****

With all of the turmoil swirling around the council, the city lost a member who, in my opinion, was the most intelligent and knowledgeable person of the group; Gary Bosworth Died in July of 2006 and was remembered at a widely attended ceremony, held in Desert Hot Springs' High School. The article speaks volumes about the man, his dedication to the city and his quiet but forceful leadership qualities:

Bosworth remembered for dedication to desert SERVICE:

The late city councilman was honored by political friends and foes at memorial event.

DESERT HOT SPRINGS - A dedicated leader, a shrewd politician and a loyal friend, Gary Bosworth was remembered as many things to many people during a memorial service Thursday.

**10:00 PM PDT on Thursday, July 20, 2006 By DAVID HERMANN and WES WOODS II
The Press-Enterprise**

About 200 of Bosworth's family members, friends, constituents and fellow political officials gathered in the theater at Desert Hot Springs High School to remember and honor the 52-year-old Desert Hot Springs city councilman and Democratic political strategist, who died unexpectedly of natural causes a week ago.

At a podium flanked by two large U.S. flags and a garden of wreaths, sprays and other floral arrangements, Hobart Bosworth recalled his brother's start in politics.

He recalled how Bosworth, who at age 13 was diagnosed with a severe arthritic condition called ankylosing spondylitis, came to live with him after hip surgery.

"He didn't know what he was going to do," the brother said.

Hobart Bosworth said he recommended that his brother get involved with the local disabled students union -- without realizing what that would lead to.

First, he brought home a picture of him being arrested at a student-protest rally, Hobart Bosworth said.

"Then he invited me to his birthday party -- it was a $100-a-plate Democratic fundraiser," he said to loud and knowing laughter.

Bosworth's dedication, integrity and statistical acumen were the focus of many speakers.

Palm Springs Mayor Pro Tem Ginny Foat said any good Democrat in the Coachella Valley would call Bosworth before they decided to run for office.

More than one speaker recalled how Bosworth would send birthday and Valentine's Day cards every year to all of Desert Hot Springs' female registered voters. They also spoke of how Bosworth generously shared his political insights and strategies with others.

"I look around this room now and there are 20 or 30 people who, like myself, have benefited from Gary's work on campaigns," said state Sen. Denise Moreno Ducheny.

Ducheny, a Democrat who represents San Diego and part of the Coachella Valley, said Bosworth was a Democrat in every sense of the word -- a skilled and dedicated political partisan and someone who encouraged everyone, regardless of party affiliation, to get involved and vote.

Ducheny also praised Bosworth, whose disease forced him to use one and sometimes two canes to walk, for his work as an advocate of the disabled.

When projects came before the council, Bosworth would always ensure developers considered issues such as wheelchair access so that buildings were accessible to everyone.

Francine Moeller, chairwoman of the state Democratic Party Disability Caucus, said Bosworth, who served as the caucus' longtime vice chairman, was an invaluable partner and advocate for the cause who always put people first.

Bosworth also had a sense of humor about his condition, Moeller said. "My spine might be crooked, but my politics aren't," she said of one of his favorite lines.

George Zander, chairman of the Desert Stonewall Democrats, the Coachella Valley's largest gay and lesbian political organization, described Bosworth as an unbending champion of his adoptive hometown who would not let anyone refer to Desert Hot Springs by its frequently used initials -- DHS.

"He loved the words Desert Hot Springs," Zander said. "You could not say the letters in his presence." Praise for Bosworth did not just come from political allies. Republicans such as Desert Hot Springs Councilwoman Mary Stephens and former Councilwoman Jan Pye spoke affectionately and emotionally of Bosworth as an honorable adversary and good friend.

Reach David Hermann at 760-837-4415 or dhermann@PE.com and Wes Woods at 760-837-4405 or wwoods@PE.com

****

Six: And the beat goes on

Meanwhile the city was being sued by the police union for having fired four policemen, including the Chief who was fired by the city manager, Jerry Hanson, who at the time was no longer the city manager, adding to problem.

All claims stated the four were fired without cause and that they wanted to be reinstated. None of this of course was conducive to bringing investors, bankers or developers to a city with so many problems, particularly when these type stories continue to play out in the media:

Former Desert Hot Springs police officer wants dead man's statements heard again in his bid to regain his job

10:00 PM PDT on Friday, April 27, 2007

By DOUGLAS QUAN
The Press-Enterprise

The alleged words of a man who shot and killed his family and himself two years ago were at the center of a courtroom debate Friday about whether the statements of a dead man could be used as evidence.

The arguments emerged at a hearing for a former Desert Hot Springs police officer who is appealing to get his job back. David Gallardo and three other officers were fired in 2003 amid accusations they covered up the circumstances of an off-duty vehicle accident involving one of the officers, though they were never charged.

Following an arbitration hearing, two of the four officers were reinstated but not Gallardo.

David McGowan, a Riverside County district attorney's investigator, was assigned to the case and had testified at the arbitration hearing in March 2005. Two months later and days before he was to testify again, McGowan took the lives of his wife, mother and three children while they slept in their Garner Valley home. He then shot himself. Investigators said they could not determine a motive and a suicide note was not found.

McGowan confided to a fellow investigator and friend in the months leading up to the murder-suicide that he had been pressured by his bosses to find criminal wrongdoing even though he believed there was none, according to documents

220

filed last week in Riverside County Superior Court by Gallardo's attorney.

Cover-Up Noted

McGowan had written in his report that there had been a cover-up in the off-duty accident and that charges could be brought against the officers, according to the documents. He considered resigning from the district attorney's office because of the pressure, former Riverside County district attorney's investigator Luis Bolanos said in a declaration supporting Gallardo's appeal.

"He felt he was stuck between doing the right thing (sticking with his findings) and being disciplined for not following orders," Bolanos said in the documents.

Bolanos was fired by the district attorney's office in 2005 amid allegations of domestic violence, though he was never convicted.

Bolanos said in an interview this week that he didn't know Gallardo or about his case until a few weeks ago when a friend mentioned Gallardo's case. That's what triggered his recollection of several statements McGowan made about a conflict he was having with his bosses, Bolanos said.

City's Response

Kathy Mount, an attorney for the city of Desert Hot Springs, argued in court that Bolanos' statements were hearsay and should be excluded from the evidence because there is no opportunity to cross-examine McGowan.

"You have one person who comes in and says (McGowan) was getting pressure to change his story. Who's going to dispute that? The guy's dead," Mount said by phone after the hearing. "The validity you can give to information like that, it's so suspect." Mount said she has been involved in a couple of cases where attorneys attempted to introduce the alleged words of dead people, ultimately without success.

Report Called Key

McGowan's alleged statements should be allowed because the police chief relied on McGowan's investigation in deciding to terminate Gallardo, his attorney, Robert Krause, said in an interview.

Judge H. Morgan Dougherty heard both arguments in an Indio courtroom Friday but did not immediately decide whether to allow Bolanos' evidence. No date for a decision was set.

Ingrid Wyatt, a spokeswoman for the district attorney's office, said she could not comment on the alleged disagreement between McGowan and his bosses because it was related to an employment action.

Grover Trask, the district attorney in 2005, said he believes Bolanos is a disgruntled former employee and doesn't put much stock in Bolanos' statements. Trask also said he doesn't recall hearing about any conflicts that McGowan was having with his superiors.

'It Was Inconclusive'

"We could never come to a conclusion as to the motivation, as to what was in his mind," said Trask referring to the murder and suicide. "It was inconclusive."

Riverside County Sheriff Bob Doyle said that he, too, had not heard that McGowan might have been upset with his bosses. The sheriff said there was nothing on McGowan's computer hinting at why he had killed his family.

"It would be nice if we had the answer as to why this happened," Doyle said.

Sandy Curl, McGowan's sister, said that she had spoken with her brother often before his death but was not aware of any problems that he may have had at work.

McGowan, described by colleagues as always calm and reasonable, shot his wife, Karen McGowan, 42; mother, Angelina McGowan, 75; son, Chase, 14; and daughters Paige, 10, and Rayne, 8. He called 911 seconds before killing himself. In the days after the murder-suicide on the family's sprawling estate in the San Jacinto Mountains, neighbors hinted at marital problems, and investigators looked into possible financial trouble. But in the end, no motive was found.

Investigators said that the only clue McGowan left was a printout of lyrics from the Los Lonely Boys song "Heaven." The lines read: "Woe is me. I'm looking forward to seeing you in my next life."

Staff writer Kimberly Trone contributed to this report. Reach Douglas Quan at 951-368-9479 or dquan@PE.com

As if there wasn't enough going on with the police department, looking for a replacement for the city manager, a recall election and the regular election coming up which could put three new people on the council, one of the members of the Desert Hot Springs Police Department became entangled in a child molestation case:

08:08 AM PDT on Friday, September 29, 2006

By DAVID RACLIN and JOHN ASBURY
The Press-Enterprise

A Desert Hot Springs police officer was arrested Thursday in Los Angeles on suspicion of aggravated sexual assault on a child.

Dennis P. Decker

Dennis P. Decker worked with Explorer Scouts and as a school resource officer at Desert Hot Springs High School and Desert

Hot Springs Middle School, according to law enforcement and school officials in the Coachella Valley.

Decker is scheduled to be arraigned Monday in Riverside Superior Court in Indio. He faces multiple felony charges, according to the Riverside County District Attorney's office.

Decker was arrested by Riverside County District Attorney's Office investigators while he was training in Los Angeles, attorney's office spokeswoman Ingrid Wyatt said Thursday evening by phone.

"We found out today," Desert Hot Springs Councilwoman Mary Stephens said Thursday evening by phone. Desert Hot Springs police told council members this morning that they had investigated Decker then passed that information along to the District Attorney's Office, Stephens said.

Desert Hot Springs Police Chief Walter McKinney said the station was "taken back" by the arrest and the charges being weighed against Decker.

McKinney said he was contacted late last week about an investigation but was not told the specifics of the charges. He said the department cooperated with district attorney's investigators while they also served search warrants on Decker's home.

"Right now we're just staying neutral," McKinney said. "We just don't know what is real and what isn't."

While with the Desert Hot Springs Police, Decker investigated juvenile offenders and created the Desert Hot Springs branch of the Explorer Scouts, a junior police program, McKinney said.

Decker worked at the high school for two years before he was reassigned in Sept. 2005, Palm Springs Unified School District Superintendent Lorri S. McCune said Thursday night by phone.

"As long as he (Decker) was with us, there was no report of anything," McCune said. Chief McKinney added that there were no complaints against Decker during the two years McKinney has been with the department.

McCune said district staff would likely try to locate any children who might have come in contact with Decker at the school and assess their needs.

Decker was arrested on suspicion of aggravated sexual assault of a child and other felony count and was being booked Thursday night into the Robert Presley Detention Center in Riverside, Wyatt said in a news release.

He was being held in lieu of $1 million bond.

Staff writer Paul DeCarlo contributed to this report.

****

The resignation of City Manager Hanson, created the immediate need for a replacement. Corky Larson, the former Desert Hot Springs City Attorney, was pressed into service on an interim basis, then Deputy City manager John Soulliere was elevated to "acting City Manager" and the search for a permanent replacement was continuing, but going very slowly with negative results. Then The Desert Sun published a provocative Editorial, chiding the city leaders to press harder and change their tactics:

Desert Hot Springs needs to start over on city manager's search

THE ISSUE
Desert Hot Springs' last three city manager finalists have question marks about their backgrounds.

WE SUGGEST: The city needs to start over on its search, either by seeking someone locally or hiring a professional search company.

WHAT DO YOU THINK? What must Desert Hot Springs do to ensure it can find the best qualified city manager?

The Desert Sun
February 26, 2006 February 26, 2006

Desert Hot Springs should start over its search for city manager. The city should look at qualified candidates in the valley who are known entities or turn to a headhunting firm that specializes in finding city managers.

Given the revelations about the latest front-runner, we are not convinced that Desert Hot Springs has found the best person for the job. The city should keep looking. Though more than six months has passed since the council began searching for a new city manager, the post remains open.

The need for Desert Hot Springs to get a quality city manager is imperative. After the Jerry Hanson contract controversy last year, the council needs someone to ensure City Hall's house is in order and to help restore residents' confidence in city government. In the long run, Desert Hot Springs needs a city manager who with the council can guide the city to realizing its full potential economically and in quality of life.

Candidates resigned past posts

227

The city manager search has been problematic. Consider the background of the three front-runners that the search has yielded so far:

The current frontrunner has held three different city manager posts in five years, has sued a previous employer for wrongful termination and resigned as deputy administrator of the Los Angeles Community Redevelopment Agency under controversy. We have questions about how long she might stay in Desert Hot Springs given she has moved on a lot in last few years. Her current mayor, however, does have good things to say about her.

A former head of San Bernardino County's redevelopment agency resigned from his job, and some have criticized him for not communicating well with residents. He has declined to comment.

A former city administrator had been forced to resign in May from his post of six years. Further controversy swirled when a city council member brought him but not his opponent to a party.

At least one council member has expressed displeasure with the search, a continuation of last autumn's aborted effort. Council member Mary Stephens rightly called the process "blemished." Stephens has been a strong advocate of the city doing the recruiting itself and is now saying it's no longer a good idea.

Among the problems in the search is that City Council members simply don't have the time to properly search for a candidate. They're part-time officials with other jobs. Recruiting is understandably not their expertise. They have many obligations as elected officials, from staying abreast of a variety of city issues to representing Desert Hot Springs on valley-wide and county panels. Indeed, based on their track record, the council either is not luring the best candidates or hasn't been able to select them from the pile of applications received. Consider that of 80 applications received for the job,

228

only 7 had municipal experience, Mayor Alex Bias told the editorial board.

Two solutions

To do a thorough job of identifying the best finalists, the council either must consider candidates with who they either are extremely familiar or hire an outside firm that can make the search its top priority several hours a day over several weeks.

Certainly there are a number of candidates working in the valley, from deputy city managers to other officials who've previously worked in such a position, who qualify for the job. For example, Deputy County Executive Officer Michael O'Connor - among the top five finalists in Desert Hot Springs' latest winnowing - previously served as Coachella's

and Ontario's city manager. We don't presume he's the best candidate but only offer his name as evidence that there are good ones in the valley. Such local candidates have a reputation that City Council members easily could turn to other trusted valley officials for verification.

Hiring a professional search firm marks a good strategy as well. The search would be conducted by professionals who keep track of quality candidates and are able to match them to Desert Hot Springs's needs and the council's vision. This search can be done speedily, sometimes as quickly as 45 days. The council always has final say about who is hired. Indio used this method last year when hiring its city manager. A search firm can be expensive, be having the best person in the job ultimately could negate that cost.

It behooves the council to start the search over and to get it done right. City Hall has been fine under Deputy City Manager John Soulliere's leadership certainly it will hold up under his tutelage for a few more weeks.

****

After pursuing several possibilities to bring commercial development into the city for over three years, a serendipitous event took place for me during a break in a city council meeting.

John Furbee, a well known wealthy resident of the city, former developer and philanthropist with large land-holdings, was telling the person sitting behind me that he had offered a ten-acre commercial site to the city for a planned community center, but they were stalling and haggling. The site was located across from City Hall and the price Furbee stated, was very low. I turned to him and said, "John, I can sell that parcel for that price in a heart beat." With that, John said "come see me tomorrow and we can talk about it." The result of that meeting was that I listed and then quickly sold that property, making John Furbee a tidy profit and me a good commission.

The buyer, Tahiti Partners, LLC proposed to build a commercial center on the site. This project was intended to be the first of many commercial ventures for spurring economic development. But unfortunately, personnel changes and ineptness on the city's planning and development staff delayed the project so long; it became trapped by the economic downturn. (Tahiti Partners just recently announced that the project is back on track and they are soliciting tenants).

By this time I had also accumulated several other listings of commercial sites throughout the city, hoping to convince commercial developers to acquire, design and build out, thereby helping improve desperately needed sales tax revenues for the city. Those dreams remain unfulfilled and are waiting for the next upswing in the economy, but only if/when Desert Hot Springs' leadership gets their act together.

Vortex Magazine, a publication of the Desert Local News, recently ran a story on John Furbee, which I thought would be appropriate to place here after receiving permission from Max Lieberman, my friend and publisher.

I want to preface the article with an explanation of its content. Max Lieberman, publisher of the Desert Local news, uses mostly volunteer "reporters" for his publication and for the most part, the articles are not edited. While the writers are well intentioned, quite often the quality of their submission is rather poor, as you may find this one to be. You will however get the point; John Furbee is, and has been a pillar in the community, a philanthropic giver of his time and money as well as a strong force in its leadership.

Should I be fortunate enough to interview John, the result will be entered in the "Interview" section of this manuscript.

John Furbee a Desert Hot Springs Icon

Desert Local News 08/2010

Vonda Pate-Davis

Exclusive: When you enter the grounds of John Furbee's home, there is a very large pool is the history of Desert Hot Springs. You are greeted by "Blitzen" a white Shepard dog who has been John's constant companion for 14+ years. Newer, and on duty as watch guard is "Kelly". You sit at the chess/dining table and look out at the BBQ pit and beyond pool is the Palms and Mountains. There is history all around you. The plaques of appreciation and awards are numerous from State, local and charitable organizations.

John came to the Coachella Valley in 1959 from West Virginia after graduating from University of West Virginia as a pharmacist. He fitted into the style of Palm Springs very well. He went to work for the Drug King drugstore and for a period of time lived in the famous "tree house" of Palm Springs. In 1969 he and a partner bought a motel in Desert Hot Springs, and started remodeling it for living quarters. The units were rented out to Canadians which proved out very well.

John Furbee

He bought the drugstore on Palm Drive near Pierson.

As the pharmacist it meant long hours so he bought the restaurant across the street. The many visitors at the hotel would go to the restaurant and Coffee's Bathhouse or events at Wardman Hall; which both facilities have been torn down and gone from history today. After closing the pharmacy for the day he could go across the street for his dinner and days count of proceeds. This became a very enjoyable part of his life. He got to know and talk to many people and to become a part of his city. This started his venture into property and business ownership. John was becoming involved with real estate purchases and development.

In 1974 John bought the Savers Drugs in Coachella. He started a drugs pick up and delivery service to the nursing homes and eventually was serving all the nrsing home in the valley. At this time he was running two pharmacies. He was first in the valley to have automatic pill count for filling orders.

232

John got into more land acquisition at auction and together with partners Jasper Huckabee and Larry Bertrand, built Casa del Sol, a 108 unit development on 2nd street. Later came 48 units Casa West next to what is now the Desert Hot Springs High School. In 1977 he sold the property which was later to become Rancho del Oro on Mission Lakes Blvd. These were the beginning of his major involvement in the development o Desert Hot Springs.

Dennis Baldwin bought the drugstore in 1977. However John stayed as relief pharmacist for a long time.

In the 1980's John, along with partners, ventured into building homes as Spa City Construction to sell at $90,000 a piece. In 1990 they built 53 homes as Sun Spring Homes. Later, John bought 288 lots in the 1990's. In 1999 they built homes to sell for $99,900, which a few years later resold for over $250,000; proving to be a very good investment for the buyers.

John has been a very active serving on the Board of the Boys and Girls Club for years and President one term. He donated land for the Angel View Foundation hoses. One of the houses was designated "Furbee House". He sold the land to the city for its future civic center and was available for help when needed for advancement of city facilities. John served on the Planning Commission and was involved with the Economic Development Committee. He has been on the Board of the chamber of Commerce several years and served on the original Downtown Development Committee.

John also serves as President of the Mission Springs Water District with a high level interest in the usage of solar energy. He has looked at the technology as the advancement for future development consideration.

John always appears at every event as he was Grand Marshal of 2006 Christmas Parade and recipient of the 2006 Senior

Inspiration Award for Desert Hot Springs. Although John did not know Cabot Yerxa; he did know Cole Eyraud, who saved Cabot's Pueblo Museum from demolition. As of 2010, he is still active in areas important to today to the city, even if just behind the scenes in our city of Desert Hot Springs.

****

The city has a new Manager

A new city manager was finally decided upon by the council. Ann Marie Gallant was chosen to be the city's ninth and newest of the string of managers hired, fired and/or quit during a relatively short cycle of time.

With the failure of the recall, our attention was directed to the coming election. Mary Stephens was running again and Hank Hohenstein wanted to retain his seat. Some of us encouraged Russell Betts to run for a council seat. Karl Baker, a very vocal and active community member through his hat in the ring once again, while as usual, Adam Sanchez, the perennial candidate waged a campaign for a seat as well.

Russ, Karl, Patrick, me and several supporters wanted to make sure that Mary and Hank wouldn't get reelected. It seemed to us that in order to get a majority on the council which would evoke change in the way things had been going in the city, Russ and Karl joining Alex would be the right mix.

We held a meeting in my home to discuss strategy and to get commitments from all concerned. Attendees were: Russ; Patrick; Karl; Gabriel; Alex; and Dean. We wanted a commitment that all candidates would support one another, and to agree that the goal was to get three of them elected. Hohenstein and Stephens weren't going to be push-over's, they were going to fight, and they were being supported and funded by the developer consortium headed by Walt Luce. The evidence came out in some news stories which we played on in the ensuing campaign:

It turned out that the all-knowing Al Schmidt, Planning Commissioner, future candidate for council, former card dealer in Reno and self styled real estate investor/guru, knew much less about what makes things work than he or others thought he did, as this article shows by his quotes and the utter failure and ultimate abandonment of the planned commercial project of Schmidt and his partners.

Desert Hot Springs primed for expansion: "If you build it they will come"

Jun 26, 2007

The "northern gateway," the new "west side," the city "corridor" are all creating the new Desert Hot Springs. The city, which has admittedly had its difficulties in the last ten years, is primed for growth.

The Village at Mission Lakes

"My partners and I happen to believe the city has finally caught on," said Al Schmidt, one of four partners opening The Village at Mission Lakes, a business development, offering 65,000 square feet of leasable space in the city's touted new "west side."

The Village at Mission Lakes will soon house a restaurant and a market, with much more to follow, according to Community Development Director Steven Mendoza.

"The city is on an upswing right now. We have a pro-development city council currently," said Mendoza.

That is clear by the number of single-family homes, approximately 14,000, on approved tentative maps, according to Schmidt, who is also chairman of te city's planning commission. Desert Hot Springs also has many approved, active developments and an influx of annexations. The city itself is sponsoring two annexations of Riverside County land. One is approximately 354 acres generally bordered by Atlantic Avenue to the west, Palm Drive to the east, 15th Avenue to the north and Dillon Road to the south. The other is about 3,494 acres generally bordered by Indian Avenue to the west, Palm Drive to the east, 15th Avenue to the north and Interstate 10 to the south.

Meanwhile developers are petitioning for their own annexations.

College of the Desert Board members have not yet decided on the location for the new west valley campus, but Mendoza and others in the city are optimistic.

"We're hoping for a positive vote [in favor of Desert Hot Springs] pretty soon," said Mendoza.

Oasis

With more people and a new educated workforce opportunities abound for commercial, retail and business space. The Oasis master planned development would be the first major shopping center on the north side of I-10. The 133-acre plan includes 518,000 square feet of commercial retail space, 430,000 square feet of office space and 690 residential units in the form of apartments, duplexes and sixplexes. Oasis is still in the maps and planning stage, according to Mendoza.

More Articles of Interest:

Pierson Professional Center

Tahiti Partners Real Estate Development Corporation plans to break ground on the Pierson Professional Center by years end, said Mendoza. The center will be located on Pierson Boulevard, the main artery of Desert Hot Springs. The development is broken into three phases, the first is a medical office building, the second and third are planned for medical emergency care facilities, professional office space, a national restaurant chain and other retail.

Pierson Boulevard Corridor

Infrastructure is also key to preparing the city for growth and development, that's why the city spent 4-million dollars renovating its new "Main Street," the Pierson Boulevard Corridor. The renovation included road construction and expansion from two lanes to four. The street now also has

parking on both sides, landscaped center medians, antique lighting and other decorative touches, all in an attempt to make a classy first impression to drivers coming into a city in progress.

The next step for this corridor: attracting new businesses. The city's redevelopment agency is dedicated to bringing in neighborhood retailers that will serve current and expected future residents, according to the city's circulating "Open for Business" brochure.

Two Bunch Palms

The city's noted "crowned jewel," Two Bunch Palms, is taking notice of the growth and expansion projects all around and doing its own. Not only is the world-renowned spa planning a makeover for itself, it is also looking to expand and include the country's first mineral springs and spa-oriented, residential-planned community. Two Bunch Palms and its developers King Ventures of San Luis Obispo is in the planning stages to build 700 residences and 600 visitor units located around mineral soaking pools and recreational facilities.

The Desert Hot Springs city counsel has already given its approval for a 121,500 square foot Healing Arts Plaza that would include specialty medical clinics, massage center, spa and fitness center, health and wellness education center, soaking mineral grotto, hydro-therapy center, theaters, meeting rooms and restaurants.

According to the city brochure, the spa's expansion is critical to the revitalization of the city's tourist-serving spa industry, enhancement of downtown and would ultimately generate numerous service-industry jobs for local residents.

New Branding

On tap for the city that boasts some of the world's best drinking water: marketing. Desert Hot Springs is branding itself as "California's Spa City" and has the facts to back the title. The renowned mineral waters flowing under the earth in the desert city have been used for healing and therapy since they were discovered. Celebrities and sun seekers from all over the world have been coming to Desert Hot Springs for a natural, tranquil retreat since the 1950s. The city offers more than 40 boutique spa resorts with a commitment to health and wellness for residents and visitors.

The city is fine-tuning its branding message and a new "Spa City" logo. It also conducted a market study of stakeholder groups to find out what attracts developers to Desert Hot Springs. The answers were these: 1) an abundance of affordable, available land; 2) a business-friendly atmosphere; 3) an uncommon opportunity.

Mendoza said the city plans to market these attributes and aggressively grow the little town that could.

****

Of course most of this was braggadocio. What did come to pass became roaring failures, as Schmidt and his partners' ill planned and poorly executed development plans for "Paradise Springs" and "The Village" projects went down in flames, leaving the city holding the bag for more than $500,000 in unpaid public improvements on "The Village", a 440 unit residential project only 20% complete, with raging home owners trying to deal with a defunct Home Owners Association and no funds to operate with. Between Hubris and the Vortex, the partners and home owners didn't have a chance.

Added to this debacle was the eye-sore of the partially completed commercial project on the very visible corner of Mission Lakes Blvd. and Little Morongo; three buildings in various stages of completion; some partly framed; one partially plastered with some clay tiles scattered on the roof, black underlayment paper blowing in the winds and haphazard piles of construction materials and waste baking in the sun, lasting until this month, (February 2011) almost four years.

"The Village" was a project that should never have been built. I spent many hours with one of the lead partners Michael Rissman, pleading with him not to break ground. This project was destined to fail when it left the drawing boards.

239

Designed to be s two story mixed retail/office complex (a death knell, as any competent commercial broker will tell you) out in the middle of the desert, with nothing remotely close by, other than a 15-year-old golf course and a residential home project of a few hundred homes and plans for homes that have never broken ground.

Had Schmidt, Rissman and the other partners been using conventional financing, they would never have received funding for the project. Financing for both "Paradise Springs" and "The Village" was provided by a firm raising money by selling fractional interest trust deeds, the principals of which are now in jail, having left more than 500 projects in the state of California in various stages of completion and thousands of investors losing millions.

I could not change his mind. Rissman was convinced (hubris is a bad thing) the project would succeed. History has proven otherwise. Developers and other experts I have attempted to interest in salvaging the project have all said the same thing: "it will take ten to fifteen years for this project to make any sense."

The defunct project was subsequently listed by a friend of mine, Craig Way of Seaway Properties, who works with bankruptcy Trustees. I tried to find someone brave enough to take a chance on it, at one time convincing Geoffrey Pane, CEO of Tahiti Partners to at least look and run the numbers, which he did, and then passed, saying it was 10 years too early and was worth way less than the asking price at the time.

The Artist's drawing and description of the project on the following page, not only describes the property, but also the tale of how it ended up not being finished, and a bit of hype about Desert Hot Springs being the "fastest growing city in Coachella Valley due to developer interest". That of course is no longer the case, and was an overstatement at the time the information was published.

The Village at Mission Lakes

64949 Mission Lakes Boulevard, Desert Hot Springs

Description

The Village at Mission Lakes is an UNAPPROVED SHORT SALE. The Village at Mission Lakes is a 51,776-square foot commercial center in West Desert Hot Springs, across from the Mission Lakes Country Club. With a Santa Barbara style architecture, the center has 44,000 square feet in Building #1, which is 90 percent complete and includes 10,000 square feet of office space, a food court of 5,200 square feet and 28,800 square feet for retail. Building #2 is approximately 50 percent completed and is envisioned as a restaurant row for two or three quality restaurants, something the City of Desert Hot Springs desperately needs. A third building of 13,000 square feet has been approved and designed but has not been built pending the successful rent up of the first two buildings. No income or expenses for Building #3 have been included in this proposal.

The property was bought in 2005 with funds from the lender, Estate Financial, Inc. Construction began in early 2006 and continued until April, 2007 when Estate Financial, Inc. informed us that they were not able to pay any more vouchers. In July, 2007, Estate Financial filed for bankruptcy. Since then, the project has been shut down

241

The City of Desert Hot Springs is a city of approximately 24,000 people. Located 100 miles from Los Angeles, 50 miles from Ontario International Airport and six miles from the Palm Springs Airport, it is the city that all experts agree will be the fastest growing city in the Valley in the years ahead due to its location, available land area and developer interest. The Village at Mission Lakes is located at the intersection of Little Morongo Road and Mission Lakes Boulevard approximately two and one half miles from the center of town on the West side of Desert Hot Springs, in the more affluent area of town. There are over 3,000 homes within five a minute drive of the center and the L.A. Times recently wrote that the West side of the Coachella Valley (Desert Hot Springs & Palm Springs) will be the fastest growing area in the next decade because of the short commute to Riverside and San Bernardino.

Once again, with a new city manager at the helm, positive statements were being made by the Desert Hot Springs city council and staff, and a new general plan was being talked about. Ann Marie Gallant looked like she would take no prisoners in setting her goals for turning the city around and promised the allusive economic prosperity the city so desperately wanted and needed. Gallant was going to become the white night everyone in the city was hoping for. At least that's what they thought.

Desert Hot Springs may channel new image

10:00 PM PDT on Monday, June 4, 2007

By JULIA GLICK
The Press-Enterprise

DESERT HOT SPRINGS - Long beset by financial woes, political infighting and blight, Desert Hot Springs is touting a new, rather New Age plan to remake itself, capitalizing on the city's mountain views, healing springs and what planners say is its status as an "energy vortex."

A plan that calls for main streets with edgy architecture and nature-based features defined by the elements of earth, water and air was unveiled and praised by city leaders last week. Members of the Desert Hot Springs City Council, planning commissioners and residents also warmed to the idea of branding the city north of Palm Springs and down-mountain from Joshua Tree National Park as "California's Spa City."

Staff is now working to put these ethereal-sounding ideas into the earthy lingo of design standards, setbacks, colors and architectural guidelines ideally by early July, said City Manager Ann Marie Gallant. Desert Hot Springs leaders are praising an urban design plan unveiled last week that would give the city a new look.

Rodrigo Peña / The Press-Enterprise

Once the council and planning commission approve the urban design plan and those standards, the city can use them to guide more than two dozen developments obtaining approvals to break ground near the city's main drags, she said. After its makeover, Desert Hot Springs officials are entertaining the idea of using the title "California's Spa City."

Power of Change

By fall, officials hope to have the newly presented plan for the corridors around Palm Drive and Pierson Boulevard incorporated into a general plan and land-use plan for the future, Gallant said."This whole thing is a microcosm of the city reinventing itself, new image, new look, new architecture,

243

new staff," Gallant said. "It is one of many things we've done to say, 'Hey look, we are not the same Desert Hot Springs.' "

The rapidly growing city of about 20,000 residents emerged from bankruptcy in 2004, and has been encouraging new development, boutique spas and attractions that appeal to health-conscious tourists.

Jerry Ogburn, of the Rancho Mirage office of The Planning Center, unveiled the new plan May 29, saying the idea is to make the city a work of art.

The plan outlines what it calls two vortexes, defined as areas where powerful earth-energy sources converge: one at the city's gateway from Interstate 10 along Palm Drive and the other at the downtown intersection of Palm Drive and Pierson Boulevard.

An energy technology park and a regional business campus would stand at the I-10 gateway, and the downtown area's two main streets would have different architectural and landscaping features.

"Earth" zones would feature desert landscaping, and would transition dramatically to adjacent "air" zones with oasis palms and plants, Ogburn said. The city's two "water" zones would encompass many of the city's boutique spas and and, the lavenders of the mountains, sunny gold and the turquoise of the city's would employ lush landscaping. The

The concept of balancing the natural elements in a city comes from the writings of Marcus Vitruvius Pollio, a Roman architect during the first century B.C., Ogburn said.

Ogburn added that Desert Hot Springs should eschew the Mediterranean, tile-roof architecture abundant in Orange County and throughout the Coachella Valley in favor of modern "true desert architecture" reminiscent of Frank Lloyd Wright's Taliesin West.

Complementary Ideas

Bruce Abney, one of the owners of the El Morocco Inn and Spa, said he is excited about the new plan and hopes to hang a copy of it in the inn for guests to see.

"It's a great talking point: 'The city is sort of rundown, but look what's coming our way,' " he said. "It's exciting, it's different and it celebrates the place we are in."

Abney, whose spa sits on the edge of the downtown vortex zone, said the New Age elements of the plan dovetail nicely with the city's emphasis on spas, healing and wellness.

Community organizer Judy Shea was also enthusiastic about the plan, but said she worries it could become another expensive document that gathers dust on city shelves.

The city must also be careful not to impose the new standards as a burden on small businesses that may not have the finances to revamp.

"Redevelopment money should be spent to help the business owners upgrade," she said.

Also under discussion is a proposal for a new and radically different city seal and logo. Mike Cheley, CEO of Palm Desert-based Graphtek, unveiled last week a draft logo and seal

featuring a water spurt framed by a desert plant, purple mountains and a golden sky.

City officials sent the consultants back to the drawing board with suggestions for improvement. Gallant said the city hopes to have a version most people can agree on by July.

Reach Julia Glick at 760-837-4418 or jglick@PE.com

Desert Hot Springs candidates want bigger tax base

10:00 PM PDT on Friday, October 12, 2007

By STEVE MOORE
The Press-Enterprise

DESERT HOT SPRINGS - Image, fiscal responsibility and more commercial development for funding public services are key issues in the upcoming City Council election.

Two incumbents, Mayor Pro Tem Mary K. Stephens and Councilman Hank Hohenstein, are seeking re-election Nov. 6, facing off against five challengers: businessman/manufacturer Russell Betts, retired businessman/teacher Karl Baker Jr., bookkeeper Sharon Sandison, business owner Terry Scheurer and Planning Commission Chairman Al Schmidt. The seven hopefuls are vying for two council seats.

Stephens, an accounting manager, has served on the council for eight years.

In a candidate's statement on the sample ballot, the councilwoman says she helped Desert Hot Springs through some very difficult times, including bringing the city out of bankruptcy. She says the city's famed spa industry has turned around with entrepreneurs buying old spas and generating more bed-tax revenue for city coffers.

"It is important that the city have continuity and that the progress continue," she wrote.

Hohenstein, in his candidate's statement, said, "Much has been done, but there is still more to do to realize our vision of becoming California's Spa city. We are on our way to being the desired health and wellness destination."

Prosperity in Desert Hot Springs requires a long-term vision, he said, citing 40 years of working with local governments on planning.

"It is not how well each person works, but how well we work together," Hohenstein wrote.

Challenger Betts says Desert Hot Springs has focused too much on outlying areas -- a situation that he says has "left our city center neglected and residential neighborhoods in disrepair," according to his candidate's statement.

He said the city lacks a "vibrant shopping district" capable of generating sales-tax revenue for funding public services such as police and code enforcement.

"I'm running for City Council to bring about that change," he wrote.

Challenger Baker is calling for "new leadership" for the city.

"I have developed a reputation as a fighter for the rights of taxpayers," he wrote in a candidate's statement.

Baker said he vigorously supports increasing the retail tax base for funding city services.

"I will push to improve our downtown and support new businesses in our city," he wrote.

Challenger Sandison says her more than 30 years in accounting, her "common sense values" as a businesswoman, homemaker and mother and her experience working for the city will help her deal with important issues affecting taxpayers.

Much could be done to improve the city's financial situation, she wrote in a candidate's statement, adding, "By so doing, a culture of confidence can rise, encouraging more businesses to come to the city, increasing tax revenue and making for a more varied and vibrant community."

Challenger Scheurer calls for improving the city's image, increasing revenue for city services, more police and fire protection and keeping a City Council log of citizen complaints/suggestions and the actions taken -- along with several other issues in a 10-point plan.

"Our city offers low housing prices with fantastic views and natural hot springs," he wrote in a candidate's statement.

Challenger Schmidt says that during his tenure on the planning commission he has been directly involved in the growth of the city, citing Skyborne and The Village at Mission at Mission Lakes Shopping Center.

"I want to see this growth continue and as your councilmember, I will be diligent in working toward that end," he wrote in a candidate statement.

Schmidt calls for managing Desert Hot Springs like a private business and creating a Citizens for Desert Hot Springs volunteer organization. The group would strive to "improve the image and perception of our city." He says one example would be eliminating "illegal" and "unsightly" signs in the city.

"We're growing and it's time to shed our small town attitude and image and take our rightful place in this valley," Schmidt wrote.

Reach Steve Moore at 760-837-4417 or stevemoore@PE.com

****

We published the article and picture below shortly after Stephen's lost her mayoral election attempt, dealing a blow to the King-makers, Walt Luce and his hired guns.

Desert Sun Photo

This picture, taken by a Desert Sun photographer, captures the essence of the inner feelings of Desert Hot Springs mayoral candidate Mary Stephens and a few of her supporters on the evening of the November 8th Election as they view the results of her loss to challenger Alex Bias.

What went wrong? What went right? For the answers to these two questions and others, watch this column over the next days and weeks as we interview candidates and share in some "Monday Morning Quarterbacking" send us an e-mail on your views and we will share them with our reader/viewers.

Yours for better government

Bill Effinger

Desert Local News

Gallant's tenure and the euphoria surrounding her predictions and take charge persona, soon took a turn for the worse with revelations of questionable decision making and financial commitments she made in her past position, and then in Desert Hot Springs. Her visionary concepts were clearly beyond the city's capacity to fulfill. Gallant's champions were starting to become her detractors. Al Schmidt however was one of Gallant's strongest supporters and allies. After her departure, it became quite clear why.

Whether a lapse of good judgment or something less seemly, Gallant agreed that the city would accept a $500,000 "letter of credit" rather than the normal Surety Bond for all of the offsite construction of city improvements. Unfortunately for the city, the letter of credit proved to be a worthless piece of paper. The shady dealings of Estate Financial, Inc., the lender for Schmidt and his Partners "The Village" project was indicted and subsequently jailed, where they remain while the State of California sifts through more than 500 other projects left in various stages of completion lay dormant. The "letter of credit" was bogus. Why Gallant accepted it as collateral for required infrastructure improvements remains a mystery. Suspicions abound about the role Schmidt may have played in Gallant's action.

'Turmoil' seen in Desert Hot Springs after personnel upheaval

250

The Vortex made me do it

11:24 PM PDT on Sunday, August 19, 2007

By JULIA GLICK
The Press-Enterprise

Under the guidance of a new city manager, Desert Hot Springs looked like it might finally claim a share of the Coachella Valley's wealth and cachet.

The city, one of the poorest in Riverside County, began projects to revamp its image and to replace blighted and trash-strewn roads with desert landscaping, crisp modern architecture and a proposed community college campus.

Just as some plans started becoming reality, their architect, City Manager Ann Marie Gallant, abruptly quit. Days later, her replacement resigned on his first day on the job.

Story continues below

Ramon Mena Owens / The Press-Enterprise

The Village at Mission Lakes, along Mission Lakes Boulevard in Desert Hot Springs, is one of the projects being built in the community. City officials have initiated projects to improve Desert Hot Springs' image.

The two resignations in less than a week this month have many residents worried the city will slide back into political

251

turmoil and economic instability. A group of residents, including several candidates for City Council, is calling for Gallant's reinstatement. Meanwhile, the City Council is promising to continue her work while searching for a lasting replacement.

'We Will Continue'

"I think that the projects that we have going will not slow down," said Councilman Hank Hohenstein. "We will continue with great vigor on all of those."

After interim City Manager John Hensley resigned Aug. 13, the City Council appointed Assistant City Manager Steven Mendoza as acting city manager. Hohenstein estimates the city will find a replacement for Gallant in three to six months, but may have to increase her salary of $155,000, which was one of the lowest for a city manager in the Coachella Valley.

Both Hensley and Gallant have declined to speak with reporters, and city officials will not comment on why Gallant left.

During her roughly 15-month tenure, she spearheaded efforts to hire a new police chief to lead the city's troubled department, which is part of an FBI inquiry.

Gallant took over a few years after the city of roughly 22,000 people recovered from bankruptcy. Early on, she laid off city employees to balance the budget.

Gallant later hired consultants to improve the city's image. The tagline "California's Spa City" was formally registered this month, and a city-sponsored Web site marketing Desert Hot Springs' boutique spa hotels came online this summer, said city consultant Catherine Rips. A redesign of the city logo, a new urban design plan and a bid for a College of the Desert west campus are all under way, Rips said.

Ramon Mena Owens / The Press-Enterprise

Downtown shops along Palm Drive in Desert Hot Springs are among the attractions the city offers.

The City Council is striving to make the transition seamless, and projects will not fall through the cracks, said Councilwoman Yvonne Parks. But some residents believe that won't be possible.

"I am really upset about the whole thing," said Dot Reed, a former councilwoman who served during the early part of Gallant's tenure. "I just feel we had come so far and were doing so well. And nobody now is going to step in and do things the way they are supposed to be done."

Reed, one of more than a dozen residents who told the council recently to rehire Gallant, said she thinks the circumstances of Gallant's departure and the high turnover of city managers over the years will discourage qualified job applicants.

Potential Harm Seen

She said she also worries that the uncertainty right now in leadership could hurt the city's bid for the college campus. School officials have said they plan to choose a site in September.

Bob Marra, president of Wheeler's Market Intelligence, which analyzes business trends in the Coachella Valley, said the turnover could hurt the city's image and potentially put off some developers from investing in the city.

"Gallant was working specifically on projects such as new identity and logo, a tagline and a way to promote the city both for tourism and economic development, issues to improve the city, and here we go with more turmoil and more question marks," he said.

The upheaval comes just a few months before elections in which the city will choose a mayor and two council members. Several challengers have called for Gallant to be rehired, but incumbents such as Hohenstein remain optimistic about a replacement and the city's prospects.

"It's a great city. The water is award-winning, the air is better here, the views are phenomenal, we'll get it together," Hohenstein said. "We'll get through this."

Then Mayor Bias became a major problem. Unfortunately for the city and Alex Bias, he became his own worst enemy, believing as mayor, he was really a King, or put another way, Alex became a wanna-be dictator, an embarrassment to the city and me personally for having worked hard to help him get elected.

For a former school teacher, he seemed to know very little about our form of government at the level he was involved. In short, Alex Bias as mayor was a total failure. Having been deeply involved in helping get elected, I took it upon myself to let him know publicly my disappointment.

This letter was published in the Desert Local News:

An open letter to Mayor Bias

Mayor Bias you were elected as mayor and as such you are a member of the council, no more and no less.

As described in California Government Code, Section 34903, and 40605: "The mayor is a member of the city council and has all of the powers and duties of a member of the city council: (but no more Mr. Mayor) And: "In general law cities where the office of mayor is an elective office pursuant to Article 5 (commencing with Section 34900) of Chapter 7 of Part 1 of Division 2 of Title 4, the mayor, with the approval of the city council, shall make all appointments to boards, commissions, and committees unless otherwise specifically provided by statute."

The action words in 40605 are: "with the approval of the city council" simply put, you are a member of the city council with no special powers not approved by your colleagues on the council.

The City Manager serves at the behest of the entire city council and answers to the entire city council, not the mayor, not the mayor pro-tem as individuals, but as a majority.

The city manager's power is described in Section 34856 of the Government Code as: The city manager may appoint and dismiss the chief of police and other subordinate appointive officers and employees except the city attorney. In other words Mr. Mayor, whether you agree or disagree with our City Manager Ann Marie Gallant and her decisions, you may not interfere with her performance unilaterally without council consent given in an open or closed session meeting.

When you were campaigning for your job, you told us that the past was forgotten and that you wanted the best for the city of Desert Hot Springs. You said you were a consensus builder and wanted to cooperate with your colleagues on the council. Your actions since being elected have proven to be far from your stated intent.

We looked the other way when you clashed with our acting City Manger Corky Larson, but we will not look the other way or stand by quietly while you attempt to interfere and micro-manage or second guess Gallant's decisions. She was hired as City Manger, to run the city as her experience and the city council (all five members or at least a voting majority) allow.

Your widely published and televised personal financial antics have become a major embarrassment to the city and the people living here. Friday morning you described yourself as having been a "Crusader Rabbit" all your life. Unfortunately your personal crusades are detrimental to the well being of the citizens of Desert Hot Springs.Please, for the good of the city during the remaining months of your term, allow Our City manger to do her job and if you have complaints, don't voice them unless you have at least the minimum of a council majority that share your views, and then only withb their permission.
Yours for a better Desert Hot Springs

Bill Effinger

My son Brian chimed in from his perch in Washington, posting a Blog on the subject, succinct and erudite as usual:

After reading and hearing much of what has gone on at City Hall in Desert Hot Springs over the past several months, however, I have to ask myself if there's nothing left to lose for residents of this city by recalling the mayor, if not entire council.

Mayor Bias appears deluded by the title he holds. In a council-manager system, he is just another vote. He is not the Grand Poobah of Desert Hot Springs. Bias' influence is dictated by the extent to which he is willing to play the hand that is dealt to him in terms of who he shares the dais with, and his ability and desire to build consensus among the other council members. Mayor Bias obviously feels that is beneath him and is attempting to get his way by sheer force of will. He is discovering, though refusing to admit, that his belligerent approach is stripping him of whatever influence he thinks he has, which, given the makeup of the council as a whole, is perpetuating the status quo -- the very thing he campaigned to shake up.

Mayor Bias does have one duty as mayor that, while not codified in the City Charter, is nonetheless vastly more important than swinging a gavel at council meetings. Mayor Bias is the face of Desert Hot Springs. For better or worse, his title, his reputation, and his representation of the city of Desert Hot Springs is the first impression that is etched in the minds of the public, potential investors, and public officials up and down the bureaucratic food chain in California. Threatening to throw people out of "his" chamber and telling a fellow councilmember to "go play with herself" tells folks all they need to know about the city of Desert Hot Springs. To that extent, he is a reflection of the values of the residents who put him there; and if that is an inaccurate assessment, voters therefore have a duty to throw Alex Bias out on his ear.

Brian Effinger

Most of us felt the same way, but decided to wait Alex's term out and make sure he didn't get elected again. The city didn't need a recall to add to the trouble caused by Bias's actions.

In fairness to Alex, the council set him off almost immediately after he was elected, by stripping him of all of the normal appointments the mayor had always made, and in general, treating him very badly in public. He fought back as anyone would, particularly someone who had served two voluntary deployments in Vietnam, as Alex had. He was a fighter, but didn't know the rules of this battle.

Ann Marie Gallant cut her tenure short by resigning after being with the city about eighteen months, negotiating a settlement of her contract and receiving several months' severance pay in the process.

Once again, the city found itself in search of a new city manager. But this time, they received help from County Supervisor Marion Ashley. Ashley and the balance of Supervisors were in fear that if something wasn't done and quickly, the county could end up having to take over the city and its problems. Should that happen, the county would inherit the city's past mistakes and debts—not a good prospect for the county.

Ashley came to the city's rescue by presenting his long time friend Rick Daniels, former Executive Director of the Salton Sea Water Authority and Executive Director of the Coachella Valley Economic Partnership, whom I had worked with as a member of that organization.

I liked Rick, and thought he was good at what he was doing and had done in the past, but I was stressing through my articles, the importance of the city's leaders not making a choice for a new manager before the new council would take their seats, thereby avoiding controversy about the un-electeds' having made the choice just weeks before a probable new council would take shape.

Following my article, I received a phone call early on a Sunday morning from Daniels asking me "why I was opposing him". I explained that I wasn't opposing him, I was opposing the current city Council's choice to make the selection 45 days before the election of what would probably be a sea-change in the council, basically robbing the new members of making a choice of the person they would be looking to manage the city for the foreseeable future.

I felt he and Ashley were creating a possible firestorm of protests from the voters when their newly elected leaders were not given the opportunity to vet and interview the new city manager. I also felt that with Supervisor Ashley's efforts, he would no doubt be selected anyway. My explanation seemed to quell his fears that I was going to blow his chances.

After a whirlwind round of meetings with the selection committee that included future candidate for council Scott Matas and Planning Commission chairman John Gerardi, Rick was hired with a salary of $235,000 plus benefits totaling another $35,000, on a three-year contract with a "Golden Parachute" of a year's salary if he was fired with or without cause.

As I had predicted, there was an uproar from a large group of citizens crying foul and chastising the "railroading" of Daniels into the manager's position prior to the coming election, and the accompanying pressure applied to the process by Supervisor Ashley. With the decision made and Daniels assuming the role of city manager, it was time for everyone to accept the fact and move on, so I published the following article in the Desert Local News in October of 2007:

A new beginning for DHS

Now that Rick Daniels is officially our new city manager I hope the entire community will support him as he begins to grapple with the myriad issues before him and the city at large. Changing the historical direction that mismanagement and poor political choices have created for the city will be a monumental task.

Frustrations over the process and timing of the city manager appointment should be voiced at the polls in November when the opportunity to make real change in the political leadership is afforded citizen voters. Until then and on into the future we should all be willing to volunteer our time and effort to help in any way we can to assist Daniels in his task.

Helping build a thriving revenue generating economic base can only happen with the cooperation of the community at large. Cleaning up the visual trash with effective code enforcement and reducing crime are top priorities which Daniels has evoked in recent media interviews. We must help Rick in all of his stated goals if the city is to rise above itself and become the good neighbor our sister cities and DHS citizens deserve.

Please join me in pledging your support to Rick Daniels, City Manager of Desert Hot Springs.

Bill Effinger

****

The article was well received by Rick, his friends and supporters as he immediately dug into the issues confronting him and the city. But as had been predicted, Daniels started out with some mistrust among some of the new council members, which lingered and festered over time.

The 2007 Election

Diana and I had great interest in the coming election and wanted to see Russell Betts get elected. He, I and Diana spent many nights on our front patio in the balmy evenings discussing his potential candidacy and what he would do if elected. We worked hard for Russ during the campaign.

Russell Betts and Karl Baker defeated Mary and Hank decisively, with Betts garnering more total votes than anyone ever received when running for office since the city had been incorporated, Yvonne Parks was elected mayor, upending

Alex's rein, and none too soon. Al Schmidt was elected by 12-votes, narrowly defeating the next closest candidate.

Karl Baker was appointed Mayor pro-tem, by Parks, which generated some resentment from council member Betts. As the largest vote-getter on the slate, including Yvonne Parks, Betts felt he should have been appointed rather than Karl because of his large vote count, but that's Politics!

We all felt the city was now poised for change. With Hank, Mary and former mayor Weyuker out of the picture, things would definitely get better—at least that's what we hoped for.

Unfortunately that wasn't to be. Soon after the election, a rift between Baker and Betts developed into a schism, splitting their votes, and Betts, being a conservative business man wanting to see the city run more efficiently and cost effectively, quite often found himself as odd man out when the issues and votes came before the council at times.

———

One of Daniel's first and most pressing problems as city manager was steering the past and present efforts of the city council away from battling the Coachella Valley Association of Governments (CVAG) over the Multi-Species Habitat Conservation Plan (MSHCP). Desert Hot Springs was the lone holdout under former mayor Matt Weyuker's misguided leadership, exposing the city to being required to pay a penalty fee of $1.3Million to CVAG for the delays it caused and the related costs to the Valley's neighboring cities.

Daniels, through some masterful negotiations and help from Supervisor Ashley, convinced the Desert Hot

Springs council and then CVAG to allow the city back into the Plan, without having to pay the assessed penalty, thereby breaking up the ten-year log-jamb created under Weyuker's leadership.

However, Daniels was running into some opposition from a few newly elected council members, as I had suspected might happen, resulting in Daniels calling me for some friendly advice, to which I replied in an e-mail as follows:

Rick:

In your call yesterday you indicated you "needed counsel" and that you didn't understand the "mistrust" you are sensing amongst the many individuals you are dealing with.

This response is coming from my experience as a former city councilman and mayor, as well as many years of working with managers and councils of a myriad of cities in California, Arizona, Nevada and Colorado, and is being given sincerely and honestly.

When someone asks me for "counsel" I take that seriously, and make the assumption that the party requesting counsel is prepared to hear what I have to say, whether it is what they want to hear or not, so here goes:

First, you will remember the Sunday morning you called me at 7:30am after you read my comments in the Desert Sun about my opposition to the rush in your being hired and pushed by Marion Ashley? During that call, I attempted to explain that you would be jeopardizing your future, and that of the city, in that the new council would take exception to the process. I told you that your inexperience in city management/government would be a target for the community and the new council. I said to wait was a much better alternative because of the probable resentment the community would have.

Well, as I also predicted, the three people that have been elected are the same three and most vocal who opposed the rushed process of your hire.

That, in a nutshell isa big part of the "mistrust" you are experiencing.

Now couple that with the fact that the new mayor is joined at the hip with Matt Weyuker and his crony crowd (read Mary, Glen Greener, Hank Hohenstein, Walt Luce) and you have the additional reasons for mistrust.

This is all just for openers. Now let's look at what your job entails. A good city manager is a master politician, top administrator of personnel, a strong fiscal manager, and must exude the embodiment of the community in which he/she serves. Add to this mix that the CM must be capable of giving solid advice to the city council he/she serves, and most important, the council must have the confidence that the manager is that capable person.

You are now faced with what I predicted would happen. You are not trusted by the majority of those you must serve for all of the reasons outlined herein.

On three occasions over the past few months I offered to arrange some good counsel for you from top city managers, which could have girded you for what you are now facing. For your own reasons, you chose not to avail yourself of the opportunity. Those doors are now closed and both are watching the ensuing drama with amusement.

Your recent actions are confusing to us all. You say you proposed the meeting last evening to show "open government" a master politician would not have set up that ridiculous stage, in light of the existing mistrust. On the heels of that, you propose to discontinue the televised meetings, which the community fought for and finally got, which seems counter to your wanting "open government" for the people. The Desert Sun jumped on that this morning as I expected they would and that issue will be given much publicity over the next few weeks I am sure. There are many more issues the council-elect have shared with me that will unfold as they come into office which you will be confronting soon enough, so I won't go into them here.

I have almost five years of my time invested in Desert Hot Springs, as well as a considerable monetary investment, and have tried to always see the glass as half full for the city's future, much to the dismay of my wife, Diana.

I would like you to succeed, because that would mean that the city is succeeding, but in my view as I told you before you accepted the job, you would be starting out on the wrong foot, and it would be hard to overcome, and I am afraid that is what is happening.

I offer these comments as a friend and to be as constructive as possible. This, then is my counsel.

Bill

****

Daniels pursued the unwinding of the MSHCP roadblock to the relief of CVAG and those of us who understood the importance of Desert Hot Springs being a part of it, concluding the arrangement with the county and CVAG.

A copy of the first page of the document is on the next page. What transpired was that the county used its leverage to offset the fine levied by CVAG on Desert Hot Springs, by crediting the city with funding it had received from a federal grant for a transportation project, which in effect, saved the county money for the project.

The county was happy; The City was happy; CVAG was happy; and all of the sister-cities of Coachella Valley were happy; a rare occurrence when everyone can get up from the table pleased at the outcome.

The Palmwood Flim-Flam

Another big issue for Daniels, was the residue of what promoters of a proposed project that had boondoggled Hohenstein, Schmidt, Parks and Stephens into believing that an 1,800 lot exclusive home subdivision and a million square feet of retail would be built around two championship golf courses in the foothills of Joshua Tree National Park, smack dab in the middle of a rare species of plant life and the designated area of the MSHCP. I was astounded at the gullibility of the council. Mayor Alex Bias was the only one on the council at the time who saw through the impossible plan, and much to his credit, he stood up to them to the bitter end taking heat all the way, including being chastised by his own council, who were being wined and dined by the developer funding the battle against the MSHCP.

The controversial project was given the name Palmwood, and Phil Mickelson was purported to be part of the development group. A major battle ensued between CVAG, Desert Hot Springs and the Palmwood group, in the local media. The developers were running full-page ads almost daily trying to power their way into getting approved. I was fighting them with my articles in the local news and in

265

every planning and council meeting I had the opportunity to speak on the subject. Brian Harnak, the development group's attorney tried several times to get me to stop fighting them in the media, but I stayed with it until it was all over. Crosby spent thousands of dollars waging a campaign of falsehoods trying to convince Desert Hot springs voters to stay out of the MSHCP.

The MSHCP Express Is Headed Straight For DHS!

The Conservation Plan is a fast moving down the road — and it's heading for Desert Hot Springs! With trains leading the way, our city's leaders should keep choosing the right amount of action for Desert Hot Springs Series, and continue to vote a resounding NO to the MSHCP at the May 16th and the May 30th City Council Meetings. Stay strong, Desert Hot Springs!

Former Desert Hot Springs Mayor
- Matt Weyuker

LEARN MORE NOW - www.ConcernedLandOwner.com

Vote NO to MSHCP
14090 Palm Drive, Suite D-106
Desert Hot Springs, CA 92240

What's the direct impact on Desert Hot Springs?

The city stands to lose a significant amount of property and sales tax revenue. Beyond that conundrum, who will pay for the city's inability to maintain its roadways and arterials? Off-site improvement fees, normally paid by developers, won't be available if the "plan" is adopted, because of the non-development aspects of the "plan." There is also a very troublesome piece to the "plan" - for every 10 acres "taken," 1 acre would be developable. How would that work, if the property under consideration for a building site should be deemed to be some critter or weed's habitat?

Kudos and much appreciation go out to Hank Hohenstein, Yvonne Parks, and Mary Stephens for putting the best interests of Desert Hot Springs first by voting NO to the Coachella Valley Multiple Species Habitat Plan (MSHCP). Your strength and wisdom will save our great city from very difficult financial times!

Former Desert Hot Springs Mayor - Matt Weyuker

Paid for by www.concernedlandowner.com
(760) 568-5898

266

Fortunately for Desert Hot Springs, the project blew up when the main player, Michael Crosby was sued by some of his investors and was proven to be a fraud, having skipped on some projects in Minnesota, leaving those investors in the lurch also. But not before leaving the city with some unpaid bills and costs for Attorney fees.

Palmwood development project investors accuse developer of fraud

By Kimberly Pierceall The Press-Enterprise, Riverside, Calif.
Publication: The Press-Enterprise (Riverside, California)
Date: Friday, February 8 2008

Feb. 8--Investors in a 1,766-acre development plan just outside Desert Hot Springs dubbed Palmwood have accused its developer, Michael Crosby, of fraud and asked the Riverside County Superior Court to allow them to intervene in an environmental lawsuit to stop the project.

At the same time, investors are attempting to oust Crosby from the project.

Officials with the project have said it would include 1,853 homes, a golf course designed by Phil Mickelson, a 400-room resort and 1 million square feet of retail space near Highway 62 and Indian Avenue once it was finished.

In a court filing, investor Ron Breckner accuses Crosby of failing to pay property taxes and income tax returns, withholding payroll taxes, and not maintaining records; and questions purchases such as a $136,000 payment for a luxury car bought in the Coachella Valley and more than $850,000 spent in an American Express account using investor funds.

"Michael denies any improprieties," said Brian Harnik, attorney for the Palmwood development. "I haven't gotten

267

into the details of it. There are inaccuracies and there are inconsistencies."

Breckner referred questions to Ben Howell, with Los Angeles law firm Munger, Tolles & Olson LLP. Howell refused to comment on pending litigation. A representative of the Breckners, David Worrell, did not respond to requests seeking comment.

Breckner is the managing member of Desert Hot Springs Properties LLC, the entity seeking to intervene in the lawsuit , which was filed against the city of Desert Hot Springs by the Center for Biological Diversity and the Sierra Club when the city approved the Palmwood project in December 2006. Breckner's company has poured millions of dollars into the project, including $17 million in loans.

The court is scheduled to hear arguments related to the request on March 24 in the Indio courthouse.

Separately, the developer also owes the city of Desert Hot Springs between $70,000 and $75,000 for legal fees in that case from the month of October, said City Manager Rick Daniels.

That amount, along with bills from November, December and January and estimates for how much it will cost to prepare arguments for the case, will be included in a letter the city intends to send early next week giving Palmwood's developer 10 days to pay the amount owed as well as a $50,000 deposit for future legal costs, Daniels said.

Last July, the county's annexation commission reversed a previous decision and refused to allow Palmwood to be included inside Desert Hot Springs boundaries.

Investors have been attempting to oust Crosby from the project by designating their limited liability company, Desert Hot Springs Properties, as the manager of the project and petitioning the Nevada court system, where Crosby's development companies are registered, to force the companies to have an election for board directors.

****

Before the battle ended, Michael Crosby asked me to have lunch with him, when it was clear I was doing everything possible to expose his plan as a pipe dream that neither could nor would happen in either of our lifetimes.

We met in the Sidewinder restaurant, across from City Hall, and had a light lunch, while he proceeded to attempt to convince me that his project had merit. When he finished, I asked him some simple, but straight forward questions: "Have you ever developed and built a major retail shopping center?" The answer was no. have you ever master planned and built a residential project anywhere near the size of what you are proposing here?" The answer was no.

The final Question was: "Have you ever developed and built a major championship golf course?" and that answer was also no—but followed with: "My investors and I will hire all the expertise we need to build and develop the project."

Then I told him I had been responsible for building all three types of projects that he had never had the experience of doing; that they were all in the City of San Diego, in the heart of one of the most densely populated and traversed sections of the county, with hundreds of thousands of people living in the vicinity, with a great deal of discretionary income to spend, none of which existed in Desert Hot Springs, nor would it for many years, if ever, and that the three projects took almost twenty years from start to finish. Continuing, I said the concept that anyone could plunk a million square feet of commercial/retail in the middle of the desert in a city that is growing at the rate of a thousand people a year, and not close to the path of progress is totally ridiculous.

I then said that the bunk he was handing out to the unsuspecting, wide eyed and hopeful council members was nothing more than hype, which I suspected was a smokescreen for his equally wide-eyed, but no doubt unsuspecting investors, and that he was going to go down in flames and I didn't want to see him dragging Desert Hot Springs down with him and his investors. They (the city) had enough problems on their plate.

After that, I got up from the table, paid for my lunch and left him sitting there with his mouth open, and no words coming out.

Soon thereafter Crosby and his investors started fighting and the entire project began unraveling when Crosby was sued. As everything started coming out in the open, it became quite evident that many people had been taken in by Michael Crosby.

Failed Palmwood golf resort hurts several MN firms

Four Burnsville-based companies involved in a failed golf-resort development in Desert Hot Springs, Calif., filed for Chapter 7 bankruptcy in St. Paul Nov. 21, claiming debts of $165 million and assets of only $17 million.

The filing is the latest turn for a project that has entangled a developer from Minneapolis, a family-owned investment firm in Burnsville, the city of Desert Hot Springs, at least two dozen creditors and investors from the Twin Cities, and PGA Tour pro Phil Mickelson's golf-course-design firm.

In January 2006, Minneapolis-based developer Michael Crosby unveiled plans to build a 1,800-acre resort on the outskirts of Desert Hot Springs, about 15 miles from Palm Springs. The project, dubbed Palmwood, called for 2,200 homes, 1.4 million square feet of retail space and two golf course designed by Mickelson.

Crosby, who is listed as an unsecured creditor in the filings, couldn't be reached for comment.

The project died due to delays related to environmental concerns and the severe housing slump. That left dozens of bills unpaid and investors with millions in losses.

One of the early backers of the project and the man now in control of the remaining assets is Ron Breckner, chairman of Data Sales Co.http://www.bizjournals.com/ - bizWatch-infoPopup Inc., a Burnsville-based computer-equipment leasing company that he and his family own.

"It's just an absolute nightmare," Breckner said of the project.

Breckner is principal of the four entities that filed for bankruptcy. He and his family hold the first mortgage for about 890 acres of the development site. He obtained control of the entities related to the development after taking Crosby to court last spring.

When his family took over the project, Breckner said, creditors began "coming out of the woodwork from way back when."

There are about 80 creditors listed in one of the bankruptcy cases. They include American

271

Bankhttp://www.bizjournals.com/ - bizWatch-infoPopup of St. Paul, U.S. Bank in Minneapolis, Wells Fargo Bankhttp://www.bizjournals.com/ - bizWatch-infoPopup in Minneapolis, Welsh Capital in Minnetonka, Cuningham Group Architecture in Minneapolis, Jebco Group Inc. in St. Paul, MidCountry Bankhttp://www.bizjournals.com/ - bizWatch-infoPopup in Minnetonka and Phil Mickelson Design, based in Woodland Hills, Calif.

Breckner said the steep decline in demand for new homes probably makes the land — the development's primary asset — worth less than half the value of the mortgages. "There are zero assets in the corporation. There's nothing to divide up."

Creditors, like Mickelson's design company, which is owed about $1.6 million, will probably get nothing, he said.

Once the development started "going sideways," Mickelson's company separated itself from the project, said T.R. Reinman, a spokesman for Scottsdale, Ariz.-based Gaylord Sports Managementhttp://www.bizjournals.com/ - bizWatch-infoPopup, which represents Mickelson.

The bankruptcy claim is just that, and Mickelson hopes to get paid, Reinman said. "It's a disappointment that there's not $1.6 million coming our way, but better that than having something that we just wouldn't want our name attached to."

Bruce Bailey, chief financial officer of Jebco, a real estate financing company, said Jebco just learned about the bankruptcy this week and is studying its legal options.

Court documents indicate that Jebco has a claim of $6.9 million that is secured by property worth $2.4 million.

This was the only project that Jebco invested in with Crosby, Bailey said.

Breckner said he got involved with Crosby after he was approached by a third party. "We checked out one project

272

that [Crosby] did, felt that turned out all right and went from there. ... We probably did less homework than we should have."

Breckner Ventures, which is the family entity that made the investment in Palmwood, is owned by Ron, his wife, Judy, and their four children, Bob, Paul and Bill Breckner and Jane Pederson. Data Sales is not affected by the bankruptcy, even though the four entities involved are based at Data Sales' headquarters.

Breckner said he's entertaining offers to sell the land where the development was planned. The city has canceled its approvals and the most likely buyer is a conservation group, he said.

He blamed Palmwood's demise on two things: the housing market's slide and environmental groups that lobbied local governments to uphold the annexation of the land until a conservation plan for the area was completed.

Such a plan was approved by local governments to protect about 15 species of animals and plants such as the Palm Springs pocket mouse, the desert tortoise and a 1-inch-tall moss called the Little San Bernardino Mountains linanthus. But the plan greatly restricts the amount of developable land on the site, Breckner said.

sblack@bizjournals.com | (612) 288-2103

****

Developer of contested Desert Hot Springs project removed

08:39 PM PDT on Monday, March 24, 2008

By KIMBERLY PIERCEALL
The Press-Enterprise

The developer of a controversial project in Desert Hot Springs that promised 1 million square feet of retail and a Phil Mickelson-designed golf course, has been ousted by his investors.

Minnesota developer Michael Crosby has responded with a lawsuit against the investors contending he was trapped into loans with unreasonable interest rates and demands and no way to pay them back.

In a complaint filed in late February, Crosby contends initial investors in Palmwood, his 1,766-acre project near Highway 62 and Indian Avenue in Desert Hot Springs, made it nearly impossible for him to pay back loans that in some cases resulted in 20 percent interest rates compounded monthly. Other lenders such as Lehman Brothers and GE Capital were unwilling to supply permanent financing when it became apparent that the project's debt from interest rates and fees alone exceeded $55 million, according to the lawsuit.

The Press-Enterprise

Investors in the Palmwood project in Desert Hot Springs have gone to court to have the developer ousted from his

274

leadership position. The project has faced financing problems and challenges over its impact on the environment.

Crosby and his lawyers did not return calls seeking comment.

The project has been plagued by environmental lawsuits since Desert Hot Springs approved it December 2006. The Center for Biological Diversity expects to settle its lawsuit against Riverside County's annexation governing body, the Local Agency Formation Commission, which had approved Palmwood's request to be included within the city of Desert Hot Springs, said Jonathan Evans, attorney for the environmental group. The agency later reconsidered and denied Palmwood's request on July 12.

The settlement would still allow the group to challenge any future attempts by developers to annex the land intended for the project.

"Thankfully, as proposed the project is dead in the water. It cannot receive the approvals it needs because Riverside LAFCO recognized Palmwood would cripple important regional plans and was a financial house of cards," Evans said in an e-mail.

"I don't believe Mr. Evans has all the facts at his disposal," said Brian Harnik, a lawyer representing Crosby and the project, but not representing Crosby in his lawsuit against investors. He said Crosby is also disputing investor attempts to oust him from the project.

The suit challenging the project approval granted by the city of Desert Hot Springs still stands.

"Until the City of Desert Hot Springs formally withdraws the 2006 approval of Palmwood, we are forced to head to court to fight this irresponsible project," Evans said.

The city is not giving up.

"We still see that there is a high-value project there that can be built and yet still respect the environmentally sensitive areas," said Rick Daniels, city manager of Desert Hot Springs.

In the meantime, the development is being led by a group of Minnesota investors who successfully petitioned a Nevada court to oust Crosby from his leadership role and take over.

Ron Breckner, owner of Data Sales Co. in Burnsville, Minn., and his family invested nearly $17 million in the project. In interviews last year, Breckner said he was dismayed when the county denied the project's annexation proposal and doubted its success as a result.

In February, Breckner filed a request to intervene in the Center for Biological Diversity case because he claimed Crosby failed to pay property taxes and income tax returns and withheld payroll taxes. He also questioned Crosby making $850,000 worth of credit card purchases and spending $136,000 of investor funds on a luxury car.

Ben Howell, a lawyer representing the Breckners, wouldn't comment on his client's current role with the project or future plans for the development because of the pending lawsuit filed by Crosby.

Reach Kimberly Pierceall at 951-368-9552 or kpierceall@PE.com

****

Seven: The more things change, the more they stay the same……..

One of the most ardent supporters of the Palmwood project, other than Hank Hohenstein, whom even after he was no longer on the council continued to promote the farce, was Councilman Al Schmidt, former chairman of the Planning Commission, real estate broker, investor and would-be developer/partner of the failed Village & Paradise Springs projects.

Schmidt ultimately resigned from the council, shortly after taking his place on the Dias, due to several of his failing business ventures throughout the city, not the least of which was the disastrous "The Village" project. After resigning, Schmidt left the city, moving back to Northern California where he had come from. It appears the Negative Energy Vortex got him good. He was given the following send off by the local "Valley Star" Newspaper:

Schmidt Parks Council Seat

NEWS ANALYSIS
by Dean Gray
March 11, 2009

He started his public service to Desert Hot Springs with an appointment to

277

the city's planning commission. It ended last week when Al Schmidt announced to Mayor Yvonne Parks that he was resigning from the city council citing family reasons.

> With the letter of resignation to Parks, Schmidt not only ended his term on the city council, he ended a long running civic relationship with Parks dating back to when they served on the planning commission together.

Ironically, so close was that relationship, that when Parks seat on the city council was vacated with her election to mayor, it was Schmidt who won her seat on the council to fill out the remaining two years of the Parks four-year council seat term.

On the planning commission, Parks and Schmidt worked closely, approving many development projects during the construction boom. Schmidt, a real estate broker by trade, noted more than once that he first brought the signature Skyborne development to the city, proudly explaining how he alone grouped small property owners together, making possible the purchase by DR Horton, the largest homebuilder in America, possible.

Schmidt's tenure in the city was not without controversy. He remains a partner in a stalled and unfinished shopping center, the Village, frequently the subject of much complaint by residents upset over the projects unsightly unfinished condition.

The Village, approved while Schmidt was chairman of the planning commission, found him with something else in common with Parks. When Schmidt could not vote on the matter before the commission and had to recuse himself from deliberations over it, it was Parks that chaired the meeting and signed the final approval on the Village.

Unfortunately for the city, the Village skated on paying over $500,000 in developer impact fees and providing a bond to guarantee off site improvements such as street improvements

278

and landscaping. Instead, a letter of credit was accepted that became worthless when the private lender securing the note was arrested on charges of fraud.

Schmidt and Parks joined forces on several key issues before the city. Both vociferously opposed and campaigned against a valley-wide environmental initiative, the Multi Species Habitat Conservation Plan (MSHCP).

That issue pitted the city against the rest of the Coachella Valley cities and other state and federal agencies.

Desert Hot Springs vote against the plan cost its valley partners over $1 million and an additional year to rewrite the plan without Desert Hot Springs included.

By that time Parks had been elected to the city council. Schmidt remained as chairman of the planning commission. That separation did not keep them apart when it came to another hotly contested issue.

In a joint city council and planning commission meeting in December 2006, commission chair Schmidt again sat with then council member Parks to approve annexation of the Palmwood development - rushed to final approval so that it would not fall under the guidelines of the MSHCP.

Ultimately the ill-fated Palmwood project became embroiled in legal suits among its partners and later the annexation was nullified in a suit brought by the Center For Biological Diversity (CBD) ending with the city ordered to pay the legal costs of CBD.

If Schmidt and Parks have ever departed company, it was finally over the MSHCP when Parks reversed her earlier vote on the environmental measure. Parks flip-flop began a process of Desert Hot Springs making a new application to join the plan. By this time, Schmidt was elected to the council. He maintained his opposition to the city joining the MSHCP.

Their separation over the MSHCP, however, did not end the close relation between Schmidt and Parks, even over the MSHCP issue. As mayor, Parks appointed Schmidt to be the city's representative on the Energy and Environment committee at the Coachella Valley Association of Governments (CVAG). That committee administers the MSHCP plan, including land purchases from affected land owners.

As a developer, Schmidt maintained several land holdings in Desert Hot Springs in addition to the Village Shopping Center. Some of that land is located in areas of the city destined to be governed by the MSHCP once the city joins the plan, forcing Schmidt to abstain from voting but enabling him to lobby for his cause.

Schmidt learned at a CVAG meeting last year that much of the land where he has an interest can not be developed due to MSCHP restrictions.

For Desert Hot Springs, the decision to first opt out of and then later rejoin the MSHCP has cost the city in excess of $350,000 for environmental reviews to rewrite the city back into the plan Parks and Schmidt had once voted against.

With Schmidt's resignation, it now seems clear he did not intend to seek re-election, an election that would have been difficult given community angst over Schmidt's failed Village shopping center and the controversy over the MSHCP.

Here again, Schmidt and Parks will be parting company. Parks has announced she is running for re-election. With Schmidt's resignation from the council, Schmidt's resignation, seven month's ahead of the election, puts greater distance between her and Schmidt over their controversial collaborations.

Despite those political considerations, however, Parks has remained close to Schmidt throughout. Even though Schmidt was on the city council, she made sure Schmidt's influence did not stray completely from the planning commission.

280

In another Parks appointment, Schmidt was appointed to serve on the planning commission design review sub-committee where project applicants first submit their plans for review prior to advancing to the full planning commission.

Schmidt enjoyed other close relations on the city council. Surprisingly it was Councilman Karl Baker, a harsh critic of past city council and planning commission business before being elected to council, who became closely aligned with Schmidt.

The alliance with Parks and Baker made time on the council easier for Schmidt, as did committee appointments he was given. Even with that, Schmidt increasingly appeared tired and seemingly distracted in the months prior to his resignation. At city council study sessions, Schmidt would often rest his head on his hands on the table as if disinterested.

Finally giving up the seat he filled for Parks, Schmidt resigned, ending the long relationship he and Parks shared at the helm of Desert Hot Springs politics. Parks and the council will now begin work to fill the vacancy left by Schmidt's resignation.

****

One would think that the Vortex was working overtime here, slaying dragons right and left. The abandonment of a commercial project that should never have been started; the demise of a hoped for, but pie-in-the-sky 1,800 unit residential project and companion one-million square foot, commercial project, including a championship golf course, a disgraced councilman/investor/developer leaving town with his tail between his legs, and who knows what else?

In this case, I don't think the Vortex had much to do with what happened here. Greed and stupidity working

together won out over common sense. But then again, maybe
that's some of what the Vortex does to people.

What I believe took place, was well intentioned
people (Al Schmidt not included) met up with some shady
people, greed got in the way of otherwise well meaning
people, and ego trumped a few elected officials. When all
elements were combined, they yielded a blow to a great
many expectations and some long lived embarrassment.

Fortunately for Desert Hot Springs, something positive, did
occur out of the Palmwood debacle however, resulting in
correlation to the Bard's famous Line in his classic "All's well
that ends well" play and making lemonade out of a lemon:

Conservation group buys part of Palmwood development for $3.9 million

By Kimberly Pierceall *The Press-Enterprise*, July 10, 2009

About a third of the land reserved for Palmwood, a proposed
development just outside Desert Hot Springs boundaries that
promised a world-class golf course among high-end homes
and a luxury hotel, has been sold at a discount to the
Coachella Valley Conservation Commission.

The 1,766-acre project near Highway 62 and Indian Avenue
across a freeway from Palm Springs, had hit environmental
and financial snags. The project's land fell inside the Coachella
Valley Multi-Species Habitat Conservation Plan - a plan in the
works since 1996 that was ultimately approved by eight
Coachella Valley cities and Riverside County in 2007 and went
into effect Oct. 2008. Before the plan was approved though,
Palmwood's developer - Michael Crosby -- ran into funding
challenges and the project's investors ousted him.

On Friday afternoon, the Coachella Valley Association of
Governments - which created the multi-species plan and
staffs the Conservation Commission - announced it had
bought 638 acres of Palmwood land for $3.9 million. That was

$1.1 million less than the land's market value, said Katie Barrows, director of environmental resources for CVAG.

Barrows said the group hopes to acquire more of the land that had been intended for Palmwood but will need more funding.

Funds that the group could have normally relied on, such as state bonds, have been frozen because of the economic recession, she said.

Construction on the Palmwood project never started and the land remains barren desert devoid of the one million-square-feet of retail space, Phil Mickelson golf course, homes and hotel originally proposed.

Just because something hasn't been developed on the land yet, doesn't mean someone wouldn't build on it in the future, Barrows said.

"To ultimately conserve land, you need to own it," she said.

Before Friday, the Conservancy Commission had bought 227 acres in the Coachella Valley for $3.45 million. Eventually, the group hopes to acquire and preserve 90,000 acres of desert land.

*****

In the final analysis, the environment and future generations won out over greed and corruption after all of the smoke cleared and wounds were healed. One could say that The Negative Energy Vortex was overpowered by the Positive Energy Vortex, and Desert Hot Springs' community members came out the better for it.......this time.

The final touch to this sorry tale of deception and crime was the arrest and indictment of the perpetrator, Michael Crosby, who's real name it turns out is Michael Krzyzaniak as this article in the Desert Sun details:

Dream of luxury resort in Desert Hot Springs ends up a nightmare

Plan mastermind charged in $20M investment scams

11:44 PM, Apr. 15, 2011

Written by

Keith Matheny
The Desert Sun

An ill-fated, high-end golf resort that ultimately cost the city of Desert Hot Springs more than $1 million was apparently based on a previously convicted Minnesota con man's scam.

"This is just a sad chapter of the city's history," said City Manager Rick Daniels.

U.S. Attorney B. Todd Jones on Thursday announced the federal indictment of Michael Joseph Krzyzaniak, 62, of Minneapolis, also known as Michael Joseph Crosby, on 30 fraud, money laundering and tax evasion charges.

The counts involved wide-ranging scams — the Palmwood golf resort project near Desert Hot Springs is one — that allegedly bilked at least $20million from people including professional golfer Phil Mickelson.

Crosby, the name by which he was known in Desert Hot Springs, allegedly told investors their money would be invested in a particular project and they could expect a substantial return, Jones said in a news release, and that each project was proceeding toward a successful conclusion having secured the necessary government approvals.

Additionally, Crosby told investors he had various financing sources available and a number of celebrity endorsements.

"All of those representations were false," Jones stated.

In addition to Palmwood, Crosby allegedly scammed investors on golf courses in other states, Internet terminals in several airports, alternative energy projects in Colorado and a NASCAR-type race track in Elko, Minn.

Envisioned as a transformative economic boost for Desert Hot Springs, the 1,766-acre Palmwood development, off Highway 62 and Indian Avenue just north of Desert Hot Springs, was to feature retail shops, a luxury hotel, high-end housing and a Mickelson-designed golf course.

Mickelson's attorney, Glenn Cohen of Jacksonville, Fla., declined to comment Friday.

Palmwood was the reason city officials balked at joining the Coachella Valley Multiple Species Habitat Protection plan in 2006, making Desert Hot Springs the lone valley city not to join. Much of the land the regional protection plan wanted to preserve for threatened plant and animal species was within the proposed resort's footprint. Desert Hot Springs officials planned to bring the resort into the city's limits through annexation.

But a county agency charged with considering annexations reversed an earlier approval of the city's plan, because of its failure to follow regional species protection plans.

What followed were unpaid legal costs to the city by Crosby, and lawsuits over the development by environmental groups.

Ultimately, Palmwood went nowhere. The city settled a lawsuit with the Sierra Club for more than $350,000, and it cost more than a quarter-million dollars for the city to have the multi-species plan reworked so they could join it, said Daniels, adding that his first actions upon becoming city manager in 2007 included "cleaning up the mess (Crosby) created."

Work by Desert Hot Springs officials to gain approval of Palmwood "completely consumed" the city for months, and the unspecified related costs were also significant, Daniels said.

Palmwood investors sued Crosby in 2008, attempting to wrest control of the development away from him.

Among their allegations at the time was that Crosby didn't pay property or other taxes for the development, instead spending $136,000 at a luxury car dealership in the Coachella Valley, made $850,000 in payments to American Express and purchased a building in downtown Minneapolis in which the investors had no involvement.

"This guy is evil and it's good he's off the street," Paul Breckner of Wayzata, Minn., told the Minneapolis Star Tribune. Breckner and his father, Ron Breckner of Prior Lake, Minn., were bilked in the Palmwood scam.

Paul Breckner declined to disclose how much money he and his father lost investing in the golf resort, telling the Star Tribune only that it was "a lot" and that Palmwood alone probably affected dozens of investors around the Twin Cities.

Ron Breckner took control of development company Landmark Midwest from Crosby and filed for Chapter 7 bankruptcy liquidation in 2008, Paul Breckner said.

The Breckners now own 884 acres of land that was going to be part of Palmwood, and are working on an alternative energy project there, Paul Breckner told the Star Tribune.

Daniels said the remaining Palmwood land that had caused the environmental controversies was sold to the Coachella Valley Conservation Commission to preserve as species habitat in 2009.

Crosby/Krzyzaniak was convicted in absentia of mail fraud in Minnesota in 1989, related to a silver medallion-selling operation. That conviction was overturned on a technicality, but Crosby/Krzyzaniak pleaded guilty to a related charge in 1993 and was sentenced to three years in federal prison.

A federal judge on Thursday ordered Crosby/Krzyzaniak held until a bond hearing next week, and appointed a public defender to represent him. Crosby/Krzyzaniak said he owns no property, stocks or bonds and has "a few hundred dollars in the bank."

If convicted, Crosby/Krzyzaniak faces a potential maximum penalty of 20 years in prison on each mail and wire fraud count, 10 years on each money-laundering count, five years on each tax evasion count and one year on each failure to file taxes count.

'I had no idea'

Among those Crosby worked with in the Coachella Valley were well-known valley advertising executive Scott Kiner and attorneys Brian Harnik and Rob Bernheimer.

Kiner said that with Harnik and Bernheimer's involvement in Palmwood — as well as Mickelson lending his name — "there was no reason for me to think there was anything wrong with what was going on."

After initially paying his bills to Kiner's firm, Kiner said Crosby ultimately failed to pay $45,000 for services rendered, money that was never recovered.

"He was very believable, acted very professional, was very passionate about the project," Kiner said of Crosby.

"If you can believe Bernie Madoff, you can believe anything."

Bernheimer, a former Indian Wells city councilman, said he hadn't spoken with Crosby in years, after representing Landmark as Palmwood was pursued.

"It certainly surprises me there was a scam," he said. "The property was real, and the folks that put all the work into the EIR (environmental impact report), that was all real work.

"Certainly I had no idea anything was out of sorts when we were working on it."

Bernheimer said he also was ultimately left unpaid for some of his services to Landmark, but declined to discuss an amount.

A message left with Harnik was not returned Friday.

Though the pursuit of Palmwood occurred under a different city manager and city council, Daniels said Desert Hot Springs is only now putting the episode behind it, currently finalizing plans to join other valley cities in the multiple species habitat protection plan.

"In retrospect, knowing what we know now, the community, the city, the region, was dealing with a professional con man — who sucked in and got to act as his surrogates some of the top attorneys, professionals and ad men in the valley," he said.

****

Left unsaid in this debacle is the one individual city councilman who was the driving force in convincing his council colleagues to support this ridiculous project from the outset. Hank Hohenstein the Pied Piper of Coachella Valley once again "woke up stupid" dragging the city with him.

Then some good things began happening to help let the world know things could get better in Desert Hot Springs, like this glowing article in the New York Times:

Near Palm Springs, a Little City Thinks Big

By DAVE CALDWELL

Published: March 31, 2006

AS you head north out of Palm Springs, Calif., late on a sunny afternoon, the rumpled brown foothills a dozen miles away cast long shadows. The houses sprinkled on those hills, part of the rapidly growing city of Desert Hot Springs, look as if they were taking a nap in the folds of a cozy old blanket.

Bill Effinger

Windmills between Desert Hot Springs and Palm Springs take advantage of the area's strong winds.

When you get to Desert Hot Springs, the view from on high isn't too bad, either.

Thousands of windmills stand sentry in the foreground, slowly generating electricity by catching the persistent desert wind. Mount San Jacinto looms over Palm Springs and the Coachella Valley, and after magnificent orange sunsets, the lights in Palm Springs begin to twinkle.

That panorama, access to aquifers of pristine spring water and temperatures that are slightly cooler than those in Palm Springs, its famous resort city neighbor, have made Desert Hot Springs a boomtown. Its year-round population has more than tripled in the last 25 years, to about 19,400 today.

Teresa Thompson, a spokeswoman for Desert Hot Springs, said there were plans to build 13,000 houses in the next decade, to be sold at a wide range of prices. Second-home buyers, real estate agents say, can afford bigger and better houses in Desert Hot Springs than in Palm Springs.

Donna Peace, an agent for Zephyr Realty, sold a four-bedroom house in Desert Hot Springs three years ago for $165,000. Ms. Peace recently put the same house on the market for $362,000. But $362,000, she said, would probably buy only a fixer-upper in Palm Springs.

Ms. Peace's office is in Palm Springs, but she said she spends twice as much time showing houses in Desert Hot Springs. After showing a house in Palm Springs, she often takes customers on a detour to Desert Hot Springs. Then, she says, she often declares, "Look at what your money can buy here." About 20 percent of residents, Mayor Alex Bias said, are part-timers.

Desert Hot Springs has struggled to catch up with its growth, and the city, which emerged from a three-year bankruptcy in 2004, is trying to change its reputation as a dusty desert outpost.

Palm Drive, the main north-south thoroughfare, is not lined with upscale shops. But Ms. Thompson said that a shopping center called the Village, which is expected to attract high-level shops, is to be built to meet those needs. Construction is expected to begin this year.

The city has no golf course or movie theater within its limits, and none are planned; the closest are in Palm Springs. "There's not a lot to do here," Mayor Bias said. "So that becomes our biggest challenge."

Work is to begin next year on widening two overpasses leading to Interstate 10, the freeway that connects Desert Hot Springs with Los Angeles, 110 miles to the west, to create better traffic flow. Completion is expected in 2009. Mayor Bias said he was confident that better access would lead to more retail opportunities and to a bigger tax base.

"It still has the remnants of a sleepy town, but it's probably not going to be sleepy for too long," said Mary Ann Hooper. Ms. Hooper, a former Los Angeles resident who lives in nearby Sky Valley and who just bought property in Desert Hot Springs, said she intended to build a two-bedroom house.

The Scene

Desert Hot Springs is not a town for shoppers. The nearest mall is in Palm Desert, 20 miles away. "Even a movie theater would be nice," said Steve Ciccarelli, who spends about six months a year in Desert Hot Springs and the rest in Minnesota.

The city has about 10 restaurants, the most notable of which is the Capri, a family-owned Italian restaurant on Palm Drive that has been in business for about 30 years. (But Palm Springs and its restaurants and nightlife are only 15 minutes away, and there does not seem to be a rush hour.)

Even on weekends, there is not much traffic on Palm Drive. Residents have playfully labeled Mountain View Road, which has even less traffic, as a bypass. Propped next to one of the new homes in town is a sheet of plywood with "Hey! Slow down!" spray-painted on it. "It's not a town for hoopla," Ms. Hooper said.

Much of what hoopla there is in Desert Hot Springs is created by desert life. Roadrunners gallivant among the cactuses in housing developments. Hummingbirds flit among the desert flowers. Tiny green lizards and desert squirrels skitter between the rocks and the hardy creosote bushes.

Pros

The view is a major selling point, and so is the weather, for most of the year. The heat can become fierce in summer, with temperatures sometimes climbing over 110 degrees. But a string of recent March days offered high temperatures in the 80's with no precipitation.

If you need to get out of your house and away from its air-conditioning in the summer swelter, there's always the option of adding a swimming pool. Ms. Hooper's house is to have a middle courtyard with a pool. And there's always a drive to a mall.

Desert Hot Springs gets an hour more sunlight in the afternoons than does Palm Springs, which sits near the foot of Mount San Jacinto. Desert Hot Springs is also windier than Palm Springs, and so it is five to eight degrees cooler.

Palm Springs is also more crowded. Erv Olssen of Seattle bought a Spanish custom-built home in Desert Hot Springs a little more than a year ago after becoming weary of Palm Springs's congestion. "I didn't like the valley floor," said Mr. Olssen, who lives in Desert Hot Springs for about half the year. "There seemed to be a lot of pollution, things like that."

The water is sublime. Municipal water comes from an aquifer and has been pure enough in the past to win awards. Spa resorts in town have access to hot mineral springs, and several developers are planning to tap into the hot-water aquifer, a huge asset.

"People love this heat, and they love this mineral water," Ms. Peace said.

Cons

Property crimes such as burglaries have been persistent, but Walter McKinney, the police chief, said that steps are being taken to help limit them. Chief McKinney said that the city plans to offer to monitor burglar alarms in new housing developments, and that the plan will eventually include every residence in town.

For years, Chief McKinney said, Desert Hot Springs had a reputation as a place where the state sent parolees. But, he said, the issue has diminished.

The Real Estate Market

Desert Hot Springs is a good place to build one house — or several. Mr. Olssen owns a two-acre plot on which he plans to build four houses. The price of land has risen dramatically. A plot that sold for $20,000 five years ago now sells for $75,000. "I just can't believe the prices," Mr. Olssen said.

The prices in Desert Hot Springs are far less intimidating than those in Palm Springs — or, for that matter, other nearby municipalities, including Rancho Mirage, southeast of Palm Springs.

****

Things on the political front were starting to change for the better, bringing a sea-change to the council. Due to the unfortunate death of council member Gary Bosworth and the November election, the city had three new council members; one appointed and two elected, and a new mayor.

———

Desert Hot Springs gets a new mayor:

When Alex Bias lost his bid for a second term, Yvonne Parks became mayor. With a new city manager and a new mayor, Desert Hot Springs leadership was once again looking to a rosy future, according to Mayor Parks, as this article projects. When you read her statements, you will see she was refuting my call for disincorparating the city to merge with Palm Springs. I wished her luck in accomplishing her goals:

Desert Hot Springs poised to catch inevitable next wave of growth, economist says

09:20 PM PDT on Saturday, July 19, 2008

The Vortex made me do it

By STEVE MOORE
The Press-Enterprise

DESERT HOT SPRINGS - The Inland area's leading
economist, John Husing, says the Spa City will start
booming in about four years as Southern California's
relentless growth pattern keeps pushing eastward,
finally reaching the tip of the Coachella Valley.

By 2010-11, the nation's struggling economy will be
on an upswing, he said.

Under the scenario, building activity in Riverside and
San Bernardino counties' "hot spots" will pick up
largely where they left off before the slowdown.

Husing said new construction will hit Beaumont,
spread through the Pass and then leapfrog over vast
sandy stretches along Interstate 10 heading for

Desert Hot Springs.

Amanda Lucidon/The Press-Enterprise

Desert Hot Springs Mayor Yvonne Parks stands in the area
near Interstate 10 that is part of a future annexation project.
Desert Hot Springs, unlike other areas, has plenty of land
available for growth.

Builders also will concentrate on the High Desert -- the Victor Valley area including Victorville, Adelanto, Hesperia and Apple Valley -- and the stretch of Interstate 215 from Moreno Valley to Murrieta, the economist predicts.

Because of heavy speculation, the Perris and Menifee Valley areas could "take longer to unwind and recover in the next cycle," Husing said.

Looking for Dirt

For builders across the Inland area, it's a perpetual quest for plentiful affordable land, something Husing calls the "dirt" theory.

"They follow the 'dirt' wherever it is," he said. "And it's going to continue. I don't see it stopping.

"Desert Hot Springs is in the unique position of being the first city in the Coachella Valley to find itself caught up in this trend of urbanizing of Southern California," he said. "Many in the valley thought they were separate from that."

Husing recently wrote a report and gave a speech titled "Desert Hot Springs Economy: Period of Adjustment, 2008" outlining the city's future -- including a population projection of almost 91,000 people by 2035.

He adds one slight caveat for the Inland region, however.

"Nothing is guaranteed in life, " Husing said. "Five-dollar gas may have some effect, but I'm skeptical. I don't see everybody rushing back to central Los Angeles."

Growth and Taxes

296

Many in Desert Hot Springs are eager for an economic uptick that could trigger a boom for this city of 26,000 residents, located north of the freeway and Palm Springs and against the Little San Bernardino Mountains.

They say the city's Desert Hot Springs' future prosperity depends on it. Desert Hot Springs has been an incorporated city since 1963.

The outside world knows the city largely for its spas and the hot mineral water bubbling to the surface.

But something new is brewing.

The Spa City is working on annexing about 3,800 acres in its sphere of influence, which could mean big sales tax revenue when name retailers come to town. Desert Hot Springs already has 11,000 lots approved and ready for builders to pull permits.

And unlike many areas of the Coachella Valley that boomed years ago, Desert Hot Springs still has plenty of available land. Only 20 percent of the city is built out, officials say.

But against those growth projections, looming financial challenges must also be factored in.

Vital tax revenues approved eight years ago will expire in two years unless voters extend them at the ballot box. Money for a special election next year has already been budgeted.

About $2.3 million a year is at stake. The money is earmarked for public safety -- police, fire, code enforcement and animal control services -- and for bond payments from Desert Hot Springs' past bankruptcy.

City leaders realize that what voters "giveth," they can "taketh away."

The Police Department could lose about one-third of its funding if the tax measures aren't extended, said City Manager Rick Daniels.

Desert Hot Springs has three years of bankruptcy bond payments set aside in a special reserve, said Mayor Yvonne Parks.

Desert Hot Springs declared bankruptcy in 2001 over a developer's lawsuit involving a mobile home park. The city settled and emerged from bankruptcy in in2004.

No Bumps

Fresh from adopting a new budget for 2008-09, Desert Hot Springs officials are now upbeat about their city's future.

A spending plan calls for $44 million in new capital improvements this year, adding four more police officers and ending a practice of using reserves for some ongoing operations.

"You just can't keep eating your seed corn," Daniels said.

City officials say they have heard what residents have said they wanted.

Every worn, bumpy street will be repaved, and many new traffic lights installed. City parks will be given major makeovers -- last year, 200 youngsters couldn't play soccer because of a shortage of fields.

In addition, there will be new money available for commercial redevelopment.

Can't Go Back

Even during the toughest times, abandoning cityhood and going back to county rule "wasn't on the table," said the mayor. And Parks said the public won't support disbanding the Desert Hot Springs Police Department and having sheriff's deputies patrol the streets under a contract.

During a recent driving tour of the city, the 71-year-old civic leader sported a big button proclaiming, "Positive energy!"

"It's a new day in Desert Hot Springs," she said. "You know the old adage from that song, 'Accentuate the positive and eliminate the negative'? That's what I've tried to bring to the city."

Barber Steven Aguirre gets an earful of small-town politics as he snips away in his shop called Hare Cutters.

"If you don't vote, don't whine," reads a sign behind his chair.

In the past, complacency and a "don't care" attitude sometimes plagued Desert Hot Springs, Aguirre said.

"That's why the community doesn't prosper or grow," he said. "But I'm starting to see a little bit of change now. "If we disincorporate, it's going backwards," he said.

Reach Steve Moore at 760-322-5738 or _stevemoore@PE.com_

****

There were also some good decisions being made about that time by the council as evidenced by this short article in the Desert sun:

Desert Hot Springs wind farm deal OK'd

February 8, 2008 by Mariecar Mendoza in The Desert Sun

Desert Hot Springs City Council on Tuesday unanimously approved a wind farm replacement project that will deposit $40,000 a year with a 2.5 percent annual increase for the life of the project into city coffers. Proposed by Energy Unlimited Inc., a family-owned energy company, the project will replace 16 old turbines that stand 115 feet tall with eight 340-foot turbines along the southern edge of the city. ...Some residents near to the wind farms, however, aren't too excited. Joyce Manley, a Whitewater resident who lives off Painted Hill Road, said she is "almost totally surrounded" by the windmills and has been fighting the installation of newer turbines since 2001.

Bigger can mean better - at least in the wind farm industry - and it's a trend making its way into the Coachella Valley with one of its first stops in Desert Hot Springs.

****

Unfortunately right about the time when things were looking to the upside for the city, the over heated housing market began to slide, bringing the Coachella Valley housing boom to an unceremonious halt, leaving several unfinished projects to bake in the sun, dashing dreams for thousands of overextended home buyers and housing developers.

One of the first casualties, locally based Mayer/Luce began unraveling. Their house of cards was disintegrating

300

rapidly, as they were caught up in the calamitous economic downturn. The Negative Energy Vortex strikes again!

Nine projects totaling several thousand houses, apartments, a resort hotel with a championship golf course and a shopping center purportedly to have a Wal-Mart, all came crashing down at the same time, leaving three partially completed condominium projects sitting empty in the blowing desert sands for the better part of three years. This was not a good thing for the city.

Mayer-Luce Development principals file for Chapter 7

10:23 PM PDT on Wednesday, June 11, 2008

By KIMBERLY PIERCEALL
The Press-Enterprise

A Desert Hot Springs-based home developer who at one point promised to build the city its first golf course eventually fell to foreclosure and has now filed for bankruptcy.

The principals of Mayer-Luce Development have chosen to liquidate their business assets, about $8.7 million worth, in Chapter 7 bankruptcy filings rather than to reorganize.

Both partners of Mayer-Luce Development -- Robert O. Mayer, of Indian Wells, and Walter W. Luce, of Bermuda Dunes -- filed for personal Chapter 7 bankruptcy protection earlier this month.

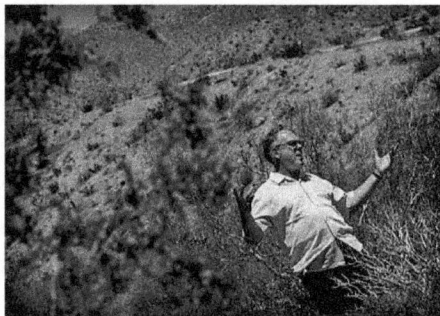

2005 / The Press-Enterprise

Walter W. Luce, one of the Mayer-Luce Development principals, is seen on the land that was to be the golf course of Mayer-Luce's proposed Tuscan Hills project. The property went into foreclosure in 2007.

Thomas Polis, a lawyer representing Mayer, Luce and their businesses, declined to comment.

In court filings, Mayer said he had $2 million in assets and $86.4 million in debts. Of his $5,616.66 monthly income, $3,000 is from a family trust. His father, H.M. Mayer, founder of the Oscar Mayer bologna empire, died in April 2007.

Luce reported personal assets of $708,278 and $85.4 million in debts.

The duo's three business entities based in Desert Hot Springs -- Mayer-Luce Development Group Inc., Mayer-Luce Builders Inc. and LTV Builders Inc. -- also filed for liquidation.

One entity claims no assets or debts. Another claims $2,022 in assets and $20,000 in debts. LTV Builders Inc. reportedly has $8.7 million in assets consisting of eight residential lots in Oakland and $10.1 million in debts.

Filing for Chapter 7 bankruptcy is typically the last alternative when all others have run out, said Marty Mueller, a partner in the Best Best & Kreiger law firm's Indian Wells office. Mueller said he hasn't seen a trend of home developers filing for Chapter 7 and doesn't expect it to become one.

In the filing, Mayer claims $6,750 in watches and jewelry and $3,600 in sports equipment should be exempt.

Individuals filing for bankruptcy are typically allowed to keep one home, depending on the value; one vehicle; the tools of their trade; and some personal items, Mueller said.

Walter W. Luce

"Expensive jewelry is not going to be exempt," Mueller said.

Luce claims in court filings that his $200 golf clubs and$5,000 worth of clothes should be exempt.

John Soulierre, a former planning director and interim city manager of Desert Hot Springs, is listed as a creditor. He bought a home in Mayer-Luce's Hacienda Heights development before he started working for the city and discovered there were air-conditioning issues, he said.

Soulierre is among the homeowners in an ongoing class-action lawsuit filed against Mayer-Luce for shoddy construction in the neighborhood.

"Life goes on, right. We will deal with what comes," he said of the bankruptcy filing that could make it unlikely that he'll be compensated. "Obviously we're not happy about it."

In 2005, Mayer and Luce proposed building Tuscan Hills, a $1 billion 550-acre project that would have included a high-end hotel, the city's first golf course and homes costing as much as $1 million each.

Soulierre said it meant a lot to the city at the time.

"The city was finally seeing the project moving forward. It had a professional golfer's name attached to it," he said.

In January 2007, the property was foreclosed on with no golf course, hotel or high-end homes yet built. Last year, Mayer said the company was scaling back but still working on commercial projects in Banning, Riverside County and Oakland.

Reach Kimberly Pierceall at 951-368-9552 or kpierceall@PE.com

Tuscan Hills plan ends in foreclosure

02:59 PM PDT on Friday, April 6, 2007

By KIMBERLY PIERCEALL
The Press-Enterprise

The hotel should've almost been built by now, but a cooling housing market has sent a barely touched 550-acre parcel in Desert Hot Springs into foreclosure.

Mayer-Luce Development had announced it would build an 18-hole golf course hotel and high-end homes, a first for Desert Hot Springs, dubbing it Tuscan Hills in mid-2005. Now the company no longer owns the project and is being sued by 52 homeowners at its other Desert Hot Springs development, Hacienda Heights, who complain of shoddy construction work.

Robert Mayer, one half of the Mayer-Luce firm, said the foreclosure sale had been arranged and agreed upon by his company and the lender last October after attorneys on both sides said it would be the best option, "to release us from the personal liability that was attached to the loans," he said.

Scripps Investments & Loans Inc., which loaned $34 million to the project, formed Scripps Tuscan Hills LLC and along with a family trust bought the property in foreclosure for $38.4 million on Jan. 26, according to Riverside County records.

"We're thinking about what we need to do. We're moving forward cautiously," said Jeffrey Lubin, president of Scripps.

Mayer said the size of the project made it difficult to find financing when the company needed it last year to pay off the $34 million loan from Scripps.

When Mayer-Luce had to start paying interest, the company realized the project wouldn't last long.

"We paid over a million dollars out of pocket to keep it going for a couple months longer," Mayer said.

In 2005, Walter Luce said that the 350- to 450-room hotel would be finished two to three years later. Last year, Luce said he was slowing down on Tuscan Hills' development to watch the housing market.

"The market up here ... went from being one of the fastest-growing cities in the state to where sales have softened dramatically," he said. "The Coachella Valley was really the last part of Southern California to feel the crunch. We thought that maybe we wouldn't be affected by it," he said.

Mayer said the company is finishing developments in Banning and Oakland and working on commercial projects in Riverside County.

"We are going forward. We're a lot leaner of a company than we were," he said.

Three weeks ago, Irvine-based attorney Ken Kasdan sued the company, accusing it of construction defects at its Hacienda Heights development including stucco and concrete foundation cracks, window leaks and roof leaks.

"Overall we're alleging very poor quality and shoddy workmanship," Kasdan said. The homeowners will likely seek about $250,000 each, which they believe is the cost to repair their homes, he said.

Mayer said it appears that most of the homeowners didn't contact the company's customer service center first to talk about construction issues.

"We're kind of skeptical as to the real impetus behind that," he said.

****

We make a bad project a good project

As an aside, four years after the Mayer/Luce debacle, I was able to help a client of mine, Hitzke Development

Corporation, acquire a 62-unit condominium that Mayer/Luce had partially built and abandoned on Hacienda in Desert Hot Springs.

We purchased the building from the FDIC, for pennies on the dollar, as the Bank that loaned the money on the project was closed by the FDIC. To the city's delight, the project was turned into a quality Affordable Housing Project. The Grand Opening of "Hacienda Heights" was held on Wednesday, February 17, 2011, as 62 happy families moved into the homes, turning what was once a very sour lemon into lemonade for the city and the projects inhabitants. I am proud to have been part of the project.

City Manager Rick Daniels came to our rescue several times during the process of piecing together the documentation required by county and federal authorities, as we attempted to assemble engineering and architectural drawings to receive building permits and loans.

———

Since becoming mayor, Yvonne Parks pushed hard for cooperation on the council and to promote a positive image for the city as the article in the Palm Springs Life Magazine illustrates. She did a good job in that regard. However, as in the past puff-pieces by Yvonne's predecessors, talking a good game is so often countered by the negative results of city council and management mistakes, the positive is overshadowed by the negative. They should never give the Vortex a chance to mess things up, but it happens.

Desert Hot Springs

A city on the move

By Pamela Bieri PHOTO BY CHRIS MILLER

Desert Hot Springs boasts the best views of the valley of majestic Mt. San Jacinto.

Desert Hot Springs, experiencing a resurgence of energy from within, is truly a "City on the Move" that is growing into its potential. The city's new Vortex Downtown Revitalization Plan was recently adopted by the City Council and includes a vision for the city that will transform Desert Hot Springs into a world-class health and wellness destination.

The city not only provided the vision, but also the resources to begin a transformation. The energy of development is clearly visible as you drive into the renovated downtown at Palm Drive and Pierson Boulevard with new streetscape and building façades. This $4 million renovation of the heart of the city included new sidewalks and curbs that frame the freshly paved road inset by stately young palms in diamond-shaped planters.

Desert-landscaped medians with stamped concrete, river rock, antique lighting, and lush desert plants now center the streets. Street signs clearly mark the way, and building façade improvements and renovations on each corner speak of a resurgence of business and civic pride in downtown.

Mayor Yvonne Parks said, "In the past two years, we have improved some 37 miles of streets throughout the City of Desert Hot Springs and completely transformed the look and feel of our downtown. Once the Vortex Plan is completed, downtown Desert Hot Springs will be a destination for residents and visitors to eat, shop, and play."

SPA CITY

Desert Hot Springs was first known for its mineral hot springs, sunshine, and refreshing cool water — a vortex of wind, sun, earth, and water energy.

Today, its boutique and historic resorts and spas such as Two Bunch Palms, El Morocco Inn and Spa, Tuscan Springs, and many others have formed the Desert Hot Springs Hotelier Association to market Desert Hot Springs as "Spa City."

The city hosts the first Wellness and World Music Festival, early 2011, with reggae icon Ziggy Marley as headliner. The event promises to "meld all aspects of wellness, healthy living, and sustainability with world music." Musical artists, inspirational speakers, treatment specialists and noted wellness leaders will share their knowledge for "living a healthy, positive and energized lifestyle." For more information, go online to www.visitdeserthotsprings.com.

"Our plan is to move forward with retail, restaurant, and commerce as the base that encourages people to stop, eat, stay, and play in Desert Hot Springs," Parks says.

Often referred to as the "shining city on the hill," the city of Desert Hot Springs is combining its plentiful natural assets of hot water, world-class drinking water, unmatched views, and cooler summer temperatures with innovative and aggressive city leaders to energetically realize its great potential and build the Coachella Valley's "City of the Future."

FOCUS ON HEALTH AND WELLNESS

"In addition to fiscal responsibility and economic development, City Council and staff are dedicated to improving the quality of life in Desert Hot Springs," says Parks. "Public health is paramount to the quality of life."

In the past, there were only 1.5 doctors for Desert Hot Springs' 26,000 residents. Now the new Desert Hot Springs Medical Center houses three additional full-time doctors to the city. In addition, Riverside County is developing 14 acres along Palm Drive for a new regional center that will include a health clinic, workforce development, and social services offices.

On the drawing board is a new community health and wellness center that will have a gymnasium, meeting rooms, and pool that the high school will use for water polo and swim meets, as well as community use. With computer and game rooms, the Boys & Girls Clubs of Coachella Valley will also use the facilities for its programs and events.

Located between the high school and City Hall, with access from Cholla Drive, the building will meet advanced standards for green practices and energy efficiency. Collaborating with private donations along with school, county, and federal agencies for funding, the center should be open by the end of next year.

All of these programs and plans support Desert Hot Springs' designation as a HEAL community (Healthy Eating, Active Living), the first valley city to win this California state designation.

"With schools and employers becoming involved in healthy eating, recycling, green programs, community gardens projects, and promoting a healthy community, we plan to keep that designation," says Parks.

COMMUNITY RENAISSANCE

The community's renaissance includes neighborhood renewal, public infrastructure improvements, and new commercial and retail projects.

The city has acquired properties on the southwest, northeast, and northwest corners of Pierson and Palm totaling some seven acres for multiuse business, residential, and hotel development. Plans call for a beautiful, functional, and vibrant downtown Desert Hot Springs.

A part of the downtown area is set aside as a natural park. Angled southwest with a dramatic view of Mt. San Jacinto, the open vista makes an aesthetically profound statement while creating a recreation area in the heart of the city.

COMMUNITY DEVELOPMENT PROJECTS

Upgrading neighborhoods helps improve property values and promotes public health and safety, as well as community pride. The Community Development Department has implemented several measures to improve and beautify neighborhoods.

A neighborhood cleanup of debris took place in October of last year and February of this year. The cleanups will be quarterly, according to Mayor Parks.

The city has bought foreclosed homes for rehabilitation and resale, promoting home ownership. New ordinances stipulate that agents managing foreclosures are now required to keep the houses looking presentable. Also, owners of multiple properties or multifamily housing are required to manage their properties in accord with a Safe Housing Program. The program is aimed at increasing safety awareness of residents and providing quality housing.

City leaders recognized that neighborhood renewal was imperative to improving the quality of life for residents. A strategic effort of ridding the city of code violations was enacted. Additionally, a graffiti abatement plan was adopted, and graffiti has been eradicated.

"There used to be a problem with graffiti. Now with our 24-hour graffiti hot line and increased code enforcement, neighborhoods are clean, and there is a new sense of pride," says Parks. The Neighborhood Renewal Program offers grants up to $15,000 for homeowners for home improvements such as new weatherization, landscape, paint and stucco repair, roofs, and installation of energy-efficient measures like new air conditioning units.

In cooperation with Riverside County, millions have been spent creating more affordable homes. The city has redeveloped several properties such as Desert Willow, a formerly failed condominium development.

Redevelopment and improvement contracts must use local labor and goods.

"Desert Hot Springs' unemployment rate is above the county average," Parks says. "Community development projects are also designed to invigorate our own economy by hiring local workers and purchasing local goods and equipment to encourage local employment."

PARKS IMPROVEMENT

"Parks and community buildings are extremely important for the health and well-being of the community, as young and old congregate for sporting events, recreation, education, and relaxation," says Parks. "Improving the quality and safety of our parks helps bring our community together.

Mission Springs Park was reconfigured from combination soccer and baseball fields to an exclusive soccer park, now offering a dedicated place for American Youth Soccer Organization clubs. A new walking path, beautiful landscaping, and smaller play areas make the park a destination for young and old.

Wardman Park was renovated with new dugouts, bleachers, and lighting, providing Little League teams a world-class baseball park.

The Tedesco Park Lozano Community Center was renovated by adding a full kitchen and meeting rooms to better serve the community. Service providers and organizations — such as Gilda's Club — use the center to offer programs to the community. The park also houses a neighborhood police office and Citizens on Patrol, establishing a strong police presence in the park and neighborhood. I-10

FREEWAY CORRIDOR EXPANDS DEVELOPMENT OPPORTUNITIES

In February, the city officially annexed 4,000 acres that connects the city to Interstate 10 at Palm Drive and at Indian Avenue. Now, when motorists exit I-10, they are in Desert Hot Springs.

Acreage alongside the interstate will also afford Desert Hot Springs new commercial possibilities for such developments as a regional auto mall, shopping centers, hotels, and industrial areas — another way to increase goods and services to residents while also increasing the city's sales tax revenue for public safety and community services.

"This affords Desert Hot Springs more opportunity for exposure along the I-10, which some 150,000 people travel daily," says Parks. "The annexation provided additional economic development opportunities by expanding the community's job base."

City officials are also working with the Coachella Valley Association Governments with respect to the Multi-Species Habitat Conservation Plan that affects a large portion of the newly annexed area by setting aside from development natural areas for threatened and endangered desert plant and wildlife species.

ADDED SAFETY MEASURES:
TOOLS FOR POLICE AND TIGHTENED CRIME PREVENTION

The City Council's top priority is to promote public safety. Over the past two years, voters overwhelmingly approved two tax measures dedicated to public safety. The measures provide funding for additional officers and the tools they need to fight crime. The city has installed 32 community cameras in key areas such as parks and major intersections. Desert Hot Springs police cars are now equipped with mobile computers connected to the cameras so that they can zoom in to see a situation in real time, pinpoint location, and respond faster and smarter.

A recent sting operation known as Operation Falling Sun removed some 125 gang leaders when 700 law enforcement officers descended upon targeted areas in Desert Hot Springs. The operation received a state award. The Riverside County District Attorney was successful in acquiring two gang injunctions that prohibit gang members from associating on public streets. Additional measures approved by the City Council are geared at ridding the city of parolees and sex offenders.

WEST VALLEY ENTERPRISE ZONE AND OTHER COALITIONS

In partnership with Cathedral City and Palm Springs, Desert Hot Springs has applied for a West Valley Enterprise Zone. The Enterprise Zone Program exists to stimulate business investment in depressed areas and create job opportunities by offering state tax credits and incentives to businesses operating within the zone and hiring new employees.

These incentives combine to form a powerful economic development tool for expanding existing and luring new businesses to the area and spurring economic growth.

The mayors of the three cities are working together to address the issues they have in common and are thinking more regionally about what benefits the west end of the
valley.

Mayor: Yvonne Parks
Mayor Pro Tem: Scott Matas
Council Members: Russell Betts, Karl Baker, Jan Pye
Year Incorporated: 1963
Population: 26,811
Median Household Income: $36,379

When such a glowing summary of accomplishments becomes overshadowed by negative publicity such as what follows, it is no wonder that people often refer to the community as "The Little Engine that Could" *"I think I can I think I can I think I can"* rather than "The Shining City on the Hill," as council member Hank Hohenstein so often referred.

One could argue that the "Gang Sweep" written about in the following article was and is a good thing for the city. Certainly driving crime out of Desert Hot Springs is of paramount importance, but the results of such notorious publicity can hurt the city's image further, unless the criminals actually are gone.

But the Chief's statistics do show a downward trend in crime for the past several months, so maybe they will get it under control—we can hope.

Major gang sweep conducted in Desert Hot Springs

The Associated Press

Posted: 03/27/2009 04:49:37 PM PDT

DESERT HOT SPRINGS, Calif.—Law enforcement officials from nearly three dozen agencies conducted perhaps the largest gang sweep in Riverside County history on Friday, arresting more than 120 people and confiscating an assortment of drugs and dozens of guns.

The sweep, which had been planned for seven months, centered on rural Desert Hot Springs and involved nearly 700 officers from local, state and federal agencies, said District Attorney Rod Pacheco.

Besides the arrests, police found 400 grams of methamphetamine, 3,000 grams of marijuana, more than 50 marijuana plants and some cocaine and heroin, he said. They also discovered an active meth lab inside the wall of a public housing unit and recovered more than 50 guns, he said.

Police also served two local gangs with a gang injunction notice. Such injunctions are used to restrict the movements and behavior of known gang members.

Pacheco said members of the gangs had committed more than 156 felonies in the past three years and violence had escalated in recent months.

The city has one of the highest crime rates in Riverside County as a result, he said.

"In the last eight or nine months, the gangs in Desert Hot Springs have been on a real tear," he said. "They're shooting at police officers, they're shooting at innocent citizens, they're committing murders. They've been even more aggressive than usual."

The sweep began at dawn in the small desert city about 110 miles southeast of Los Angeles.

****

West Drive Locos gang of Desert Hot Springs home torn down.

Posted March 28, 2009

Crews tear down a house that police say was used by the West Drive Locos gang of Desert Hot Springs Friday after a massive multi-agency anti-gang injunction The home on Estrella Avenue at Palm Drive was turned to rubble within minutes as government officials and city residents cheered. "The symbol we're about to provide is, we're taking back this community, even if it involves tearing down the playground of

317

the West Drive Locos," Riverside County District Attorney Rod Pacheco said during a news conference just before the home was destroyed.

Whether standing behind brick walls or sitting on nearby rooftops, residents watched as construction equipment tore into the home that was tagged with gang symbols and sat in a vacant lot littered with debris."You couldn't drive by at night without seeing guys hanging out or making noise," Desert Hot Springs resident George Hansen, 57, said after the news conference.

"I'm glad it's gone. It's one less place for gang members to congregate. They know (law enforcement officers) are coming after them."

****

This is not exactly the kind of publicity conducive to enticing vacationers to come to your town, or new business ventures either. On the other hand, maybe the crooks are starting to get the message. If so, and the current Police Chief can get his arms around the problem to succeed in driving the parolees and their convict friends out of the city, maybe, just maybe Desert Hot Springs will "move forward" as Mayor Parks has declared it will.

Using the Locos Gang home as a metaphoric message to felon parolees and other gang members was a good idea. Following through with other methods at the disposal of the police and sheriff's department to keep the pressure on, will eventually stem the tide of crime in the city. How long "eventually" will be, is the sixty-four dollar question. It's here that everyone should wish for the Positive Energy Vortex to take over.

The following excerpt from a Los Angeles Times article points out the locals' focus on the powers of the Vortex in a quote from one of the spa owners, Jeffery Bowman, which I placed in bold for emphasis:

Desert Hot Springs is fighting for its life

A military-style police operation has put a dent in crime. The next job is revitalizing the city.

Los Angeles Times

August 25, 2009 | David Kelly

City boosters are busy touting Desert Hot Springs' advantages over ritzier neighbors like Palm Springs and Palm Desert. They note the magnificent mountain views, cooler temperatures and the fact that nearly 80% of the town is undeveloped. And there is that vast pool of hot water lying just beneath the sand that feeds the spas.

"There is a vibe here, maybe it's the vortex we are sitting on," said Jeffrey Bowman, relaxing at his clothing optional Living Waters Spa. "You have heat above, heat below, mountain ranges, clean air, and it has a wonderful power."

But poverty remains. Unemployment stands at 18.5%, and in July 1,544 homes – 7.2% of all housing units – were in foreclosure, more than twice the state average, according to Realty Track, which monitors foreclosure rates. Aside from spas and a few restaurants, there is little local industry, and some 7,000 people a day commute out of town for work, officials say.

The city hopes to win a $1-million federal grant to begin refurbishing its infrastructure, create jobs and start intervention programs for at-risk youth.

"All the kids coming in here are at risk," said Jeanette Jaime-Quinonez, who runs a life skills program at the cramped Boys and Girls Club. "Most come from domestic violence, drug abuse or from broken families."

As she spoke, Ron and John Lange walked through the door.

The 14-year-old twins hung out with a rough crowd until their friend, Luis Lopez Jr., 16, was gunned down by gang members two years ago. Seeing his body at the funeral shook them up and set them both on a different path.

They worked on their soccer skills and were recruited for a team that recently played in Guadalajara, Mexico. Now they hope to turn professional.

Jaime-Quinonez, a former gang member paralyzed in a drive-by shooting, said they are the exceptions.

"What really happens to kids like this is they end up in jail," she said.

In addition to gangs, parolees attracted by cheap rents remain a concern.

"Gov. [Arnold] Schwarzenegger says he is going to release 43,000 prisoners, and when they get out they'll be coming right out here," said Jesse Sanchez, pastor of Living Word in the Desert Church in Indio who runs half-way houses for parolees in and around Desert Hot Springs. "They send them to the streets rather than to programs like ours."

Sanchez, 34, has a personal stake in ridding the area of crime. When he was 14, he said, he and some friends started the Brownstown gang, the oldest in Desert Hot Springs.

"I feel like I have blood on my hands. I made all this trouble, but the gang keeps going and going," he said. "That's why I feel so passionately about helping."

He knows many of those arrested in Operation Falling Sun.

"The D.A. took in people who had jobs and were trying to change their lives," he said. "He should have been more strategic and gone after the big dogs. The gangs will lay low for a few months and strategize. You can't kill a gang, you have to change the way they think."

But most residents applaud the crackdown as a watershed moment when a beleaguered town stood up to bullies and won – for now.

"They arrested a lot of people and intimidated a lot more," said John Furbee, 79, who has lived in Desert Hot Springs since 1969. "I think the tide has now turned. Everyone is on the same page. It's the criminals against us, and us is bigger."

****

The Desert Hot Springs Boys & Girls club has also been waging a battle against local gangs also, with the help of the Police department, trying to teach and train their young members to stay away from gangs.

Boys & Girls Club fights to keep kids out of gangs

6:56 PM, Mar. 2, 2011 Written by**Ron Houston**
Special to The Desert Sun

Boys & Girls Club of Coachella Valley is the grateful recipient of several recent grants. These awards have recognized and galvanized our efforts to become the premier development organization for youth in the Southern California desert and the best Boys & Girls Club in the country.

Based in Palm Desert with clubhouses in Coachella, Desert Hot Springs, Indio and La Quinta (and another coming to Mecca in the fall), Boys & Girls Club of Coachella Valley contributes to the quality of life we enjoy here. More than creating after-school diversions, it's our mission to reach out

321

passionately not only to enhance our kids' lives but to save them.

Funding grants foster growth

Boys & Girls Club of Coachella Valley's expansion into Desert Hot Springs last year was rewarded in October with a $45,000 donation from the city's nonprofit Mission Springs Foundation. It will help fund the construction of the new Desert Hot Springs Clubhouse and enable our organization — after 43 years of serving the east valley — to reach children in a previously under-served area.

This fall also brought us a string of good fortune in the form of grants from the Houston Family Foundation, CalGRIP and the Bank of America Charitable Foundation, which recognized us through its Neighborhood Excellence Initiative.

Among our programs
benefiting is Choices, a
multiperspective, personal
experience-based school and
community center program
stressing gang and drug
prevention. As the program's
co-founder and links
coordinator, based at the
Indio Clubhouse, I ensure
that it delivers real-life
cautionary tales to students
about gangs, drugs and
other dangers from the perspectives of law enforcers, ex-convicts and victims. The program encourages young people to make better choices for themselves.

Gang-prevention focus in DHS

The Bank of America grant and a grant from the city of Indian Wells have enabled Boys & Girls Club of Coachella Valley to hire a new director of community services, Jeanette Jaime, at our recently acquired Desert Hot Springs Clubhouse. A five-year resident of the city, Jeanette was previously affiliated with its independent Boys & Girls Club and has been providing the victim's viewpoint on gang violence in our Choices program. After a drive-by shooting left her a paraplegic at age 17, Jeanette, who also spent 13 years working with gang violence victims through the Oakland-based organization Youth Alive!, developed a passion for assisting kids similarly impacted.

In Desert Hot Springs, Jeanette is administering the Choices program and other programs deployed nationally by Boys & Girls Clubs of America. Her position is unique because no other major organization has availed a youth-specific community services outreach worker to the city.

Beyond our defined duties, each employee of Boys & Girls Club of Coachella Valley — which has a membership numbering some 6,000 children 7 to 18 — typically takes one club member in dire need of mentoring under his or her wing. I myself have helped divert a teenager from heavy gang involvement and got him enrolled in a college prep class. He's now working to shake off the gang lifestyle completely.

People in our organization say, "If you can make a positive difference in the life of just one individual, you've done your job." What's wonderful is that I don't know a single colleague in Boys & Girls Club of Coachella Valley who would settle for helping just one.

> Ron Houston is co-founder and links coordinator of the Boys & Girls Club of Coachella Valley's Choices program. He can be reached at (760) 347-5712. E-mail him via dean@cvstrat.com

****

An introduction to the current council

The current council, three of whom will be up for election in November 2011 is dedicated to attempting to raise the city's image, and addressing the issues most important in the minds of their constituents, and that is no easy task. Currently the city is embroiled in the controversy of what was to be the World Health & Wellness Festival, which will be explained further on these pages.

The five members are truly representative of the population of Desert Hot Springs: Mayor Yvonne Parks moved to the city to retire with her husband; Mayor Pro-tem Betts moved with his wife to be closer to his aging parents who live in the Mission Lakes Country Club area; Council Member Baker came to the city to retire from teaching; Council Member Matas was born and raised in the city, and Council Member Jan Pye came to join her friends and attend College of the Desert, to get her Masters Degree in Finance.

Meet Mayor Yvonne Parks

Yvonne Parks, Mayor
Parks_Yvonne@hotmail.com

Current Term: November 2011
Serving since March 2007.

Welcome to the Desert Hot Springs City Website. This

324

wonderful City, with it's magnificent views, clean air, unique Spas and awarding winning drinking water, is on the brink of economic prosperity. We have many new residential developments and increased commercial development is just around the corner. We are home to many unique intimate Spas as well as larger Hotel/Spas and the infamous Two Bunch Palms Resort and Spa. In addition we have our Cabot's Old Indian Pueblo Museum, a historical site in honor of Cabot Yerxa that homesteaded 160 acres which is now known as Desert Hot Springs. Our current population is approximately 24,000 and growing.

I have been a resident of Desert Hot Springs since 1994. We chose Desert Hot Springs because of the clean air, the beautiful views and the fact that we always have an afternoon breeze to cool us down during the hot summer months. We have found the people here to be wonderful caring individuals.

In November 2005, I was honored to be elected to the City Council from a field of eight candidates. I have been active in the community since moving here in 1994. The Desert Hot Springs Women's Club holds a special place in my heart. The primary goal of this organization is to provide scholarships to deserving Desert Hot Springs students to provide them with an incentive to continue into higher education. I encourage you women that are reviewing this website to consider joining this worthwhile organization.

I have also been a member of the Chamber of Commerce and held an executive office on the Board of Directors since 1999-2005. I was appointed to the Planning Commission twice. The first time in 1997 and again in 2004, where I sat as Vice-Chairman until elected to the City Council

I lost my husband to cancer in 2006. My consolation was to devote full time to working to make Desert Hot Springs the best that it can be.

In 2007, I decided to run for Mayor and was elected. My goal is still to make Desert Hot Springs the best City in the

Coachella Valley.

It is an exciting time for all of us living and working in Desert Hot Springs. This City Council has an opportunity, through carefully considered decision making, to move gracefully into the 21st century. We have a much needed Health and Wellness Medical Campus coming in the near future, the future prospect of a beautifully designed and much needed Community Civic Center, developing a Comprehensive General Plan utilizing a "smart growth" plan, and bringing the desired commercial growth to enable our residents the opportunity to work and shop in Desert Hot Springs.

Because of my nearly 25 years in State government, working with all segments of the population. I believe I understand the needs and desires of individuals, business owners, entrepreneurs, developers as well as the City staff. My goal is to always keep this in mind when making decisions that affect our community.

Our City staff and Chamber of Commerce are eager to help you in any way they can.

If you would like to contact me personally, I can be reached at the following numbers:

(760) 902-6655 (cell

326

phone)

(760) 329-1146 Fax

Current Term: November 2011

Meet Mayor Pro-Tem Russell Betts

Russell Betts, Mayor Pro-Tem
Current Term: November 2011

Serving since December 2007

The economic benefits of downtown revitalization and economic development are well documented. Local residents enjoy better shopping and more jobs close to home. They have more cultural and social activities to choose from, as do their children.

Housing values improve as our city becomes more attractive.

Retail business owners get an improved image, increased sales and more customer traffic, as do professionals who operate from downtown offices and new business centers. The overall pride of our city rises when our downtown is re-energized and we grow our economic base.

The economy, of course, is the main concern. More retail storefronts, more shoppers mean more sales tax revenue for our city. That means less reliance on other less desirable taxes and more money to fight crime, new residential streets and sidewalks. It means more of the city services our residents expect.

For our youth, a healthy business climate means first time jobs and for others it means good jobs right here at home. Instead of our residents leaving the city to find work, the rush will be to come and enjoy Desert Hot Springs.

That is my hope for a better Desert Hot Springs and my commitment to work towards it as your city councilman.

Best Regards,

Russell Betts, Mayor Pro-Tem

Meet Councilmember Karl Baker

Karl Baker, Jr., Councilmember
kbaker@cityofdhs.org

Current Term: November 2011
Serving since December 2007

Meet Council Member Scott Matas

Scott Matas, Councilmember
swmatas@roadrunner.com

329

Current Term: November 2013

*Serving since March 2007*Welcome to the City of Desert Hot Springs website and Thank you for wanting to learn about the city.

I am a life time resident of Desert Hot Springs -- born and raised, attending school here and I am now raising my own family here in our town. My wife and I have three children, one in high school and 2 in elementary school. I own a small business and belong to the Desert Hot Springs Rotary Club and Chamber of Commerce. Plus I've been a volunteer firefighter for 17 years.

My vision is straightforward: I am currently working to bridge the concerns of our small business owners, parks & youth programs, public safety needs, and our tourist industry. We have a great downtown that with some TLC will become a perfect dining, shopping, and small business experience. Our parks are transitioning to becoming more modernized and community oriented. Our youth is a vital part of this community and our schools have the largest student population in our school district. Consequently we as a city need to promote, protect and encourage our youth to reach their dreams. Public safety is a concern in every city across America and so won't come as a surprise that our city is in need of more police officers, firefighters and code enforcement. Our police department is operated by a true professional: Chief Pat Williams. His vision is on track with our current city council to provide the highest level of public safety needs to our community. The tourist industry is the most vital industry to our community; bringing in the tax dollars and tourist revenue to fund all of the issues I just wrote about. We have the best views in the Coachella Valley, award winning and therapeutic mineral waters, the cleanest air and some of the best health and wellness spas in the country. Our tourists can relax in our spas for a day, a week or snowbird for the winter! While visiting our city a "must see" is our own California Historical Site – Cabot's Museum. Cabot's Museum will soon have trails leading into the Joshua Tree

330

National Monument with views you will not be able to find anywhere else in the Coachella Valley.

Our community is close to 25,000 but still holds that small town feeling. Please feel free to contact me and thank you again for taking the time to read about me and the city I truly love. Please come visit Desert Hot Springs and see the beauty we have to offer.

Councilmember for the City of Desert Hot Springs
swmatas@roadrunner.com
(760) 200-7428

Meet Councilmember Jan Pye

Jan Pye, Councilmember

jpye@cityofdhs.org

Current Term: November 2013
Serving since March 2009

Most everyone living in California is from somewhere else, in my generation. I came to California from Minnesota, my wife came from Michigan. Finding anyone born before 1940 who was born and raised in the same town and still living their in California is rare.

We met two people living in Desert Hot Springs who had lived their most of their lives and were schoolmates all through elementary, middle and high school. One was Mary Huthchison the other, Scott Matas; they were schoolmates during their formative years, both living in Desert Hot Springs.

My personal relationships with the council:

Mayor Yvonne Parks

I first met Yvonne, during the first visioning meeting I attended in 2003, she was a member of the Planning commission at the time. Unfortunately, our relationship has been strained since her efforts to promote Palmwood and torpedo the MSHCP ran counter to my position and outspoken articles on the subject. I admire her forceful leadership qualities and the fact that she has shown that she has the energy to lead the city, even though we differ on many issues.

Scott Matas

I first met Scott in Rotary and was impressed. He was a volunteer firefighter, member of the Public Safety Commission, and involved in several charity groups, clearly a young man on the move. Scott had purchased the local UPS Store Franchise, and was respected by the old-timers.

Scott was a true home-town boy, raised from early childhood in Desert Hot Springs and never left; rare, indeed. After being elected to fill Gary Bosworth's seat on the council, and by all accounts, is doing a great job. Assuming he runs again, Councilman Matas will be judged on his merits and record over the last four years, as will his fellow incumbents, come November's Election.

332

I have had many conversations with Scott, and judge him to be extremely honest and forthright, and as a "hometown boy" making sure his family, friends, neighbors, former school chums and all the members of his constituency get a fair shake. In the scheme of things, that's all we can ask of our representatives. We wish him luck.

Russell Betts

I first met Russ shortly after beginning my writing activities with the Valley Breeze, and I liked him as a person,. as did my wife Diana. Russ's wife Miena, is a hair dresser, and after moving to the city, Diana became one of many customers in her shop on Palm Drive.

Much of my relationship and joint activities with Russ are contained in other parts of this manuscript, but needless to say, Diana and I have been strong supporters of him and what he has continued to try to do for the city. We speak by phone and exchange e-mails regularly. We consider Russ a true friend.

Karl Baker

I first met Karl Baker at my home when our political group met with Alex Bias to discuss the issues and decide if we were going to support Bias in his run for Mayor. I was impressed with Karl's intellect and his knowledge of the inner workings of the city. He was well informed and erudite in his speech and mannerisms. During that same meeting, we decided to support Karl as well as Alex and Russ. I enjoyed the many conversations Karl and I have had over Breakfast in what we called the "Cave" Café of the now defunct Hotel Spa, La Tuscana.

Jan Pye

I first met Jan Pye while attending one of the council meetings during the time I was commuting from San Marcos to Desert Hot Springs and before we lived there. Subsequently, we met again during a meeting in Patrick Gillespie's office to plan the recall and convince her to run for Mayor. Jan had been on the council, but crossed swords with Mayor Weyuker and rather than fight, she left the council and went back to school to get her Masters Degree in finance.

Jan would not run, because she had committed to support Alex Bias in his run for Mayor.

Now that you have met all of the members of the current council, and learned my connection to them, it's time for me to get on with what I set out to do, recount the history of Desert Hot Springs; the purpose being to help us all learn from past mistakes and hope they are not repeated.

The promises of past candidates as far back as we can document, have been made many times before, and follow this general pattern. While campaigning, the candidates promise to:

- Develop better police protection.

- Stop in-migration of felon parolees.

- Promote commercial and industrial development.

- Establish better code enforcement.

- Create jobs.

- Promote "Health & Wellness" promoting Mineral Spas.

- Create a better management team.

- Change the city's image in relation to its neighbors.

I expect the 2011 season's group of candidates, both incumbents and the first timers (or 2nd, 3rd and 4th-time perennial candidates, as it were) to offer similar pledges, as these have always been the pressing needs of the community, and probably a few more. As stated earlier the problem in the past has been that the promises have nearly always fallen by the wayside and are left for the next administration to state them once again.

This reminds one of setting up pins in a bowling alley. The pins get knocked over, put back up, and knocked over again and again and nothing changes but the players. Such it is with the promises made by candidates in Desert Hot Springs since its incorporation, 48-years ago.

However, in politics anything can happen. The democratic form of government can sometimes surprise us all as it plays out in our city, county, state and federal arenas.

As an example, the city of San Marcos where my wife and I currently live incorporated in 1963, the same year as Desert Hot Springs and was on the verge of bankruptcy ten-years later, only to have the good fortune of hiring a hard driving Marine ex-colonel with an entrepreneurial bent, as city manager, who led the city to becoming the most fiscally sound city in all of San Diego County. I believe Rick Daniels has the ability to do the same for Desert Hot Springs.

A good idea turns bad:

City manager Rick Daniels, needing someone to spearhead the long contemplated redevelopment of the city's commercial core centered at the intersection of Pierson and Palm Drive, hired Palm Desert resident Rudy Acosta to become Director of Development, and Redevelopment. The concept, originated under Ann Marie Gallant's short tenure

335

was to assemble and acquire properties extending out from the four corners of the intersection and create a central theme following the "Vortex Plan".

Several properties were acquired as the process began in earnest, when Christian Minister Steven Mesarch-turned Jewish Rabbi Alon Barak, offered to sell the temple for an outlandishly overpriced amount. When the city agreed to the price, public outcry ensued, resulting in the city backing off, until an appraisal could be obtained (what a concept!).

Soon what had started out as a relatively good idea suddenly went terribly wrong—and not all the fault of those involved from the city's side.

$1.4 City Purchase Justification Found

by Dean Gray
February 2, 2010

"Having a new fire station occupying the site would mean only part of it would have to be demolished," said Rick Daniels, City Manager. "The structural safety requirements of the building for use by the fire department are different than that required for use by the general public so only half would have to be torn down."

City officials have found a use for spending $1.4 million dollars purchasing the Jewish Temple nearly two years ago. It was later found unfit for occupancy. The purchase occurred just prior to the fall of the economy and came at a high price for a building that could not be used.

City leaders and Riverside County Fire officials have been working on plans to move Fire Station 37 there as an interim use until a new eastern station is built in years to come. Station 37 is currently on the corner of Pierson and West.

Desert Hot Springs officials has been struggling to find a use for the former Temple building. The purchase came at a price in excess of the value of raw land. Original plans targeting the building's use as a community center for youth and service programs plus a community theatre were sunk when a building inspection recommended demolition. The inspection was performed after the purchase, leaving officials scrambling to find an alternative use.

An attempt to transform the rambling 1950's facility into a health clinic fell through when a grant was denied for the Borego Springs Health Clinic to operate there. A health clinic is much needed in the city due to having only 2 doctors for over 25,000 people.

"A new fire station located east of Pierson would more evenly distribute fire and paramedic response," said Daniels.

The city's second and nearly newest fire station (on Karen Avenue) is located on the outskirts of the city – way out on Pierson next to the Skyborne development. Daniels explained that Station 36 is now fully operational and providing better servicing of the city's west side where future development is anticipated.

Station 36 is surrounded by vast acres of yet to be developed subdivisions, some already inside city limits plus other properties awaiting incorporation.

Moving Fire Station 37 would be paid for by the city that has bankrolled around $900,000 in development impact fees that must be used for fire related facilities. The decision goes before the city council Feb. 16 after the public safety commission recommended it. It is too early to know the cost but construction could be completed before the end of the year said Daniels.

Volunteers are expected to continue to operate the station on West and Pierson. However, the Jewish Temple location would only be short lived as a major facility is planned ultimately on the far east of the city near Long Canyon 6 to 7 years down the road.

"Putting the building to good use will benefit the city," said Councilman Scott Matas, a former volunteer fireman. Matas was instrumental in the city acquiring the property.

****

The Jewish Temple Saga

by Dean Gray and Andrew Morales
July 8, 2010

Over the last two years, the Desert Valley Star reported on the Jewish temple in Desert Hot Springs. This story took a lot of surprising twists and turns, which still aren't over. Events unfolded suggesting a conspiracy or at the very least, sloppy management of city funds used for the purchase. Follow our story through the timeline of events climaxing in the city's ultimate decision of the future of the temple.

PART I
City Buys Community Center Again – August 27, 2008
The old Jewish temple sitting abandoned on Pierson St. is on the verge of being bought by the city to renovate it to become a community center.

PART II
Money Machine Intrigue – April 30, 2009
A string of unusual real estate transactions cause the new rabbi/minister of the Jewish temple to become Desert Hot

338

Springs' newest millionaire.

PART III
Temple Purchase Tribulations – May 6, 2009
Gone unchecked, the million-dollar conspiracy is finally taken
to the city council. The shocking vote of the city council brings
this supposed conspiracy into a new light.

PART IV
Temple Demolition Proposed – May 12, 2009
The safety engineers tell the city council that the renovation
project is not a good idea and demolition must proceed. At
this point, the cost of renovation is more than the cost of the
building back in 2008.

PART V
Another "Ooopsie" For the City – June 26, 2009
The city contends the engineer's inspection in May about the
demolition of the Jewish temple, but they didn't have to wait
for long to figure out who came clean.

PART VI
County May Shift Health
Clinic Location – July 13,
2009
A $7 million health clinic
land purchase by Riverside
County seems to have gone
out the window when their
eyes become fixed on the
controversial temple.

PART VII
Jewish Temple Becomes a
Fire Station – February 2,

2010

The city's fire department takes the Jewish temple under their wings, but Councilman Matas is the driving force behind this acquisition.

The continuation of the Jewish Temple Saga is coming to the Desert Valley Star website VERY soon.

****

The building was then declared unfit for habitation and demolished. The property now stands vacant, as a reminder of the unfortunate circumstances surrounding a reckless expenditure of Redevelopment funds, which could have been used for other more pressing needs.

The city's plans for the area are detailed in a 2008 article in the Desert Valley Star newspaper. Acquisition of blighted properties is a major part of redevelopment efforts in every city. As a matter of fact, the premise of funding these projects is based on helping revitalize run down areas, to help build new vitality and spawn increased revenues by helping create new businesses in the rebuilt business districts.

To my knowledge, nobody in Desert Hot Springs quarreled with the concept, just the execution and wild overspending in the process of acquiring the targeted properties.

Several other purchases of properties were executed during the time when values were plummeting, and the city was paying top dollar for the sites, much to the consternation of some council members and members of the public.

Some time later, this story broke on the local news channel, causing concern among members of the council and public:

Palm Desert, Desert Hot Springs Redevelopment Funds Put Into Question

To be fair, everything worth doing must start with a plan. Once that plan is put on paper though, the cost estimates for that plan should be added to the feasibility studies and assuming all things are plausible, the plan then enters pre-construction and on to the construction phases. Putting time money and talent together to reach a desired completion relies on the management staff of the city to reach the end goal—a revitalized Downtown. We wish Desert Hot Springs success in their venture.

However, historically speaking, strong management has always been the Achilles heel of Desert Hot Springs. When plans are projected to be implemented over a period of years, stable management is an important and integral part of the plan. When chinks in management begin to appear, red flags go up (or at least should go up). One such chink appeared at the most inopportune time in the city's planned program of revitalization.

Late in 2009, the city manager was pitched by a self-styled "producer/promoter" Tony Clarke, who proposed to put together a Health & Wellness Music Festival which would purportedly "put Desert Hot Springs on the map". The proposal was strongly supported by community leader Dot

Reed, chairperson of the Cultural Affairs Commission, chair of the local Soroptimist Club and a one-time fill-in on the city council for a short period of time. With the recommendation from City Manager Daniels and the urging of Reed, the council voted 4-1 to enter into a contract with promoter Clarke to produce the festival in the spring of 2010, the lone dissenter being Councilman Russell Betts.

But things began to unravel, as delays in the program's schedule slipped and some bad decisions of management staff began to leak to the public. Two things impacting the Festival planning occurred in rapid succession. Rick Daniels checked himself into rehab for alcoholism, and his immediate absence, and the firing of his executive assistant/project manager Laura Green.

****

Eight: Dark Clouds on the Horizon

A mini crisis strikes:

This is not what you would like to wake up to in the morning if you are a city councilmember in Desert Hot Springs: **Desert Hot Springs' Rick Daniels takes leave to check into rehab**

In 20 years in high-profile business and public service jobs, Rick Daniels has built a reputation as a fixer, a powerful force for getting things done………

****

Unfortunately, that's the news that Parks, Betts, Baker, Matas and Pye did wake up to, and within hours their first action was to fire Laura Green, Rick's trusted right arm for many years, well before coming to Desert Hot Springs. To this day, no reason has been given. But the council did give Green a healthy severance of $99,000.00 as she waved goodbye to the city, while Rick Daniels was in rehab. Shortly after Green's departure, this article appeared in the Desert Sun for readers to decipher:

They Fired My Project Manager

Daniels Explains Why He Considered Smith For Festival Gig
by Dean Gray
February 20, 2011

DESERT HOT SPRINGS, CA - In an email to Desert Valley Star, City Manager Rick Daniels explained why he suggested a former police commander be hired as a consultant to manage the World Wellness and Music Festival.

"Read the Council packet document again," wrote Daniels. "It said that I was considering hiring Ed since the Council had terminated the project manager while I was gone." The project manager Daniels refers to is former Community Services Director, Laura Green. The City terminated Green's employment while Daniels was "gone" in rehab for alcohol abuse.

Daniels' email was sent to Desert Valley Star in response to a February 13 story about former Desert Hot Springs Police Commander Ed Smith's involvement with the struggling World Wellness and Music Festival and how Smith came to be hired by Tony Clarke and Tresed Ventures, the event promoter. Daniels requested a correction by the Desert Valley Star.

343

The "document packet" item Daniels referred to above was the agenda for the December 21, 2010 city council meeting where the canceled music festival was on the agenda. It is there that Daniels first notified the city council of his intention to hire Smith under a consulting agreement paying Smith $24,000 over six months.

In that document packet, Daniels wrote, "Additionally I will be looking to retain Edwin Smith as the City's Project Manager on this event. Ed's past involvement with the logistics planning for this festival to date and festivals and major events in the Carmel/Monterey area uniquely qualify him to represent the City's interest in assuring the success of the venture. Ed retires from the City's Police Department this month."

Daniels went on to explain that any consulting agreement with Smith "will be presented to your Council at a future date, if required." Our February 13 story pointed out that Daniels could hire Smith without council authorization as the city manager has a spending authority threshold of $30,000 without requiring council approval.

Smith was a police commander for Desert Hot Springs with

one of his assignments while on the city payroll was preparing the city for the event. Smith worked on traffic, parking, and police preparations. On January 2, 2011 Smith retired and announced he would immediately begin working with Tony Clark.

Daniels says his only intention was to seek council input on Smith's consulting agreement but that his use of the phrase "to retain" apparently now did not at all mean he was expressing interest in "hiring" Smith.

Daniels explained in his email to Desert Valley Star, "I was merely sharing my thoughts in a very transparent manner with the Council. Regardless of the spending threshold I was taking the matter to the Council to seek their input in a public meeting. The matter, while disclosed was never discussed." Daniels made it clear in the most recent email that the only reason that Smith was considered for the position was Green had been terminated.

The last contact Daniels had with Green was at an event both attended in San Diego. Days later Daniels entered rehab and Green's employment was terminated with the signing of an agreement that she would not sue the City. Any other details remain secret. For several years Green had worked under Daniels in other positions prior to their working together for the City of Desert Hot Springs.

Regarding Smith and how he became involved post-retirement with Tony Clarke and Tresed Ventures, Smith said in a phone interview, "Rick and I discussed this. We were brainstorming about how to solve the problem."

"The problem" being Green's termination by the council and Daniels' cancellation of the 2010 music festival just weeks prior to the scheduled date. However, Daniels disagrees with Smith, saying the matter was never discussed with Smith and that he [Daniels] wrote the memo proposing the idea of Smith working as project manager without any discussion with Smith. But - before it came before the council - Daniels suddenly withdrew the proposal.

"After further internal discussions with Jason [Simpson] I concluded that the City did not have the additional resources and instead the City would manage the project within existing resources. I never sought nor received a proposal from Ed. There was no discussion between Ed and me on this topic. I had nothing to do with his decision to work on the festival after he left City employment. I know nothing of what Ed is doing other than what I read in the newspaper."

Smith, when asked how he came to work for Clarke said, "that is confidential." It is not known if Clarke approached him or if Smith made the proposal to Clarke that he should be hired. Clarke has always remained totally silent about all matters relating to the quarter million dollars and the music festival, refusing to comment to anyone of the media since Daniels canceled the event.

Meanwhile, the City continues discussing filing a lawsuit against Clarke and his company, Tresed Ventures, to recover $250,000 the City paid Clarke. It is not known if others will be named in the lawsuit or if Smith will be able to rescue the event or if Smith will be working with Clarke to defend a lawsuit by the city. The city council has held four closed door meetings in 2011 on the music festival under an agenda item titled, "Initiation of Litigation."

EPILOG: *Ed Smith continues working for Clarke. Laura Green, wife of former The Desert Sun Editor Rick Green won a $99,328.16 settlement agreement from the City before relocating to Ohio where her husband was reassigned shortly after the settlement. Daniels last month won a three-year*

346

contract extension paying over $250,000 annually (with benefits). It is also not known if Clarke has any money left from the $250,000 to produce the event. The city council and the city manager are pushing to hold the music festival in October, just before the November election in an effort to correct the situation; thereby dispelling any doubt they made a mistake.

****

Desert Hot Springs City Manager on Medical Leave for Alcoholism

As he(sic) contract renewal is being discussed, Desert Hot Springs City Manager Rick Daniels has announced he's checking himself into a rehab facility for alcohol abuse.

Daniels sent KPSP Local 2 this statement Thursday morning:

> *"I have come to the conclusion that I have abused alcohol in the past and as a result it is affecting my health and my relationships with my family and closest friends that I love the most. Tomorrow I will voluntarily enter a residential treatment facility and will return to the City in 30 days. I look forward to returning and continue the long term work to help the Community*

347

reach its greatest potential."

Desert Hot Springs Police Chief Patrick Williams and Assistant City Manager Jason Simpson will be acting City Manager, according to the mayor's office. "Rick is a great City Manager," said Mayor Yvonne Parks. "We all wish him and his family the best in his treatment and recovery."

Earlier this month the Desert Hot Springs city council decided to renew Daniels' contract for another five years. His current base salary is $217,000 annually. Mayor Parks says contract discussions and a decision on whether to renew will occur when Daniels returns.

"I would admire a man willing to ask for help," said a Desert Hot Springs resident and recovering alcoholic, who wanted to be identified only as Floyd. "Just the fact that he's willing to admit there's a problem is a big step forward. What we need to do now is watch and see if he does anything with it (treatment).

****

Upon Daniel's return to his office, things did not go back to normal, due to growing concerns over the planned Festival, a battle with the promoter, the council, the promoter's partners and myriad issues connected to the production ensued. Infighting on the council, replete with accusations flying back and forth over who did what and why, quickly hit the news media. All of this was breaking while Daniels was in Rehab.

The next thing to appear in the media was an interview piece published in the Desert Sun, with Daniels speaking against Alcoholism, which no doubt was a part of his recovery regimen.

City Manager Rick Daniels Speaks Out About Alcoholism

Reported by: Kate Cagle
Email: katec@kpsplocal2.com
Created: 3/07 5:15 pm
Last Update: 3/07 6:21 pm

Rick Daniels Desert Hot Springs city manager Rick Daniels spoke publicly Monday for the first time since returning from rehab for alcohol abuse.

"I feel to some degree that I've been through boot camp for life," Daniels told KPSP Local 2 Mobile Journalist Kate Cagle. "I wish this would have happened 40 years ago but it happened today and it happened for today for a reason."

Just over a month ago Daniels admitted he had a problem with alcohol and entered into a 30 day rehab program outside of the Coachella Valley. Daniels took a very public leave of absence from his job amid contract negotiations.

"While that has added its own layer of pain through all this, perhaps people can realize that they don't have to suffer this alone. That there is help, there's a way out and today I approach life with the most optimistic attitude," Daniels said.

Daniels says his in-patient treatment has given him a new outlook on life and that he feels more relaxed than he has for years. While he used to dread the repercussions that would stem from admitting to himself and his family that he's an alcoholic, Daniels now thinks taking the first step to getting help was the best thing he's ever done.

349

He's not just optimistic about his own life, but also about the future of the city he runs; a city where the residents spend 65% of their income elsewhere. Daniels and the city council have been working to improve shopping along Palm Drive and decrease crime by expanding the local Boys and Girls Club program.

"I'm not a role model," Daniels said. "I'm merely a human being trying to do the best they can with what they have."

Returning on the job, Daniels says he is happier than ever and grateful for the support he's received over the past week.

"People - some of (whom) I don't even know - came up to me and congratulated me for admitting my mistake. Admitting my flaws, of which we all have plenty."

Daniels is back at work on a part time basis. His temporary contract will expire in January, but he's confident the city council will give him another chance to run the city he loves.

****

Upon Rick's return to his office, I sent him this message by e-mail:

Hello Rick

Sorry to hear of your issue, but very pleased to see you have taken the right steps. It takes great courage to do what you are doing and more, when you go public as a person in the public eye. I wish you the best, and we will be pulling for you and your quick recovery. Your leadership has brought DHS from the brink and they need you to return in good health. Good luck!

He then responded with this:

It was notes and cards like this and that gave me the strength to get through this. God has me by the hand now and guiding me. I am so touched that in the middle of your challenges that you would think of mine.

I am back to work today. I am much better today than 34 days ago because of the prayers and these well wishes that I received. I am a better man, husband, friend, and City Manager because of it.

Thank you, my friend

****

Now you might be wondering, how I can be deriding him for some things and pumping him up for others. We all have our priorities. With me, friendship and character transcends the everyday minutia of our work environment and most things attached to it. I can fight with you over issues I disagree on and laugh and hug you for those we agree on.

Friendship runs deeper than words in an article or on a web site. Friendship is about caring deeply for one another, while maintaining our own integrity and self respect. If you are my friend, you may not like what I tell you on an issue, but if I didn't tell you what I thought truthfully, I wouldn't be a friend worth having. And it goes both ways. When a person calls me his or her friend, I expect them to be honest with me and tell me what they think, not what they think I might want to hear.

As a father, grandfather and great-grandfather, I can only hope my family lives by those same rules, as they have served me well over the years, with very few exceptions.

At one level, I am very upset with Rick for some issues we have been involved in and others quite pleased. I have made him aware of both, and will continue along the same path as we progress into the future. I have clients to answer to, and he has the council and a city to answer to. Neither is more important than the other.

Much remains to be done in Desert Hot Springs, and Daniels has shown on many occasions he has the talent to accomplish the tasks at hand. However, questions linger on his most recent decisions relative to the monumental errors in judgment concerning the up-front payments made to the Health & Wellness Festival promoter Clarke and the on again off again proposals to fast track an impossible schedule in an attempt to produce the festival in 2001.

Knee-jerk decisions tend to go awry more often than not. All city councils are entitled to guidance from their city manager and city attorney. When one fails them, it is not good. When both fail them it can create a disaster, and that seems to be what happened here. I believe both Attorney Ruben Duran and City Manager Rick Daniels failed their council in the matter of the Health & Wellness Festival planning and implementation.

Whether Daniels can recover from these errors remains to be seen. What the city doesn't need at this time is another change in city management. Hopefully that can be avoided.

Notwithstanding the improbable short time frame given to produce the festival, what wasn't made public until it became obvious after several postponed dates, was the fact that Clarke, operating under a quickly formed LLC named "Tresed Ventures" (Tresed, being Desert spelled backwards) which seems appropriate for such a ridiculously structured plan and resultant contract. Clarke then partnered with two other individuals and their company: "Baruch/Gayton Entertainment Group". Clarke was paid the full amount of the contract of $250,000, including an additional $15,000 for a self serving "feasibility study" prepared by Clarke, suggesting the festival would be a success. Not surprising, the debacle has unraveled and once again Desert Hot Springs became embroiled in a legal battle over a bad plan gone very bad.

Adding to this tableau was the claim from Baruch/Gayton Entertainment Group that they had not been paid by Clarke, further complicating the issue. Will this group of city leaders ever learn? One can only feel sorry for the many unsuspecting citizens of Desert Hot Springs as they dutifully pay their taxes, only to watch their money being frittered away by their elected and appointed city officials.

Following this story, one wonders how a city manager, city attorney, a mayor and three council members could have become so blind and loose with the city's $265,000 dollars. (Three because councilmember Russell Betts was a strong no-vote each and every time this fiasco came before the council). Never once it seems, did the council read the fine print in their own contract before blindly advancing such large sums to someone, which the city manager now admits was not vetted properly before doing business with Clarke.

Invariably, when government enters into negotiated contracts rather than using the open bid process, money disappears either through overpaying or mismanagement. In this case, it seems both elements were in play.

Daniels has accomplished many things for the city under the most trying of circumstances. Securing $40Million in Redevelopment funds to repair and replace most of the streets in the city and beginning a re-facing program for the center of the existing business district is one example. For this and many other accomplishments, he should be applauded. However, on the issue of the Festival, there can be no mistake; the handling of the contract was a major blunder under his hand.

Unfortunately, these negatives tend to whittle away at Daniel's credibility. Is it possible that the Negative Energy Vortex is at work here? Don't laugh—something is going on that is not easy to explain.

The articles on the following pages detail the issues quite effectively, incredible as they may seem. Daniels was under some major stress at the time the contract was negotiated, and about the time the planned Festival started coming apart, is when he checked himself into rehab for alcoholism. There are some things that can happen to you which are worse than the Vortex at times.

Fortunately for us all, we live in a country where second and even third chances are commonplace. We are a populace that wants to give everyone the benefit of the doubt. I suspect that Daniels will be given the chance to redeem himself by allowing him to continue with the job of rehabilitating Desert Hot Springs community assets.

A big step forward will be the completion of the Boys & Girls Club facility and Community Center near city hall. But first let's see what transpired with the planned Health and Wellness festival after Rick's return to city hall amid the swirling controversy.

Desert Hot Springs looking to sever ties with Wellness and World Music Festival promoter

Desert Hot Springs officials still hope to eventually put on a music festival

12:09 AM, Mar. 10, 2011

More than 15 months after Desert Hot Springs signed a $250,000 contract with a promoter, city leaders are acknowledging that work on the inaugural Wellness and World Music Festival has halted.

They also say they could be close to a deal that would fire controversial producer Tony Clarke or change his contract to allow the city to move ahead without him.

"It is no secret that the City Council and the community has lost faith in this guy's ability to deliver the event. I still believe the value of the idea is still sound," City Manager Rick Daniels said.

Several city leaders confirmed the push to sever ties with Clarke, but declined to provide details publicly Wednesday, citing closed-door discussions of a potential lawsuit and ongoing negotiations with him.

The contract, which expires in June, gives Clarke exclusive rights to the festival for one more year if the city fires him. That means the city would be barred from hiring another promoter.

If the contract expires or is changed to remove that clause, the city could hand over plans to one of the 15 promoters who have approached the city about taking over the twice-delayed festival.

The city hopes to build on what already has been accomplished to avoid spending additional money.

"My own personal opinion is that any festival that we have in the fall will have nothing to do with Tony Clarke," Councilman Karl Baker said Wednesday.

Neither Clarke nor a spokesman for Tresed Ventures, his company, returned calls Wednesday.

The city first signed the $250,000 contract with Clarke in December 2009. It is an agreement only for "pre-production" and specifically states there is no guarantee the festival will happen.

The city did not solicit bids for the contract or verify Clarke's claims of being an internationally known producer.

The city also paid Clarke an additional $15,000 to conduct a feasibility report on whether the festival was realistic.

The festival — originally slated for Oct. 9-10, 2010 — was heavily promoted as a chance for the city to boost its local economy and build its brand by promoting its signature mineral springs.

On Sept. 7, with weeks until show time and no performance lineups or ticket information released, though, the city delayed the festival. It was postponed a second time in December.

No new details — including dates, music performers or ticket information — have been released since.

On Jan. 4, the City Council chided Clarke for his failure to provide substantive updates.

Producers Baruch/Gayton Entertainment Group, which signed on to co-produce, backed out the same day.

"There have been financial problems with Tony. He owes us money. He owes others money, who we have brought into the project," Wayne Baruch, co-owner of Baruch/Gayton, told The Desert Sun at the time.

The council began meeting in closed session on Jan. 18 to consider a lawsuit against Clarke.

"I, for one, am disappointed that we haven't moved faster, but legal constraints being what they are, that's the way it is," Baker said.

The council on Tuesday will hear — once again in closed session — from City Attorney Ruben Duran about documents Clarke has submitted since a Jan. 18 city-imposed deadline detailing how he spent the city's $250,000.

"I'm still waiting to see the documents and the records that we were promised so we can get this complete," Mayor Pro Tem Russell Betts said. "I have not had anything put in front me of that I can read and review."

The city has more than 100 pages of paperwork, including contracts with performers and financial records.

Citing his ongoing review, Duran declined to share the documents with The Desert Sun, which requested them under California's open records laws.

Once optimistic the festival would happen under Clarke as planned, Daniels now says he "would do a lot of things different" if he could.

That includes seeking multiple bids for the project, hiring an experienced project manager on the city's behalf and not hiring Clarke to conduct the feasibility report.

"If I were to do it again differently, knowing what I know today, I would have done much more due diligence on who the city was getting into a relationship with," Daniels said.

Kate McGinty is a reporter for The Desert Sun. She can be reached at (760) 778-6451 or kate.mcginty@thedesertsun.com.

****

Everybody got into the act on the Festival issues.

Our former next door neighbor Bruce Barrett jumped into the fray, defending Clarke, a long time friend and business associate of Barrett's, as being an accomplished entertainment promoter. In truth, it appears the fault lies with the city in agreeing to enter into such a one-sided agreement containing only downside risk for the city against a limited upside. Also, Clarke was never properly vetted. The Negative Energy Vortex was working overtime here.

Barrett Issues Music Festival Warning
City Stuck With Clark Until June 1

by Dean Gray
February 20, 2011

DESERT HOT SPRINGS, CA - A close associate and long time friend of World Wellness and Music Festival promoter Tony Clarke has issued a sober warning to city officials contemplating a lawsuit against Clarke. "He has the contract until June. Technically they can't do s–t to him until June," said Bruce Barrett. "People should just keep quite until June. Tony could say May 31 that they will have a concert in October and they can't do nothing to him, nothing. Until then everything they say can be used by Tony against them for preventing him from doing what he has a contract to do." At a January city council meeting where Clarke appeared to provide an update to the council, Councilman Karl Baker likened Clarke to "an emperor that has no clothes" and saying he had lost all confidence in Clarke. Baker said the city should immediately severe all ties with Clarke and take action to recover $250,000 the city paid to Clarke to put on the event. Two conditions loom over

59

the City's decision to litigate.

> The city council has been meeting in closed session on four occasions in the past four weeks to study the possibility of filing a lawsuit against Clarke over the struggling music festival that was to have taken place October 9 & 10, 2010 but was canceled by City Manager Rick Daniels just a month before the event was to take place.
> 1. Clarke's contract with the city does not expire until June 2011. Even then, a non-performance clause in the contract says Clarke is actually under no obligation to put on the event. Clarke did not cancel previous dates – cancellation was done by the city manager.

> 2. Also confounding to city officials, as Barrett's warning makes clear, Clarke's contract specificially prohibits the city from engaging the services of any other alternative event promoter for a period of one year after Clarke's contract ends.

> This predicament leaves a divided city council continuing to discuss litigation while also expressing confidence in the often canceled music festival some are now saying will happen October 2011.

> Barrett, a resident of Desert Hot Springs who worked with Clarke in the early stages of the music festival, has an association with Clarke dating back to high school where both were graduates of Beverly Hills High School class of 1973.

****

Burnt Bridges

How Music Festival Screwed One Local Business
by Dean GrayFebruary 20, 2011

DESERT HOT SPRINGS, CA - A few weeks ago a prominent Los Angeles area production company associated with the music festival in Desert Hot Springs announced it was pulling out of the event because it and other vendors it works with had not been paid. Now one local business explains how it was stiffed by the city's promoter, Tony Clarke.

Max Lieberman who owns and publishes the *Desert Local News* servicing Desert Hot Springs and surrounding communities through its online publication says he was asked by Clarke to be a media partner for the music festival, including running ads and providing promotional articles for the event.

Lieberman says he did all that - running advertisements for over a year in support of the World Wellness and Music Festival. As a media partner, Lieberman also was provided advance notice of promotional announcements that he ran prominently in his publication.

Like Baruch Gayton, the Los Angeles production company that announced they quit working with Clarke, Lieberman says he's through with the much promised but never delivered music festival. An optimistic Lieberman kept the faith for the last six months even after the October 2010 event was canceled by city manager Rick Daniels in September 2010.

When doubts first starting to surface about the music festival Lieberman kept the advertising running even though another media company responsible for updating the music festival's website stopped all work on the project over non-payment.Lieberman's public relations work did not go unnoticed and was used to prop up Clarke when concerns of confidence were expressed at official meetings.

At a Community and Cultural Affairs Commission meeting June 9, 2010, Commissioner Mary Stephens said she was looking to get information from Clarke, reminding Clarke during the meeting that the city had entered an agreement with a different promoter a decade before who promised to bring a major music festival to the city. That event never took place, leaving the city out money it never got back.

In response, Commission Chairwoman Dot Reed pointed to *Desert Local News*, saying there were ads in every issue of Lieberman's publication, as proof of Clarke's legitimacy.

Lieberman says promises of payment came from both Clarke and City Manager Rick Daniels. Yet Daniels rejects Lieberman's claims of city involvement and says he's done everything possible to get Lieberman paid.

"As to Max's [Max Lieberman's issue, He came to me complaining that he had done work for Tresed for which he was not paid. I was upset at what Max told me. I relayed that concern to Tresed with the strongest admonishment for him to pay any and all outstanding obligations to local businesses," said Daniels in an email to *Desert Valley Star*.

"After a few weeks of Max repeating his claim, I again requested Tresed to pay Max what it owed him. Max, in an attempt to quantify his claim provided me with invoices in August or September. I reiterated to Max (as a local business) my intent to do what I could to get his payment from Tresed, but in no way was the City liable for the obligations of a private party. The City did not seek, order or any other way request or authorize any work by Max to promote the Festival." Lieberman disagrees.

"In order for me to answer that without getting into trouble I'm going to be careful about what I say," Lieberman said . "I just talked to Rick Daniels a couple days ago and told him again I was disappointed. He seems to have forgotten what he first promised me. It was before he went to rehab at a break at a city council meeting when I first got a chance to talk to Daniels for a minute when I first told him I got an order from Tony to do advertising."

"Daniels said then he promised me I would get paid and that he personally would make sure I was taken care of. He said, 'Max, you are going to get paid.' He may have forgotten about it when he was in rehab. It was eerie," Lieberman said.

Lieberman says he is now being told he does not have a contract compelling the city or Clarke to pay him as promised.

"I have every invoice for roughly $6,500 I sent it to Jason Simpson [Desert Hot Springs Assistant City Manager]. We even had a three way phone conversation with the music festival people, Jason Simpson and myself. I trusted Clarke. My feeling was if the city was paying him a quarter million he was OK," said Lieberman.

"Up till a couple of weeks ago he said he would take care of me and pay me. Now nothing. He promised me 'you will get paid.' I already had several meetings with Tony Clarke in the back of UPS store. Clark said the same thing - that I was going to get paid," said Lieberman [The *Desert Local News* office was located behind the UPS Store in Desert Hot Springs]

"This was not the first time I did something the City wanted. They wanted me to write something to counter-act suspicions circulating that the music festival was not going to happen and have us send stuff to the New York Times. We did. They wanted us to play ball. We did and I'm sorry we did. I was hanging on, just waiting to get paid."

Lieberman said he recently made an offer to cut the amount owed him in half. "I am still waiting on their response. As recently as two weeks ago I was approached by Clarke asking me to do things for him, to create good news stories. All I can do is wait and hope the city will do the right thing."

Max Lieberman was awarded business person of the year by the DHS Chamber of Commerce and has published www.desertlocalnews.com *for over 6 years.*

Baffled with Bull....January 6, 2011

By Dean Gray

364

Councilman On Warpath

"I was duped by staff," said Karl Baker, the Desert Hot Springs city council member who voted yes to give Tony Clarke $250,000 to create a music festival. Baker has since changed his tune. "Tony Clarke should change his name to Professor Harold Hill" [referring to The Music Man about a big-talking out-of-town promoter bamboozling a small town.] We got baffled with bullshit."

"A good lawyer can do wonders," said Baker. "It remains to be seen if we have a good city attorney."

According to Baker it is the responsibility of the city attorney and the city manager to make good recommendations to the council. When Tony Clarke the promoter of the Wellness and World Music Festival finally appeared before the council meeting last Tuesday Baker let loose, chiding Clarke and expressing critical remarks.

Clarke had canceled two previous council dates and on Tuesday made remarks of no substance to the council. Then Clarke rushed away when television and other news reporters sought answers. There is still no date for the festival and no acts lined up and Clarke is not answering phone calls and email.

"I'm embarrassed by my lack of due diligence," Baker said, "Technically it is not our job. We are not supposed to be micro managers. We are paying big bucks to these folks to give us good advice."

"We should have been informed he was operating out of a post office box," Baker said.

"We paid the city attorney something like $400,000 last year," Baker said "From this point forward anything our city attorney brings before us I will look closely at. Plus, I am going to request as soon as possible a review of the city attorney's performance and propose renegotiation. It has been five years. This might be a good time to look around and see what's out there."

"I only know what was in the agenda," said Baker admitting he did not read the contract before voting to give $250,000 to Clarke for the music festival that has been canceled three times. Councilman Russel Betts voted "no" to the 2009 funding for Clarke's music festival. However, at the last city council meeting when Baker made a motion to sever the relationship with Clarke and get the money back, Betts chose not to second the motion and it died.

The rest of the council appears unwilling to act. Council member Jan Pye remarked that the entire council "had eggs on their faces and it is up to Clarke to wipe it off." Two council members, Mayor Yvonne Parks and council member Scott Matas, continue to express confidence in Clarke.

Baker says the council has "collective naivety" and suggests there might be a way to get the money back even though the contract specifically paid Clarke for consultation services and specifically states there is no guarantee of Clarke producing a music festival.

"It's been so long since I read the contract I'm not really sure of the specifics," Baker said, "But I'm aware there was no performance clause. It's the job of the city attorney and the city manager make sure of that." Baker spoke of a plan to get the money back.

"We must go after the deep pockets of Baruch Gayton," said Baker, "Tony Clarke was their agent but I don't exactly know their pay arrangement. I wanted the council to act on this, to find out where the money went. But I couldn't get a second on my motion." Baker said he was "very interested" in the city exercising its authority to review Clarke's financial records.

"It would be wonderful to get the council together with an excellent strategy to move on this," Baker said. "I've been encouraged by the emails I have received. At least 2 of the vendors that were to have been paid have not been paid. All this is spreading ill will in the community against us. I am beating myself up over the head for having not more thoughtfully investigated this when it came before us."

The councilman also spoke of the Pink Flamingo Hotel project with the city losing another $250, 000 (Baker was the only "no" vote on the project) and his "yes" vote approving the $1.4 million purchase of the Jewish Temple intended to be a community center. After the property was purchased by the city the city inspection determined it unsafe for occupancy and demolished most of the building, leaving a vacant lot worth only the value of the dirt.

"I was swayed by political emotion that in hind site was unfounded," Baker said. "However I'm quite certain now we will get our money back."

****

The Festival affair came to a head, Monday, March 14th 2011 during the city council meeting in Desert Hot Springs, according to this article in the morning paper:

Bill Effinger

Desert Hot Springs: Music festival will go on minus controversial promoter Tony Clarke

Sources: Clarke will be fired at meeting today

10:13 PM, Mar. 14, 2011

Desert Hot Springs likely will announce a deal tonight that would allow the city to move ahead with its controversial music festival without the producer who has been paid $250,000 in taxpayer dollars.

Attorneys were finalizing a deal late Monday that would end the city's contract with producer Tony Clarke, several insiders confirmed to The Desert Sun. They asked not to be named, citing the ongoing negotiations.

An announcement that the city and Clarke have mutually agreed to end the contract likely will be made tonight during the City Council meeting.

If the deal is signed as expected, the city plans to hand any completed work over to a new promoter quickly and host the inaugural Wellness and World Music Festival this fall.

"We're anxious to get the event scheduled and marketed, and we're anxious for people to come see the vast improvements that we've done to Desert Hot Springs," City Manager Rick Daniels said.

"Will it occur with the current promoter? No."

Clarke did not return e-mail or phone messages Monday. A spokesman for his company, Tresed Ventures, declined to comment on the specifics of the negotiations.

"We acknowledge that we are still talking with the city and trying to finalize an agreement," spokesman Ed Smith said. "We hope for a quick resolution."

The contract, which expires June 4, prohibits the city from hiring another promoter until then. It gives Clarke exclusive rights to the festival for a year if the city fires him.

The city has negotiated to end the contract with Clarke early because it wants to hand over festival planning to a new producer immediately and host the festival by October.

Mayor Yvonne Parks, Mayor Pro Tem Russell Betts and Councilman Karl Baker are up for re-election Nov. 8.

Betts, who voted against signing the contract with Clarke, has publicly called for the city to slow down its plans to host the inaugural festival by the fall.

"October seems like a very quick date to pull everything together. Setting a date and then bending everything else around that isn't the way I would plan for an event," Betts said.

In the meantime, Desert Hot Springs leaders also want to account for the $250,000 the city paid Clarke over seven installments to see whether there is any money to recoup.

Clarke previously told The Desert Sun the money had been spent "honorably, verifiably," but declined to say how.

City Attorney Ruben Duran has collected more than 100 pages of paperwork, including contracts with performers and financial records, from Clarke.

Duran has declined to provide the documents to The Desert Sun, which requested them under California's open records laws, citing his ongoing review.

The contract

The $250,000 contract with Clarke dates back to December 2009. It is an agreement only for "pre-production" and specifically states there is no guarantee the festival will happen.

The city did not solicit bids for the contract or verify Clarke's claims of being an internationally known producer.

It also paid Clarke another $15,000 to conduct a feasibility report on whether the festival was realistic.

The festival, originally slated for Oct. 9-10, 2010, was heavily promoted as a chance for the city to boost its local economy and build its brand by promoting its signature mineral springs.

On Sept. 7, with weeks until Showtime and no performance lineups or ticket information released, though, the city delayed the festival. It was postponed a second time in December.

No new details, including dates, music performers or ticket information, have been released since.

Producers Baruch/Gayton Entertainment Group, which signed on to co-produce the festival, backed out Jan. 4, the same day the council rebuked Clarke for a lack of substantive updates.

The city would consider working with Baruch/Gayton Entertainment Group, a Burbank-based duo that claims Clarke did not pay them as agreed upon, on the festival, Daniels said.

The city has vowed to use the plans already developed and not pay any additional money to a new promoter.

The total festival would cost about $1.5 million, with the remaining cost paid by sponsors, according to the proposal Clarke wrote.

The council meets at 5 p.m. today in the Carl May Community Center, 11-711 West Drive.

Kate McGinty is a reporter for The Desert Sun. She can be reached at (760) 778-6451 or

Desert Hot Springs: Wellness and World Music Festival promoter Tony Clarke agrees to end contract

Clarke agrees to audit

5:39 PM, Mar. 15, 2011 |

Written by **Kate McGinty**

As part of the agreement, Clarke will hand over all work on the festival. That includes parking, security and staging plans, as well as deposits on unspecified key talent and sponsors.

He also agreed to an audit of the $250,000 in taxpayer money the city paid him, and will return any money not legitimately spent on the festival, Mayor Yvonne Parks said in announcing the deal.

Clarke previously told The Desert Sun the money had been spent "honorably, verifiably" but declined to say how.

The city will keep the rights to the name and logos of the festival, Parks said.

"The city looks forward to the festival happening as soon as feasible," she added.

The City Council approved the deal in closed session, 2-0. Parks and Councilman Scott Matas approved it. Mayor Pro Tem Russell Betts abstained.

Betts' abstention was not immediately explained. He previously voted against giving a contract to Clarke.

The remaining two council members were excused from tonight's meeting.

Clarke did not attend.

As The Desert Sun first reported last week, the city had been in negotiations to end its contract with Clarke as soon as possible.

With the deal now signed, the city plans to hand any completed work over to a new promoter, and host the festival this fall.

City leaders would not immediately say who will produce the festival, whether they will seek proposals or when a new agreement will be reached.

Clarke, who ownsTresed Ventures, did not return e-mail or phone messages Monday.

The contract, which would have expired June 4, gave Clarke exclusive rights to the festival for one more year if the city fired him. That meant the city would be barred from hiring another promoter.

The city wanted to end the contract, though, because it wants to hire a new producer in time to host a festival by October, officials said.

"We're anxious to get the event scheduled and marketed, and we're anxious for people to come see the vast improvements that we've done over Desert Hot Springs over the last three years," Daniels told The Desert Sun Monday.

372

City Attorney Ruben Duran has collected more than 100 pages of paperwork, including contracts with performers and financial records.

Citing his own ongoing review, Duran has declined to provide the documents to The Desert Sun, which requested them under California's open records laws.

The city first signed the $250,000 contract with Clarke in December 2009. It is an agreement only for "pre-production" and specifically states there is no guarantee the festival will happen.

The city did not solicit bids for the contract or verify Clarke's claims of being an internationally known producer. It also paid Clarke an additional $15,000 to conduct a feasibility report on whether such a festival was a realistic moneymaker for Desert Hot Springs.

The festival — originally slated for Oct. 9-10, 2010 — was heavily promoted as a chance for the city to boost its local economy and build its brand by promoting its signature mineral springs.

On Sept. 7, with weeks until show time and no performance lineups or ticket information released, the city delayed the festival. It was postponed a second time in December.

Since then, no new details — including dates, music performers or ticket information — have been released.

Producers Baruch/Gayton Entertainment Group, which is named in the contract to co-produce the festival, backed out Jan. 4, the same day the City Council rebuked Clarke for a lack of substantive updates.

Betts, who voted against the contract, has called for the city to slow its plans for an October festival.

"October seems like a very quick date to pull everything together. Setting a date and then bending everything else around -- that isn't the way I would plan for an event," he said Monday.

Betts, Parks and Councilman Karl Baker are up for re-election Nov. 8.

The city has vowed to use the plans already developed and not pay any additional money for an October festival.

The event would cost about $1.5 million, with the remaining cost paid by sponsors, according to the proposal Clarke wrote.

****

This follow-on article published the next morning, after the reporter had a chance to interview the mayor, suggests that maybe, just maybe, some realism was coming into play concerning the city's pursuit of staging the Festival in the Fall of 2011. Trying to do so, many community members said, would be a fools errand.

Desert Hot Springs fires World Music Festival promoter

Agreement requires Clarke to account for how he spent $250,000

11:43 PM, Mar. 15, 2011

Less than two hours after Desert Hot Springs announced it ended a deal with controversial promoter Tony Clarke that cost the city $250,000 in taxpayer funds, city leaders did not know if they would seek proposals for a new promoter.

Clarke signed an agreement Tuesday to hand over all work on the inaugural Wellness and World Music Festival.

He also agreed to an audit of how he spent the $250,000 the city paid him and to return any money not legitimately spent on the festival, Mayor Yvonne Parks said.

The announcement was made after the City Council met in closed session to consider a lawsuit against Clarke, who had been executive producer of the twice-delayed festival.

Clarke did not attend Tuesday's meeting.

Ed Smith, a spokesman for Clarke's company, Tresed Ventures, said Clarke is satisfied with the agreement after amicable negotiations. Smith also said he does not expect the city will recoup any of the $250,000.

"There aren't any funds remaining because the money has been spent on the production thus far," Smith said. "I don't believe there would be any reason, any cause for anybody to say it was illegitimately spent."

City Attorney Ruben Duran declined to release a copy of the termination agreement, pending his final review and a signature from Parks.

Once the agreement is signed, Clarke will have 15 days to turn over all the work done on the festival, Duran said.

The City Council approved the deal 2-0 with Parks and Councilman Scott Matas voting in favor of it. Mayor Pro Tem

Russell Betts abstained, citing a lack of time to review the agreement.

The remaining two council members were excused from the meeting.

Betts, who voted against signing the original December 2009 deal with Clarke, said the latest agreement was handed to council members Tuesday only moments before they were asked to vote on it. He wanted to see the city attorney review it more closely.

Though the city has previously said it would quickly replace Clarke and move forward with the festival under a new promoter, Betts wonders if that's the right thing to do.

"I want to see this go out for bid as I've always said it should, and key going forward is whether or not this is even a feasible venture for this city," he said.

Days before Clarke's termination was finalized, the city had planned to hand any completed work over to a new promoter quickly and host the festival this fall.

City Manager Rick Daniels previously told The Desert Sun he had about 15 promoters who had contacted him about taking over the festival.

After the meeting on Tuesday, though, council members said they had not decided how or when they would seek out a new promoter.

"We haven't made a decision yet as a council but I would think the best route would really be to do (a request for qualifications), and I think that to really get them competing with one another," Parks said.

Asked whether the city needed to do anything differently moving forward, Parks responded, "vetting. Complete and proper, total vetting."

The city did not solicit bids for its contract with Clarke or verify his claims of being an internationally known producer. It also paid Clarke an additional $15,000 to conduct a feasibility report on the festival.

Matas, who said he is hopeful the city will still put on a festival in October, expects the city to produce a staff report with recommendations on finding a replacement promoter.

Daniels, who will likely write the staff report, said he would "absolutely" consider hiring Baruch/Gayton Entertainment Group, which was named in the original contract to co-produce the festival.

"I would talk to anybody who would cause this event to happen as soon as possible," Daniels said.

On Jan. 4, the Burbank-based duo backed out of the festival saying Clarke had not paid them or others their agreed-upon fees.

Wayne Baruch, co-owner of the production company, declined to say Tuesday whether he would enter negotiations with the city to now take over the festival.

"It's all in the city's hands at this point," Baruch said "That's really all we can say."

The festival was originally slated for Oct. 9-10, 2010.

On Sept. 7, with weeks to go and no performance lineups or ticket information released, the city delayed the festival. It was postponed a second time in December. Since then, no new details have been released.

In the meantime, Duran is still reviewing more than 100 pages of paperwork, including contracts with performers and financial records, that Clarke submitted to the city earlier this year. The city had requested the documents to account for how the $250,000 was spent. Duran has declined to provide the documents to The Desert Sun, which requested them under California's open records laws, citing his ongoing review.

The festival is expected to cost about $1.5 million, with the remaining cost paid by sponsors, according to the proposal Clarke wrote.

****

And now for the capper--- That was the good news. The bad news was that while Russell Betts was in the council chambers and his wife, Miena was working in her hair salon, their home was broken into, and they were robbed. How's that for a Vortex happening?

The better news and further proving the new Police Chief is running a much more tight operation, the thieves were caught quickly.

Teenagers connected to recent burglaries arrested

11:18 PM, Mar. 17, 2011

Written byBrian Indrelunas

Desert Hot Springs police have arrested two boys in connection with four burglaries. Officers looking into a break-in reported Tuesday at a home in the 65-000 block of Avenida Dorado found the boys using surveillance video, officials said.

The boys, ages 16 and 17, were arrested and detained at juvenile hall. Items taken from the home on Avenida Dorado were recovered.

The boys' names were not released because of their ages.

If I were to make a guess, I would say the Negative Energy Vortex had taken the festival project over, and the best thing the council could have done was to let it run its course without getting in the way. If not careful, they could have been swept up in a cloud of swirling desert sand by the unseen hand of the Energy Vortex and deposited in a land of make believe, even more bazaar than the one they had found themselves in, like Alice in Wonderland.

The Desert Sun Editorial board seemed to have the same intuitive feeling, as they posted this Opinion the day after the council vote:

Rushing the Wellness Festival is ill-advised

7:57 PM, Mar. 16, 2011

Written by **The Desert Sun Editorial Board**

The city of Desert Hot Springs made the right decision Tuesday to part ways with Tony Clarke, who was under contract to create an inaugural Wellness and World Music Festival in the city.

Things haven't gone as planned, we can understate.

The city now is asking itself whether the show must go on but with a different producer, whether it can be further delayed or whether to move on.

We wish the city success in making this event happen — at some point.

But the city, which has already invested about $265,000 in taxpayer funding and additional manpower in the effort, would be wise not to rush this. It's more important to do this right.

Put the contract out to bid and make sure the right promoter is found to make this event successful.

This event has a lot of potential and it's imperative that the first event make a great impression on those who take part and attend.

Rushing the event to arrive in October — conveniently before the November election — isn't the right tack here, particularly because of public perception.

Asked what the city should do different this time around, Desert Hot Springs Mayor Yvonne Parks put it best: "Complete and proper, total vetting."

The city can ill-afford to make any major mistakes on this event moving forward. Times are tough and no money at any public agency can be wasted.

The city should definitely put the event out to bid this time around as well.

The city did not solicit bids for its contract with Clarke or verify his claims of being an internationally known producer.

It also paid Clarke an additional $15,000 to conduct a feasibility report on the festival. How the latter made sense still boggles the mind.

Meanwhile, we look forward to the findings of an audit that City Attorney Ruben Duran is conducting.

Being reviewed are more than 100 pages of paperwork, including contracts with performers and financial records, that Clarke submitted to the city earlier this year.

The city had requested the documents to account for how the $250,000 was spent. Duran has declined to provide the documents to The Desert Sun, which requested them under California's open records laws, citing his ongoing review.

The festival is expected to cost about $1.5 million, with the remaining cost paid by sponsors, according to Clarke's proposal.

The Wellness and World Music Festival is a great idea. Let's do it right.

****

Quickly the mayor and council majority leaped into action, scheduling a meeting for the following Tuesday, March 22nd to immediately act on the agenda item pertaining to the Festival which seemed equally bazaar relative to their previous knee-jerk decisions:

Bids to take over music festival on council agenda

11:14 PM, Mar. 17, 2011 Written by **Kate McGinty**

Desert Hot Springs should solicit bids to take over its Wellness and World Music Festival, according to a recommendation that will be discussed Tuesday.

The city released an agenda Thursday for its City Council study session.

381

It suggests giving potential promoters 10 days to turn in proposals, which must be limited to 10 pages.

"City will organize a committee of industry experts to review the proposals and select three for interview within five days," the agenda said.

The agenda does not state who will identify and select the industry experts.

The City Council ended its $250,000 agreement Tuesday with controversial promoter Tony Clarke after the festival was twice delayed.

No dates, performers or ticket sale details had been announced.

The council will meet at 5 p.m. Tuesday at Carl May Community Center, 11-711 West Drive.

****

The Desert Sun digs in

As you might expect, there were major detractors to this rush. Trouble was still brewing as the Desert Sun continued its investigation. The Desert Sun on many occasions has proven to have a desire of fulfilling their role as a Public watchdog when government steps over the line, as Desert Hot Springs had been doing with the Festival, continually digging themselves into an ever deeper hole.

The Desert Sun's reporter Kate McGinty began to dig deeper into the story by searching the city's municipal code, and pressing Daniels for a response, which he apparently consented to by e-mail. His response and the article address the possible violations of the city's own code:

Desert Hot Springs veered from code in seeking festival promoter

11:53 PM, Mar. 18, 2011 Written by**Kate McGinty**

Desert Hot Springs strayed from its own city code when it gave a $250,000 contract to a festival promoter without soliciting other bids.

The city skipped a series of steps outlined in its municipal code that call for a competitive recruitment process and thorough vetting of potential contractors before signing a consulting or professional services contract.

The Desert Sun reviewed the code and spotted the violation days before the City Council is expected to consider what city staff has called "an abbreviated open solicitation" to replace Tony Clarke.

Last week, the city ended its contract with Clarke, who was paid $250,000 in taxpayer funds to produce the twice-delayed Wellness and World Music Festival.

The city did not solicit bids before hiring Clarke in December 2009 and did not verify his claims of being an internationally known producer.

Under the plan to replace him recommended by city staff, potential promoters will have 10 days to submit their proposals for how they would produce such a festival.

This is a significantly shorter amount of time than the six-week solicitation period the city offered for its most recent project that went out to bid, the Community Health and Wellness Center.

"When you're trying to fast-track something that has already started off on the wrong foot, you're almost inviting a problem," said Judy Nadler, former mayor of Santa Clara and a senior fellow in Government Ethics at Santa Clara University.

Desert Hot Springs City Manager Rick Daniels — who recommended the council skip the bidding process in 2009 and is now recommending the quick solicitation period — says the city "satisfied the intent of the code" by discussing the festival at a series of open council sessions.

"To hang the failure on detailed compliance with a municipal code provision misses so much, including the bad economy for all entertainment, let alone a first-time one," Daniels wrote in an email Friday to The Desert Sun.

"Knowing now what we do, with 18 months of history, would the city do it differently? Of course. Is the city going forward with a better approach? Of course."

City Attorney Ruben Duran declined to comment on whether the city violated its own code or what penalties the city could face.

About the code

The city missed "very important due diligence" and "raised some pretty significant red flags" by skipping the bidding process, said Nadler.

As a graduate of Harvard's John F. Kennedy School of Government, Nadler speaks on public contracting and city ethics to groups like the League of California Cities and the U.S. Conference of Mayors.

"I'm just very curious as to how it is that the city decided they would forgo this," she said. "It doesn't make sense, I can't see what the circumstance would be for doing that," she added.

On Oct. 20, 2009, concerns about skipping the bid process were raised, but overruled, when the council first gave Daniels authority to begin negotiating a contract with Clarke.

It was also the same day the council reviewed a 12-page feasibility report Clarke was paid $15,000 to write.

Mayor Pro Tem Russell Betts, who cast the lone dissenting vote against negotiations with Clarke, cited a need to solicit other bids.

Other promoters had expressed interest, Betts said, and the city needed to see what it could get for its $250,000 before signing the deal.

"As I view my role (I am) trying to watch and make sure the taxpayers' dollar is safeguarded. We have not gone through this process," Betts said before the vote.

That process, as outlined in the municipal code, calls for city staff to circulate a request for proposals to all companies that could be qualified.

The request should ask for background information about the contractor, including a list of completed projects and description of the largest project within the past five years, the code stipulates.

The firm also should have references ready to prove its "high ethical and professional standing," the code stipulates.

The city did not require background information or references from Clarke.

Sufficient notice

Since the festival was first postponed in September, Daniels has offered varying explanations for why he did not solicit bids.

On Thursday, in an email to The Desert Sun, he said interested promoters had sufficient notice because of the media coverage of the festival.

"That resulted in far greater coverage than a posting on the city webpage or an ad in some trade journal," Daniels wrote.

"It was no secret that the city was undertaking this effort and anyone could come forward and identify themselves as qualified and interested. They did not."

At least one potential promoter, however, says he did contact Daniels but was turned away.

Richard DeSantis — a well-known producer of Coachella Valley events — was surprised and disappointed Desert Hot Springs did not want a competitive bid process, he told The Desert Sun.

In prior comments, Daniels said he did not recommend the city solicit bids because the Community and Cultural Affairs Commission had approved of Clarke's company, Tresed Ventures.

The commission is a five-person panel appointed by the council. It meets monthly to recommend community services, public art and recreational programs.

It is Daniels, not the committee, that is hired to be the expert for the city, Nadler said.

"Somehow sort of shifting the responsibility back to the well-intentioned, but not necessarily well-informed citizens'

386

advisory committee does not give you a free pass. It doesn't get you off the hook," Nadler said. "As the city manager, you are responsible."

At least one citizen says he's made note.

"Most residents of Desert Hot Springs are just appalled at the city leadership for getting us into this ridiculous situation. Our city is way too poor to be throwing away $265,000," resident Randy Rice wrote in an email to The Desert Sun.

"Rest assured we will all remember this come election time."

Betts, Mayor Yvonne Parks and Councilman Karl Baker are up for re-election Nov. 8.

Public trust has already been shattered by the city's handling of the contract, and the decision to go with a shortened solicitation process now does not make sense, Nadler said. "With the burden right now, I would suggest to go, if you will, beyond what might be required and actually look at what would restore the public's confidence," she said.

Erica Felci of The Desert Sun contributed to this report.

The entire episode of the Health & Wellness Festival caused much angst among the city's citizenry, stimulating calls for the removal of Daniels. Rightly, the McGinty article points out the responsibility Daniels had as the expert advisor to his bosses, the city council in matters such as the Festival. The historical toxic makeup of Desert Hot Springs politics was sure to boil over, and predictably could end Daniel's career with the city, which would be unfortunate for both him and the city, as he has accomplished a great many positive things since becoming manager. But when calls for his head begin to appear, pressure can build and the citizens will vent the only way they can.

————

The Negative Energy Vortex seemed to have been back in play again. Mystic powers or dumb mistakes, whatever the cause, Desert Hot Springs once again was the center of negative publicity throughout Coachella Valley, unable to shed its reputation as the city on the wrong side of the tracks.

Daniels had covered himself nicely with a golden parachute clause in his contract that will give him a full year's salary and benefits on his departure, should his departure take place. To repeat myself; another change in management however, would not be the best thing for the city.

The resultant embarrassment of the council and city as a whole in the matter of the Festival roused the electorate, who expressed their displeasure publicly in the media and during the council meeting. So much so, that the council got the message; backed down and agreed to postpone the Festival indefinitely until they can develop a plan for putting the project out to bid.

Desert Hot Springs residents to city: Don't rush festival

11:16 PM, Mar. 22, 2011 Written by**Kate McGinty**
The Desert Sun

Desert Hot Springs will consider delaying its controversial Wellness and World Music Festival until late 2012 after residents demanded city leaders stop rushing to host the festival by this fall.

Five residents wrote to the council or spoke during council session Tuesday, most calling for a thorough planning process before moving forward.

Lorraine Becker, resident and president of Cabot's Museum Foundation board, implored the city to "push the pause button" before hiring a new promoter.

"We have one chance in this valley to get it right. This entire valley is looking at our planning, our follow-through and implementation," Becker said.

The City Council agreed it should slow down the process when it met Tuesday to discuss how to replace the festival's promoter, who signed legal paperwork last week to end his contract with the city.

Tony Clarke and his company, Tresed Ventures, were paid $250,000 in taxpayer funds to put on the twice-delayed festival. No dates, performers or ticket details had been announced.

The city is now auditing how that money was spent.

In its search for a replacement promoter, Desert Hot Springs staff will solicit résumés from interested promoters, the council decided Tuesday.

The council will select industry experts and stakeholders in the festival, including public safety leaders, to sit on a committee that will review candidates and recommend a new promoter.

The timeline for that was not finalized Tuesday.

City leaders previously aimed to host the festival by October.

But after hearing resident concerns, council members seemed to change their minds.

"I think it all translates down into two words: Slow down," Councilman Karl Baker said.

When it eventually does hire a new promoter, the city should also include a performance clause in its contract and hire an entertainment attorney to review the contract, Mayor Yvonne Parks said.

When the city first signed the $250,000 contract with Tresed Ventures in December 2009, the agreement was only for "pre-production."

It stated there was no guarantee the festival would happen.

The city also did not solicit bids for that contract, despite the city's municipal code.

It also did not verify Clarke's claims of being an internationally known producer.

It paid Clarke an additional $15,000 to conduct a feasibility report on whether such a festival was a realistic moneymaker for Desert Hot Springs.

"A funny thing happened on the way to a wellness festival. It crashed and burned, but we learned one heck of a lot of stuff," Baker said.

The new promoter could use the work already completed — such as parking and site plans and a list of potential sponsors — if they still work, the council said.

The promoter the city selects should also weigh in on the date, place and theme of the festival.

Kate McGinty is a reporter for The Desert Sun. She can be reached at (760) 778-6451 or kate.mcginty@thedesertsun.com.

****

A sampling of the voices from the constituency pretty well established the feelings of the majority on the issue. Assuming the mayor and council follow through, the city won't see this come up again for some time. One does wonder where and how they will pay anyone now that $265,000 has been spent with relatively nothing to show for it, the depleted city coffers because of it and the Governor's threat of taking away redevelopment funds. Mystery of all mysteries, how do they continue to repeat their mistakes? The Vortex made them do it, is the only viable answer.

There is little question that the issue of the Festival will overshadow much of what has preceded it in the way of positive accomplishments by the current administration, come election time. The fact that the Festival production was postponed indefinitely may help some.

About now, you may be wondering, as I and many of our friends do, what else could happen to the city that hasn't already happened? Well, how about this?

Desert Hot Springs city leaders deny misuse of funds

Report asserts that redevelopment money was spent improperly

10:21 PM, Mar. 9, 2011

The city of Desert Hot Springs has demanded a retraction from the state for listing it among five cities statewide that "misappropriated" redevelopment funds.

State Controller John Chiang released the report Monday, accusing the city of improperly spending $162,600 in affordable housing funds on code enforcement.

The city agrees it initially billed its redevelopment agency for code enforcement officers, an expenditure the city defends as proper because it was related to cleaning up blight.

The city finance director canceled the $162,600 bill to the redevelopment agency five weeks later, during a standard review of accounting clerks' work, City Manager Rick Daniels contends.

The $162,600 in question was paid instead through the city's general fund, and not the redevelopment agency, he said.

The auditor missed that in his review and erroneously reported that Desert Hot Springs has misused the money by paying with redevelopment dollars, Daniels said.

"We take this very seriously that every nickel is where it is supposed to be, that every nickel is spent in the way it's allowed to be spent," he said.

"We have a reputation to protect, and I'm not going to accept the bruise."

The controller's office, however, rejected the calls for a correction Tuesday following a second review of the case.

Desert Hot Springs was given a draft of the state's report last week and had an opportunity to refute any findings.

The city argued only that its bill to the redevelopment agency was an acceptable use of the money, not that the $162,600 charge was later retracted, state spokesman Jacob Roper said.

"They're changing their tune at this point," Roper said.

"I can understand why they would be defensive, given everything that's going on with redevelopment agencies right now, but we have to stand by this report 100 percent."

The state Legislature is poised to vote on whether to dissolve the redevelopment agencies.

The city did miss an opportunity to catch the error, but Finance Director Jason Simpson noticed the reversal of charges only after the state released its report, Daniels said.

Daniels was frustrated that Desert Hot Springs has been labeled statewide as an agency that improperly uses money.

"There's no penalty we're going to face, no jail, but it's libelous," he said. "It is besmirching and blemishing the good name of the people running this place."

The report released Monday reviewed 18 redevelopment agencies around the state that had been selected for a five-week review.

Palm Desert's spending of more than $900,000 of redevelopment funding for the Desert Willow Golf Resort course was also questioned in the report.

Palm Desert city leaders have said the money was used to upgrade the golf course so it can attract tourists and boost the local economy, which is within the law governing the use of such funds.

Kate McGinty is a reporter for The Desert Sun. She can be reached at (760) 778-6451 or

When will this kind of thing quit happening? The good people of Desert Hot Springs deserve better.

With the election of three incumbents coming up in the fall, once again the chance to change or retain the direction of the city hangs in the balance. This time, in my view that kind of change at this time in its history is not what the city needs. The best thing to have happen would be the reelection of all three the incumbents, assuming they are all running.

A change in the council could mean a change in management as well. This would be like de ja vue all over again, and was the scenario the year we moved to Desert Hot Springs. What the city needs now is another election retaining its current leadership and management. Consistency, even with some mistakes is better than reverting to the instability of the revolving door of the past.

The job of guiding the policies of the city is in the hands of the current manager, mayor and councilmember's. They will be judged by the electorate, as to what kind of a job they have done while in office, that's the citizens' responsibility. A few years back, a disgruntled member of the Desert Hot Springs community suggested there should be a test for each candidate before allowing him or her to run. While many of us might agree, it would be a good idea; once again my son Brian chimed in with the best answer on the subject I have recently read:

A DLN editorial on Aug. 5, (2007) suggests that aspirants for City Council ought to take and pass some form of aptitude test as a prerequisite for becoming candidates for a seat on the Council. Given the recent performance of the Council as a whole, one can empathize with that sentiment. As a practical matter, however, your state constitution prohibits any other oath, declaration, or TEST, to be required as a qualification for any public office, other than those enumerated in the oath elected officials take upon assuming their office, at every level of government within the state. You'd have to have the constitution amended to allow for this.

As a philosophical matter, this sort of litmus test is anathema to the spirit and intent of both the State and Federal Constitution, which encourage the participation and election of citizen legislators. Who shall we assign to establish the benchmarks for passing such a test? And what's the guarantee that such a person, board, or body wouldn't purposely bend those benchmarks toward any political agenda they themselves might have? At the very least, it sets up elected officials as elites who gain a privilege denied to every other citizen who can't meet this arbitrary standard, and limits the choices of the voters. Additionally, no matter what sort of test that is used to measure the competency of an elected official, it is no guarantee that government will operate any better than it does now. Legislators are there to steer public policy; the X's and O's of carrying out that policy is in the hands of the public officers and employees hired to do the job. There's no guarantee that a smart legislator will legislate smartly. It's the nature of politics.

That puts the responsibility for electing competent individuals squarely in the hands of an informed electorate, as it should be. In a nation with a free press, especially in the Age of the Internet and Lexis/Nexus, there is no shortage of information out there from which voters can determine for themselves whether a candidate is qualified, based not on some arbitrary test, but on what they want from a candidate and what they feel the candidate can deliver. That is the only true test of their merit.

Shall we then set up a test for qualifying a voter? Sorry, can't do that. Legislation such as the Voting Rights Act has long since done away with literacy tests and the like as a means to disenfranchise certain voters; besides, while a number of us can argue that some voters have no business voting, if it's that easy to limit who votes, you yourself could easily get caught up in an effort to weed out your vote on the basis of some standard employed by the elites of society. That's bad juju, and the public wouldn't stand for it.

The Declaration of Independence held certain truths to be self-evident, not the least of which was that "Governments are instituted among Men, deriving their just powers from the **consent of the governed**." Let's not shirk our responsibility for good governance; let's do our homework instead of leaving the merit of candidates and incumbents to the elites.

Brian Effinger

We will be watching the results of the 2011 Election from here in San Marcos with great interest in seeing who will be running. Will the incumbents win another term? Continuity can be a good thing. Will there be new players wanting to step in the arena? Will the perennial candidates try one more time? Most importantly, will the members of the community come out in much larger numbers than in past elections? As someone has said, "we get the government we don't vote for". A citizen who doesn't vote has no right to complain and will get the government he or she deserves.

Nine: Good News Helps

Good news for a business can come in many ways. When it comes unsolicited, it's even better as this article attests, although the writer seems a bit ambivalent about the area's Vortex and "Healing Powers" but like Sam Snead once said: "say anything you want, just spell my name right". That's what counts. In the following article Owner William Dailey, rare book seller and Hacienda Hot Springs are both spelled right:

Caught in an Energy Vortex: Retreating to Hacienda Hot Springs

06/9/10

The outdoor hot springs at the Hacienda

Desert Hot Springs, California is famous for being a "positive energy vortex." But does it really live up to the spiritual hype?

When the opportunity arose for me to visit Hacienda Hot Springs in Desert Hot Springs, California, the first thing I did was check it out online.

I saw the beautiful pictures, read about the hot springs and how they are supposed to bring "a sense of deep relaxation, rejuvenation, and well being." It looked like a lovely resort in the middle of the desert, and I had high expectations.

After the long drive out in the famous California rush hour traffic, I arrived in the city of Desert Hot Springs, and it was – you guessed it – hot, dry, and dusty. There were shopping centers and chain restaurants lining the streets.

'It'll be nice to get out of this town and to the resort,' I thought to myself as I turned and passed a Carl's Jr. I drove down the road a bit and even though my odometer told me I was getting closer, I was still in a residential area.

After a couple of more turns, I pulled into Hacienda Hot Springs, walked up to a wall with a wooden door and pressed an intercom to be let in. So far, I wasn't quite sure I'd gotten away.

Sipping a beverage by the tub

Energy Vortex

Desert Hot Springs has been considered a "positive energy vortex" (which Roger Sunpath defines as a "power spot where a great concentration of energy emits from the planet") for thousands of years.

It is a location where several Earth powers converge – earthquake faults (from the San Andreas fault), geothermal underground water, the alignment of the mountain peaks of the Little San Bernadino(sic) Mountains, wind, and sun.

Pilgrimages were made by ancient and native peoples to positive energy vortexes, as they believed them to be sacred sites, ripe for intense healing rituals and ceremonies. These particular hot springs are also one of very few in the world that have no sulfuric smell, and are pure and clean right out of the ground.

With that in mind, I decided to test out the Jacuzzi not long after I got there. Fifteen minutes in the 90 degree Fahrenheit water, I felt more dizzy then relaxed. Native Americans went there to heal, so maybe I just didn't get it – maybe I was missing something.

Or maybe the energy vortex doesn't have the effect that it once did since modernization has occurred in the area. Maybe the strip malls and fast food joints have jammed up the positive energy?

Hot Springs History

Outdoor breakfast nook

The next day, I had the opportunity to talk to the owner, rare book dealer William Dailey, to find out what his motivation was behind the landscaping and the room décor, which had old postcards and maps on the walls and a collection of out of print books on the bookshelf.

It turns out that Dailey has always been fascinated and interested in books about the desert and the hot springs, so when the property was up for sale, he combined the two and started working to complete his vision of a hotel with a "romantic, Old California" style. With only six rooms in the hotel, it was easy to personalize the style of each room with a few rare pieces.

While I was visiting, I only saw 3 or 4 other guests, so I was able to enjoy the Jacuzzi that morning without it being crowded. As I was sitting in the Jacuzzi, I heard cars going by outside and found it difficult to forget that I was behind four walls in a busy desert city.

Don't get me wrong – the beautiful landscaping, the warm wind, and the pure natural waters were very relaxing and rejuvenating, but it was still a small resort in the middle of a desert city. I almost felt like the walls were there because I needed to be protected from something outside, or as if it created a physical barrier between us, the "spa-goers", and them, the "people who live out there."

For a spa experience, it fit the bill. For a profound spiritual experience, it left a bit to be desired.

Thanks to Laura Grover and Bill Dailey for coordinating my stay at Hacienda Hot Springs. The opinions expressed are all my own.

****

Sometimes advertising can come free and in different forms, maybe not appealing to some, but these days there seems to be a market for just about anything, and when a touch of sex is involved, it gets ink and attention from almost everyone. And in the prologue, I did promise you some "illicit sex" so, here goes.........

Desert Hot Springs to Draft New Ordinance On Sex Spas

KESQ

DESERT HOT SPRINGS -- After our recent investigation exposed a Sea Mountain Spa employee sharing exactly what goes on inside, Desert Hot Springs Councilman Russell Betts confirms he has asked Desert Hot Springs City Manager Rick Daniels and the City's Attorney Ruben Durran to draft sample ordinances for presentation to and consideration by the city council that will limit, restrict and/or prohibit adult sex spas and clubs permitted in Desert Hot Springs.

In the memo dated May 27th to the two city officials, Betts states, "We have worked hard over the past few years to build a reputation for Desert Hot Springs as The Spa City. It is not in Desert Hot Springs' best interests to be known as The Sex Spa City. It is certainly not what I want to see as our future. Our emphasis should remain on building upon our world-renown traditional hot mineral water spas."

Betts says the drafting of the ordinance will take some time.

Stay with News Channel 3 for the very latest.

Meantime, the owners of the Sea Mountain Inn and Spa have responded to KESQ's story:

Allow is to clear up some real misconceptions and Sea Mountain Hotel.

At no time does our hotel legally licensed as a nude resort call itself a sex spa. The Hotel is a Nude Hotel and spa resort. The clientele are from all walks of life, class and income and does have guests with alternative lifestyles.

A great many of our guests are from the Lesbian community and they were quite taken by the assault, and we have many letters from around the world of support. The hotel has many guests who are in no way "swingers" which is a term that we do not ever use.

This note is in response to false assumptions of KESQ reports about our Hotel Sea Mountain Inn.

The Sea Mountain Inn does not market as a "sex spa",we never have used those words to promote our business. The awarded Sea Mountain Inn is first and foremost a hotel.

We have never used the term sex spa or sex club.

Our policy page on our site http://www.seamountaininn.com/policies.html and the membership agreement states that the hotel does not CONDONE public sex. The hotel is for members only –it is for couples and not for the public in any way as it is also a private association and club.

The Sea Mountain Inn does market to alternative lifestyles and is the only lesbian friendly and lifestyles hotel.

The KESQ news report made several inaccurate suggestions. The Sea Mountain Inn is a lifestyles friendly hotel for couples and females over the age of 21.The Sea Mountain Hotel is not unlike other gay hotels which operate and do not tolerate discrimination. The property of the Sea Mountain Hotel has been there for 30 years ,which is before 90 percent of the homes were built in the area and the prior use was a lifestyles nude hotel. The Sea Mountain Hotel has an intense concern for our neighborhood and city. In fact the owners have bought a home on Palm Drive. And we can show many couples from around the world have bought homes in this city to be close to their favorite resort.

The Sea Mountain Hotel is awarded for being a hotel not for being a "sex spa" No one can enter the hotel property without being a member of Sea Mountain Hotel Association. The hotel is not open to the general public at any time.

The Sea Mountain Inn has a dance pole in our party area-(we do belong to BMI And ASCAP)and pay annual dues. There are dance poles in most Las Vegas clubs and casinos and there are pole dance lessons throughout the California region and our Valley.

The Sea Mountain Hotel amenity basket includes condoms and lubricant, as a product placement from Trigg Labs corporation. The Sea Mountain does not sell or give away these items to spa guests and there is no area where there are buckets of these products for use by guests. Many hotels in the USA do have these in rooms including 5 star resorts such as Shutters and Montage and 4 Seasons properties and they sell them too.

The Sea Mountain Hotel does not sell any alcohol at any time and no one can pay any money extra for alcoholic beverages. There are many places on our web sites and letters to guests and membership forms which state this policy.

The Sea Mountain has a lounge, it is not a bar and some may refer to it as a play area which is not unusual in any way. The Sea Mountain has a Nude Resort license with the city. And every upscale boutique hotel has lounges for laughter and social behavior.

The Sea Mountain does have quieter areas that are more private in our gardens, however each of these areas are open to view from all areas of the resort and there are no private or locked areas that are not hotel rooms. There are no private rooms or lounges that have locked doors and are not visible from other guests. It's a romantic hotel. The Sea Mountain Inn does not allow more than one couple in the private hotel rooms. Guests can be evicted from the property and their membership revoked for having any overnight guests in their hotel room, which is stated on our membership agreement.

The report interviewed DHS residents who had no idea the hotel existed which should show that the hotel is discrete in its dealings with our residents and it was odd they would interview what may or may not be legal residents who have no idea of the hotel. There would be a massive outcry if there were such problems. We are very concerned about the city and the residents.

The Sea Mountain Hotel has had no violations except for parking issues that the hotel has been seeking resolution with and those issues are to be resolved with the city in a matter of days. The County health department has inspections that deal with pools and any health issues and come unannounced for their inspections of which SMI Hotel shows perfect compliance. The fire department comes to inspect several times per year and shows all hotel rooms have all proper smoke detectors and all fire exits are clear and all fire extinguishers' are checked twice yearly and show a 100 percent compliance rating.

The Sea Mountain has had complaint of noise always from one home in 4 years and if asked for the music to be lowered the Sea Mountain Hotel always will comply and has met with this difficult couple on many occasions to seek resolution to this issue too. SMI hotel seeks to blend with the city and does not want to be a noise problem nor make our city of Desert Hot Springs a pariah for slander.

The Sea Mountain Hotel has now had 7 guests purchase homes in DHS because of the proximity to the hotel and we shown thousands of upscale individuals a positive side of Desert Hot Springs and they spend money in all areas of DHS and assist in this economy. They shop at all the local stores and eat at the _estaurants in our city, and also stay at local hotels to be close to SMI when we are sold out of our rooms.

The Sea Mountain hotel has a zero tolerance for any drugs on the premises or intoxicated members of our association. All members have signed membership agreements which state many of the above issues.

You may of course call for a phone interview if you have further issues. The posts on KESQ seem to be quite in the favor of our hotel. We do hope you can see another side to one of the greatest hotels in our Coachella Valley.

Sincerely,Julie and Dew Wohl

Sea Mountain Inn and Spa Hotel

"Seeing another side" is probably what many people would want to do when visiting Sea Mountain Inn and Spa. Joking aside, this points out the difficulties the council and manager have in attempting to keep from interfering with business, while maintaining law and order in a free society, which seems to be getting freer everyday.

I am not sure how the Energy Vortex fits into the nude scene. Maybe when you have no clothes on, the vibes have more power. I think I will do some research on the subject by paying a visit to Sea Mountain Spa and test the concept. (However, my wife is my editor, and when she sees this, my research project might be axed).

———

Here is an interesting side story about the "healing medicinal qualities" of the mineral waters in Desert Hot Springs and the closed La Toscana, Hotel Spa that few know

406

about: The owner/operator at the time was a member of the local Rotary Club and a retired entrepreneur, Ms. Aleene Jackson, the world famous inventor/producer of the popular Aleene's Fabric Glue. Aleene had purchased the hotel as an investment for her son to manage. During a Rotary meeting, we were sitting next to each other, and she shared this interesting bit of information, as she was telling me she intended to sue the seller over what she termed a "swindle".

It seems that during the process of some renovations, her contractors discovered that the hot spring well had not been functioning for several years, and was being filled with tap water and then heated. Even though the pool was filled with drinking water, visitors continued to proclaim the waters' "healing effects" so she was unaware until they discovered the flaw after escrow closed on her purchase. Imagination is a wonderful thing.

After repairing the well and completing renovations, Aleene sold the hotel and the subsequent owners were foreclosed on shortly afterwards. The hotel remains closed and decaying waiting to be rescued. Aleene and her three beautiful daughters are pictured below, followed by a brief anecdote showing what an active senior she

Aleene Jackson Craft Museum

is.

We're going to see if we can get Mom to stop dancing at

the senior center long enough to add some amusing stories

to our Aleene Jackson Craft Museum. Yep! That's right,

Mom turned 87 in January 2011 and she is still dancing up a
storm!

Removing an eye-sore:

The Village" returned in the News after three years of
baking in the hot sun waiting to be rescued and completed. A
doctor from Palm Desert was the successful bidder on the
derelict project, hoping to bring it back to life. Certainly the

families living within eyesight of the project were deserving of having the project cleaned up and put in habitable condition, but Dr. Shah, the new owner was already running into obstacles, as the following article indicates:

Desert Hot Springs council nixes request from Village project

10:24 PM, Feb. 15, 2011

The Village at Mission Lakes, a long-delayed city project, hit a stumbling block Tuesday.

The City Council voted unanimously to reject new project developer Shah Management's request to pay $259,512 in development impact fees in payments over three years.

The Palm Desert-based developer took over the shopping center about six months ago, more than three years after construction stalled and its financial backer, Estate Financial Inc., declared bankruptcy.

New developer Suresh Shah is now building at the Desert Hot Springs site after paying nearly $21,000 in permit reactivation fees to the city.

During an extended debate Tuesday, City Council members questioned how the city could set up a payment plan for development impact fees when no such policy exists, and told Shah he always knew he would have to pay up.

"If we do this for you, then (other developers) will assume we will do this for them, and I don't know if I'm willing to set a precedent that we will do this," Mayor Yvonne Parks said.

The council rejected his request, 5-0, and said he must pay the bill in one payment.

Shah did not say how the project could be affected by the council's denial.

When it was first proposed more than five years ago, the 6.6-acre Village at Mission Lakes was supposed to provide much-needed shopping to the city's west end. Instead, construction stalled in late 2007 and the project's financier declared bankruptcy in July 2008. It has since languished incomplete at the corner of Mission Lakes Boulevard and Little Morongo Drive.

"It has been a constant nuisance to the city," City Manager Rick Daniels said. "It has been a source of considerable code enforcement activity to try to keep the external impacts of that project under control."Shah contended he will need to funnel about $3 million into improvements and needs to begin recouping his investment. He had offered to submit a letter of credit to guarantee the city would eventually be paid the entire $259,512 sum.

"I want just some time as I lease the places and I make some of my investment back," he told the council. "I think I'm doing a good thing for the city, and you should be part of the success story." Construction should take about four months, he said.

In other news from the meeting, the City Council met in closed session for at least the fourth time to consider a lawsuit against Tony Clarke, the promoter of the twice-delayed Wellness and World Music Festival.

No action was taken, and the discussion will continue when the council meets behind closed doors again today.

****

Dr. Shah's request was denied by the council 5-0, who were not about to get burned twice. But he paid the full fee the following week. It looks like the council was learning. Dr. Shah, on the other hand, has some learning to do. He has undertaken what many experts have told me is a money-loosing proposition, which when reconstruction of the project is completed, will take many years before any return on his investment will be realized.

The residents of Mission Lakes Country Club will certainly welcome convenience stores and a coffee shop. The real question is can any businesses survive out there so far away from the center of town? We wish Dr. Shah only the best.

I couldn't seem to finish this book:

The bad news in Desert Hot Springs just kept coming. I had originally intended to start and end this manuscript with the attention- getting headline of the former mayor's wife being arrested, but the blunders kept multiplying. The book still ends the way it was planned, it just became longer than what I intended.

There is hope, however on another front. The council authorized the city manager to engage a consultant to study and make recommendations on what the city should do to attract commercial and industrial development, in an effort to develop much needed tax revenues.

411

Bill Effinger

Strategic plan for city calls recruitment of retailers vital

1:52 AM, Mar. 14, 2011

Desert Hot Springs should attract a movie theater and entertainment complex and recruit businesses like CVS, Payless Shoe Source and grocery stores.

Those are among the highest priorities for the city this year, according to a 71-page document that advises the city how to boost its economy over the next five to 10 years.

The document — an economic strategic plan — is expected to be approved Tuesday by the City Council.

The council, which reviewed the presentation in a special study session on Dec. 13, will also be asked to refer the plan to the Planning Commission to be included in the city's General Plan.

The strategic plan includes a thorough analysis of the city's demographics, as well as advice on the community image, how to promote home ownership and recommendations for regional partnerships.

It also offers extensive lists of businesses that could be recruited, as well as some companies that are "actively expanding" in California and could be well-suited for Desert Hot Springs.

"The city of Desert Hot Springs currently does not have enough retail establishments for which to serve the community, meaning the demand outweighs supply," Michael Bracken, managing partner of Development Management Group, wrote in the study.

412

Among those suggested stores are Kohl's, Petco and Target, as well as restaurants like Buffalo Wild Wings and Sonic Drive In.

Only 52 percent of the money spent by Desert Hot Springs residents or visitors is actually spent within the city now, according to the study.

If the city met its demand, it would generate an additional $196 million in retail sales — and pick up $2 million in sales tax revenue, Bracken added.

The plan also pushes for homeownership through first-time home-buyer programs or a rental tax, which would require any person renting or leasing to another person to get a special permit from the city.

That money would be used for code enforcement and annual inspections.

About 48 percent of units in Desert Hot Springs are lived in by the homeowner, significantly less than the valleywide average of about 66 percent, the study reports.

The council will consider the plan when it meets at 5 p.m. Tuesday at the Carl May Community Center, 11-711 West Drive.

****

Having a plan to work to is essential, but if the only thing that ever happens is developing a plan which is never implemented, as has been the history of Desert Hot

413

Springs' past performance, then wasting the community and staff time and money and energy is an exercise in futility ultimately leading to mass frustration.

Maybe the community should adopt the Nike company motto: "Just do it!" and repeat it at every council and planning commission meeting until the message gets across. The local chamber of commerce could have the motto printed on flyers and banners and post them all over town. This might sound a bit off the wall, but something sure needs to be done.

After reviewing the Strategic Plan, particularly the proposed implementation of the plan, it appears the leaders are being pointed in the right direction to once and for all, effect real change for the city. Whether the council acts on the proposals remains to be seen.

Apparently there are others who agree that the city is working its way toward a better living and working environment as the following articles reveal:

Desert Hot Springs wins award for economic strategic plan

11:56 PM, Apr. 30, 2011

The city of Desert Hot Springs earned statewide kudos for its economic strategic plan at a conference this week.

The award of merit is for the plan the city commissioned from Development Management Group.

The 71-page document advises the city how to boost its economy over the next five to 10 years and market its city.

The award was presented during the annual conference of California Association for Local Economic Development, held Wednesday and Thursday in Sacramento.

The top awards in the economic development programs category went to the cities of Fremont and Santa Clarita.

Desert Hot Springs looks at land deal with Wessman

Property would be location of new library complex

7:20 PM, May. 1, 2011

Desert Hot Springs will begin negotiating this week with developer John Wessman to buy a key piece of land or swap him for buildings downtown.

The value of the land has already prompted questions days before the City Council heads into a closed session Tuesday to weigh how to proceed.

The city wants the land — nearly nine acres at the northeast corner of Pierson Boulevard and Cholla Drive — as part a larger plan to build a city complex with a library and park.

Under the proposal up for consideration, the city could buy the vacant land from Palm Springs-based Wessman Development or trade it for four buildings the city owns at the southwest corner of Pierson Boulevard and Palm Drive.

Both sides have appraised the land but presented estimates that are "significantly apart," City Manager Rick Daniels said. Both Daniels and Wessman Development declined to release the appraisals.

Wessman owns commercial properties across the Coachella Valley and is presently working with Palm Springs to reach an agreement on rebuilding the long-vacant Desert Fashion Plaza.

That project has ignited heated public debate, particularly after a public-private partnership was proposed earlier this year.

Though the details haven't been worked out, Palm Springs voters will likely be asked to vote on a tax increase plan later this year that would partially fund the mall reconstruction project.

Known as a blunt-talking and stubborn negotiator, Wessman has described himself as simply a businessman trying to get a fair price for his property.

"John is a very astute business person, and we believe that we are as well," Daniels said. "There are deals that work out on paper whether it's John Wessman or Elmer Fudd. It's not the who; it's the what."

In the case of the Desert Hot Spring land, Wessman bought it in the 1970s and has left it vacant.

Wessman would prefer cash for the land but would consider a trade for the other property.

"We are listening right now ... but no commitment has been made from either side," said Michael Braun, senior vice president of Wessman Development.

If the deal works out, the city of Desert Hot Springs would use the land as part of an area targeted for public buildings to be built in the future.

The land is also next to the planned Community Health and Wellness Center, complete with a 25-meter pool, healthy living programs for residents and a new Boys & Girls Club facility.

"We already have so much public investment there, and what we're trying to do is create an opportunity, so if you have to deal with city government, that it's all generally in one place," Daniels said.

He's prepared to find a backup plan if the negotiations with Wessman fall through.

"We'll get a good deal, or we don't do a deal," Daniels said. "It is not critical. It would be nice. It would round out that ownership, but if we didn't do it there, we could put the library somewhere else."

Kate McGinty is a reporter for The Desert Sun. She can be reached at (760) 778-6451 or kate.mcginty@thedesertsun.com.

———

And should you get the impression that everything is bad in Desert Hot Springs, here is one of best kept secrets in all of Coachella Valley:

Desert Hot Springs Capri Restaurant Serving Generations' Worth of Red-Checkered Italian Hospitality!

Desert Sun Kimberly NicholsFrom age ten to fourteen, the highlight of my week was the Friday night trip to Capri Restaurant in Desert Hot Springs with my parents and my sister. John and Mindy, the hosts whose parents owned and ran the restaurant, would always seat us at our favorite table in the plain and completely homestyle, non-pretentious place, and bring us the long narrow glass of skinny breadsticks and warm basket of butter-saturated garlic bread.

My stepfather, who perpetually encouraged a sophisticated palate in us desert rat kids, introduced us to the veal marsala entree one day after realizing that all we ever ordered was the ravioli with the big fat meatball, and my sister and I completely fell in love.

Tender slices of veal that could be cut with a fork drenched in a sweet marsala wine sauce and dotted with thick, plump and juicy mushrooms...and the best part, soaking up all the extra sauce with that insanely-garlic-saturated bread at the end of the dish. Our second favorite thing was the cappucinno ice cream, which was black and dotted with chewy pieces of dark chocolate covered espresso beans. This was our weekly Friday meal for years.

The fact that Capri was located in a city known more for its crime and sordid history than fine culinary arts made the restaurant even better: those all over the Coachella Valley who knew about it, considered it their cherished little secret.

Over twenty years later, my friend Chef Aaron Kiefer of East Meets West Catering, discovered Capri and called to rave enthusiastically about it to me. Osso Buco! Grey Goose Martinis! He could hardly contain his excitement and we decided to eat there once a month. My first time there, now as an adult, I saw that nothing had changed, and the staff, owners and even some of the customers were the same.

You know a restaurant is good when chefs want to eat there and when you see the same faces at the tables twenty years later.

Apparently the Positive Energy Vortex has been flowing toward the Capri restaurant for many years. We can certainly vouch for the food and positive attitude of the Santucci family, owner/operators from the Restaurant's beginning. They are always there, fathers and sons all working the bar, serving the food and preparing the scrumptious specialties in the kitchen, greeting most every customer by name as they enter.

John Santucci (Owner/Manager) recently told me he was in the first Desert Hot Springs Elementary School kindergarten class consisting of five children including himself. There was no middle school or high school as John progressed in grade levels, so in order to get through middle and high school, he and his classmates had to be taken to Palm Springs.

Currently all of the schools located in Desert Hot Springs are incorporated in the Palm Springs Unified School District, but the city is not represented on the board. There have never been enough voters who go to the poles in Desert Hot Springs to elect those that have tried. As a result, some decisions, such as school locations have not been to the liking of city leaders and residents, but they have been powerless to do anything about it. There goes that Negative Energy Vortex again. What to do?

One would hope that sooner rather than later, someone capable of garnering enough votes and voters will step up to the plate and attempt to gain a seat on the PSUSD that will represent the interests of the children and families of Desert Hot Springs.

An unfortunate after-story to the Santucci family's Capri Restaurant, three-months after my son kirk and I met with John Santucci to set up an interview with his parents, the restaurant was forced to close its doors and the building remains empty. A sad end to a Coachella Valley Icon.

However, ever the entrepreneur and opportunist, Mike Bickford, owner the Miracle Springs Resort & Spa arranged for the Capri to reopen inside of the hotel, replacing a less than average restaurant with the Capri family's chefs. This is truly a better ending than could have been for both the city, the Santucci family and its many dedicated patrons.

****

Ten: What is the answer?

How can an area, first discovered in 1908, settled in 1913 and formally founded in 1963, continue to be what neighboring city residents in 2011 refer to as "that place on the wrong side of the tracks"? How can a city with a

420

population grown to its current size of almost 27,000 people, continue to make so many wrong moves, constantly shooting itself in the foot at almost every turn?

What is the solution? Who or what will change the chaotic conditions that smite every attempt made to change things for the better in this hapless community? As we ponder the question, the familiar quote "there must be a pony somewhere under all this horse manure" comes to mind.

Or, is there no solution because the majority of the city's residents enjoy living in "splendid isolation" as Paul Krassner has suggested in his essay, believing Desert Hot Springs is "Heaven" because it is isolated?

Should this be the case, the city government and its leaders might as well pack everything in boxes, put it all in storage, sit back and let the Energy Vortex do its thing. I don't think isolationism is a condition of the majority, at least not those that Diana and I have come into contact with over the years.

I have pointed to the geographic constraints the city is confronted with which does give one the sense that Desert Hot Springs, *is* in fact somewhat isolated from the rest of the valley. Even with the recent 4000-acre annexation of the properties south of Dillon Road, and west of Palm Drive, and north of I-10, the city remains an island.

However, the annexed properties do offer potential economic growth for the revenue strapped city.

My view is that most of the annexed properties should be zoned industrial and promoted to major industrial corporations nationwide. Coachella valley has an abundance of blue collar labor available for manufacturing jobs, when

421

and if industry comes into the area. Also, land values in Desert Hot Springs are much lower than anywhere else in Southern California, allowing manufacturing plants to be constructed much less expensively.

Low-cost labor and low land costs equate to low initial start up costs for the manufacturers. These tangible assets should be made known to industries throughout the country in a professional marketing campaign while the economy remains slow, allowing ample time for corporate planners to do their feasibility studies.

When manufacturers begin to locate in Desert Hot Springs, demand for housing and convenience stores will increase, directing related property tax and sales tax revenues into city coffers. This can happen. But if the city leaders and its citizens choose to sit back and let the world go by as in the past, then they can always say.........

"The Vortex made me do it" while remaining in "Splendid Isolation".

Writing the history of this small town in the Imperial Desert of California over the past few months and attempting to describe its citizens' hopes and dreams, has been a challenge. What started out to be my writing a review of the history and mysteries of Desert Hot Springs, became a running narrative of current events as a constant stream of political and management issues within the city were being created and publicized almost daily. The controversies kept coming into view almost as fast as I was able to write.

During the flurry of those news articles, I again asked myself, "how is this possible? How does this town keep making these blunders"?

I have to say, looking at the repetitive challenges community members of Desert Hot Springs and their elected representatives have had to address over the years and their relative inability to lift themselves up and out of the morass, is absolutely a puzzle challenging the Rubik's Cube.

On the other hand, I also believe as several experts have pointed out, geography and meteorology have a great deal to do with many of the city's problems. As we say in the world of real estate, "it's location, location, location". In this particular situation, the mysteries of the Desert Hot Springs Energy Vortex also seem to be working powers that are juxtaposed to what believers within the city's boundaries, claim should be happening.

In other words, the Energy Vortex must be emitting Negative Energy Flows, as described in the articles in part one of this manuscript. The Energy Vortex, if one believes in its existence, (and many of the city dwellers do) seems to be bringing chaos and upheavals, rather than the positive flow of energy purported to be the result of a Positive Energy Vortex Flow.

Mayor Parks and the city council must believe in the powers and existence of the Energy Vortex, as they have named their new downtown master plan, the **"Vortex Downtown Revitalization Plan"** I suggest if the Vortex is working, it must be working negatively and something should be done to get positive energy flowing.

Reading Roger Sunpath's explanation of the Energy Vortex in Part One, he says the streets of Desert Hot Springs were laid out contrary to the energy flow of the Vortex: *"It is unfortunate that the founding fathers of the city were unaware of this energy alignment. If they had constructed the city streets on a Northwest by Southeast axis, the general*

423

population would be calmer." Calmer would be good, but smarter would also help.

Should Sunpath's analysis prove to be fact and what he says factual, then "The Vortex Made Me Do It" may not be far from the truth. Whatever has been happening in Desert Hot Springs for more than 100-years is far from normal.

But there is always hope.....

Maintaining a "glass half full" attitude, Mayor Parks delivered the annual 2011 "state of the city" address to the faithful, extolling the council's accomplishments of the past, and her promises for the future.

Desert Hot Springs mayor spotlights goals, challenges in address

Mar 24, 2011

Desert Hot Springs Mayor Yvonne Parks delivers the annual State of the City address

R. Bruce Montgomery

Written by **Kate McGinty The Desert Sun**

Desert Hot Springs Mayor Yvonne Parks was given a standing ovation Wednesday after she spoke about challenges the city has overcome and the projects residents can look forward to seeing.

About 75 people filed into the ballroom at the Miracle Springs Resort and Spa, 10-625 Palm Drive, to hear her State of the City address.

Parks, who is in her second term as mayor, spoke about the city's efforts to clean up Desert Hot Springs and displayed numbers of citations issued and abandoned property collected.

Code enforcement cleaned more than 300,000 square feet of graffiti last year, she said.

During the past year, the city has also faced budget constraints because of declining property values.

It slashed its staff nearly in half over the past five years, but continued to place public safety as its No. 1 priority.

Parks pointed to the 34 officers the police department is allocated, a figure that is higher than the number of non-sworn city staff.

"She covered a lot of stuff the city has done in a positive way as well as some of the things that haven't worked out the way the city wanted it to. I think she was very honest and up-front with people," Chamber of Commerce board President Russ Augustine said.

The city will push ahead with its plans for a new visitors' center and to build a 25,000-square-foot medical clinic that could introduce as many as 10 new doctors to the city.

It has also secured $250,000 in grant money from the Safe Routes to Schools program and $100,000 for work at the Cabot's Pueblo Museum.

Kate McGinty is a reporter for The Desert Sun. She can be reached at (760) 778-6451 or kate.mcginty@thedesertsun.com.

****

There is little question that positive things are finally happening in the city. The most important issue remaining is that the steps going forward are not overshadowed by mistakes as they have always seemed to be in the past. For some assurances on this issue, I decided to meet with the city leaders and check out their commitment to change.

My son Kirk and I met with Rick Daniels on Wednesday afternoon, the 13th of April at 2pm. We discussed the recently released Strategic Development Plan for the city, the anticipated contract letting for the Boys & Girls Club, the new General Plan and what Daniels saw for the recently approved 4000-acre annexation and other matters concerning growth and development of the city.

I explained that I had three goals for this book; the first being to introduce the city to those that have not yet visited; the second by narrating the city's history, and its mysteries, to help create enough curiosity within the reader to prompt a visit; and third to issue a challenge to the reader to help explain what he/she likes or dislikes about the city and whether the Energy Vortex has unexplained powers affecting the city, its visitors and inhabitants.

Rick's immediately declared that the city had suffered form "Two decades of irrational thinking"; to which I said, what a great line for the book, and it immediately became the

426

title for chapter two when I returned home to the manuscript. In reviewing my notes, that twenty-year span would have to have started around 1985 and continued to 2005.

As to how to fix things, Daniels referred us to the new Strategic Plan, which I had already uploaded. The 73-page plan lays out in detail the demographics of the city and the relationship of those figures to the rest of the valley. The Strategic Plan ends with a proposal from the consultants to enter into an implementation program, which is currently being considered by the council, and follows:

PROPOSAL TO CREATE THE CITY OF DESERT HOT SPRINGS ECONOMIC DEVELOPMENT IMPLEMENTATION PLAN

Objective

To create and implement a long-term sustainable economic development program that assesses the current economic status of the City, provides training and education to all persons which can positively impact economic development efforts and produces tangible benefits (jobs, investment and improved economic related demographics) for the City of Desert Hot Springs, its residents and businesses.

Module System

Successful economic development plans are built as long-term sustainable programs that assess current economic conditions, foster a long-term economic vision, determine and utilize available regional partnerships, provide training for various persons and groups within a region and include a quarterly activity based implementation plan that can be quantifiable evaluated. Below are the seventeen (17) identified modules for this program and the corresponding amount of professional hours estimated to complete the specific module:

Module 1: Current Economic Conditions

The first step to any long-term economic development strategic plan is to understand the current economicconditions and community attributes. DMG, Inc. proposes to complete the following as a first step to this project:

Research and Compile Relevant Economic Data about the City of Desert Hot Springs:

A. Demographic Analysis

B. Inventory of Businesses

C. Inventory of Employees

D. Survey of Businesses and Employees (understand why they are located in community)

E. Retail Sales, Leakage and Opportunity Analysis

E. Inventory of Existing and Available Buildings and Land Opportunities

F. Assessment of Current Economic Development Activities being Implemented

by City Staff, Chamber of Commerce and Other Groups

G. Assess Professional Services (private and public) Available to Residents and Businesses to Determine if there are any Gaps

H. Identify other Important Economic Development Resources/Attributes within Community

Module 2: Available Regional Partnerships and Programs

Module 2 will include an assessment of the Coachella Valley Economic Partnership Economic Blueprint and determine which economic opportunities are most compatible with the City of Desert Hot Springs along with specific steps that the community must take for maximum benefit of said opportunities.

Additionally, a similar analysis of specific programs and projects available through the Palm Springs Desert Resorts Convention and Visitors Bureau (CVA), Film Commission and other identified economic development partners will be completed with recommendations regarding projects that are the best fit and what steps the Cityof Desert Hot Springs and community can take to receive the greatest economic impact.

Module 3: Create and Implement Economic Development Training for Persons & Groups inDesert Hot Springs

Design and provide appropriate economic development training to a variety of persons and groups with an economic development interest in Desert Hot Springs. The Economic Development Training Program will include (but is not limited to) the following elements:

a) Defined Economic Development

b) Provide Examples of Economic Development

c) List the Tools of Economic Development

d) Discuss Various Community & Regional Partners in Economic Development

c) Explain Importance of Economic Development and Benefits to Each Group of People within Community

d) Help Define Roles and Responsibilities of Each Person/Group within Community

e) Define How to Assess Effectiveness of an Economic Development Program (Measurement)

City Council / Chamber of Commerce Economic Development Certificated Program are proposed to be offered to the following persons having an interest in Economic Development:

A. City Staff (all levels of staff)

B. City Council and Commissioners

C. Chamber of Commerce

D. Residents

E. Employees of Various Businesses within Community

F. High School Students / Middle School Students

This project shall include the design of the actual "Economic Development Training Course" and the instruction of said course (including course materials) for up to five (5) group training sessions, at the discretion of the Cityof Desert Hot Springs.

The City of Desert Hot Springs shall be responsible for providing appropriate group meeting space forconducting said course within City limits.

Module 4: Generate Long-Term Community Economic Profile and Vision

Utilizing information researched in previous modules; generate both a community profile and long-term economic vision for the City of Desert Hot Springs. The community profile will include both demographic/market information and
430

a compilation of business and economic opportunities for potential investors. The long-term economic vision will provide a written statement of goals and objectives for the City along with economic demographic improvements and investment attraction goals.

Appendix D. Qualifications of Consultant

Development Management Group, Incorporated (DMG, Inc.) specializes in services related to economic development and redevelopment. Such services include site selection and analysis, economic development strategic planning and implementation, development management, market/development feasibility, fiscal & economic analysis, entitlement/permit processing and project financing.

Over the past eight years, DMG, Inc. has assisted over three dozen companies with their site selection and entitlement/permit processing. These companies have created over 2,500 new jobs and invested over $100 million within the communities where they are located. In addition, DMG, Inc. has assisted a number of public agencies and economic development corporations with fiscal & economic impact analysis, strategic planning, marketing and other business recruitment projects creating the administrative and operational infrastructure to enable them to grow their economies.

****

The city council adopted the Strategic Plan and will soon consider the implementation plan. When doing so they will be taking the first step in creating a viable economic future for their constituents which has been way too long in coming to fruition. I am convinced that without the leadership shown by manager Daniels; this would not have come to pass.

We also met with council member Russell Betts; council member Karl Baker and council member Scott Matas the same day, asking them the prepared interview questions we had e-mailed earlier and which follow this section.

While meeting with Karl for lunch in the Capri, John Santucci, co-owner/manager Overheard our discussion and offered to have his mother and father come up to be interviewed, which I readily agreed to do on my next trip up, as they have a world of knowledge on Desert Hot Springs' history.

On the drive back, Kirk and I shared our thoughts on the conversations we had with everyone and speculating on what the future holds for the city. Kirk's history with San Marcos, the city we both live in, goes back twenty-seven years and he remembers the political and growth problems it had before turning the corner.

Mentioned earlier, San Marcos was incorporated in 1963, the same year as Desert Hot Springs when North San Diego County was mostly farm country. Today the city is a successful bustling epicenter of commerce, industry and education, and home to five college campuses. After our conversations with Daniels and the council members, we both agreed there is hope for Desert Hot Springs.

Another positive for the city occurred before the manuscript went to press, Desert Hot springs was given an award of merit by the California Association for Local Economic Development for their new Strategic Plan. Maybe the Energy Vortex is turning positive after all these years of causing such chaos for the residents.

Desert Hot Springs wins award for economic strategic plan

11:56 PM, Apr. 30, 2011

The city of Desert Hot Springs earned statewide kudos for its economic strategic plan at a conference this week.

The award of merit is for the plan the city commissioned from Development Management Group.

The 71-page document advises the city how to boost its economy over the next five to 10 years and market its city.

The award was presented during the annual conference of California Association for Local Economic Development, held Wednesday and Thursday in Sacramento.

The top awards in the economic development programs category went to the cities of Fremont and Santa Clarita.

———

Perhaps the answers to our questions of Desert Hot Springs' civic and business leaders as well as its residents and visitors will give us some meaningful projections for the city's future. After all, it is the people living in the city and the perceptions of those who come to visit who will and have formed the city's image.

Interviews:

I sent out questionnaires to a number of people who have been active in the community over the past several years, asking them questions about topics contained in this manuscript in an effort to seek possible solutions to our question: **What is the Answer?**

These were the questions and answers in the order received:

Dean Gray; Publisher, Valley Star newspaper: Answers for Book Interview (you will note the city's citizens are not without humor)

- When did you move to Desert Hot Springs? *2001*
- How did you hear about the city? *Girlfriend, now wife, soon to be ex-wife*
- Why did you choose Desert Hot Springs over all of the other Valley cities? *Same as above*
- Do you believe in the medicinal value of the Mineral Springs? **Yes**
- How often do you go to one of the Spas in DHS? *For soaking - 12 times a year or more*
- How often do you go to one of the Spas in other Valley Spa Cities? *Zero*
- Where do you do most of your shopping for Household goods & Services? *Palm Springs*
- Where do you do most of your grocery shopping? **Desert Hot Springs**
- What organizations do you belong to in Desert Hot Springs? *Church of Fun*
- How often do you attend council meetings? Planning meetings? *Council meetings every other month or so. Planning   Commission meetings 3-4 times a year, community and Cultural Affairs Commission meetings 3-4 times a year*

- If you attend church, which do you attend? *Church of fnn*

- Do you believe in the powers of the Energy Vortex? *Obviously*
- If the answer is yes to the above, have you had any personal experiences? *I have observed the Vortex in action spinning people around and magnifying their actions similar to the whirling dervish or the practice of Sufism. Those that are circling counter clockwise are affected in a negative way by the energy vortex amplifying their revolutions and increasing their lying and deceptive behavior. Those that are circling clockwise receive the benefits of amplifying their good behavior.*
- Explain: *Four out of five members of the current city council are spinning counter clockwise.*
- Are you satisfied, unsatisfied or dissatisfied with the overall living environment within Desert Hot Springs? *Absolutely not.*
- Do you plan to live out the remainder of your life in Desert Hot Springs? *Yes because of all the above plus the great stories here and its central location to the entire high and low desert.*
- If you were King, what would you do to improve/change the living environment of Desert Hot Springs? *Since I cannot be Gabriel King (now a truck driver) I would elect to be Chancelor... then I would banish (or incarcerate after trial) the miscreants from the city. This would include all the wrong spinning civic "leaders."*
- *Then I would use emergency powers to immediately remove the triangles from downtown in order to save lives. The downtown has been ruined so best to ignore it and relocate community services to a new civic center adjacent to the freeway between Palm and Indian where retail would attract drive by traffic. This would enable the city to have a fresh start away from the powers of the vortex.*
- *I would then raise the pay for council positions because you get what you pay for. Apparently low*
- *pay only attracts idiots for the job. Then I would annex the Mission Lakes Country Club so they could*

vote. There is a lot of brain power and academic and business leaders hiding out there and this would enlist their support - no ifs, ands or buts about it.New city manager and new redevelopment manager, obviously. And I would publish a weekly newspaper with 64 pages instead of 24 because there is more news to print than I have pages.

Max Lieberman; Publisher, Desert Local news: Questions for Book Interviews

- When did you move to Desert Hot Springs? *2000 from Palm Springs*
- How did you hear about the city? *Real Estate friend Colleen Farber*
- Valley Why did you choose Desert Hot Springs over all of the other cities? *I was drinking then, ha*
- Do you believe in the medicinal value of the Mineral Springs? *no*
- How often do you go to one of the Spas in DHS? *never*
- How often do you go to one of the Spas in other Valley Spa Cities? *never*
- Where do you do most of your shopping for Household goods & Services? *Food, Gas always local DHS, clothes, and computers etc. Palm Desert. Palm Springs*
- Where do you do most of your grocery shopping? *Von's –Save a lot end of the month*
- What organizations do you belong to in Desert Hot Springs? *The poor people!*
- How often do you attend council meetings? Planning meetings? *Every time, at least watch it at home via Time Warner*
- If you attend church, which do you attend? *Only go to church, when someone dies*
- Do you believe in the powers of the Energy Vortex? *No, but it is a good concept*
- If the answer is yes to the above, have you had any personal experiences? *No*

- Explain *NA*
- Are you satisfied, unsatisfied or dissatisfied with the overall living environment within Desert Hot Springs? *I love my house, my little pool, and my animals. The people suck, special the leadership.*
- Do you plan to live out the remainder of your life in Desert Hot Springs? *I have no other choice*
- If you were King, what would you do to improve/change the living environment of Desert Hot Springs? *Burn it down and rebuild. This could be the greatest town, but this generation has to go. I have some great friends here, they support and care for me, but there is something wrong with this town, Desert Hot Springs has no feeling, no atmosphere…you ever go to a town and say vow… no vow[sic] facture here. It does not have nightlife nor is it family friendly. Everyone coming to this city has f…..d up somewhere else… Good luck with your book, my regards to your family. Max*

———

Lane Sarasohn; Writer: Questions for Book Interviews

- When did you move to Desert Hot Springs? *2000*
- How did you hear about the city? *We started going to Two Bunch Palms for special vacations in 1978*
- Why did you choose Desert Hot Springs over all of the other Valley cities? *When we bought our house in 1999 we could afford a condo in Palm Springs or Rancho Mirage or a house in DHS. We chose to buy a house.*
- Do you believe in the medicinal value of the Mineral Springs? *At the very least they are wonderfully relaxing and certainly relieve aching joints and muscles.*
- How often do you go to one of the Spas in DHS? *Almost never. We have a hot tub that we use often.*
- How often do you go to one of the Spas in other
- Valley Spa Cities? *Never.*

- Where do you do most of your shopping for Household goods & Services? *In DHS if what we want is available here, but we shop regularly at Trader Joe's and Target in Cathedral City, Best Buy in Palm Desert, Home Depot in Palm Springs.*
- Where do you do most of your grocery shopping? *Vons, Stater Brothers, Trader Joe's, Save A Lot, Farmer in the Dale*
- What organizations do you belong to in Desert Hot Springs? *DHS Rotary*
- How often do you attend council meetings? Planning meetings? *Never.*
- If you attend church, which do you attend? *Don't attend church.*
- Do you believe in the powers of the Energy Vortex? *No.*
- If the answer is yes to the above, have you had any personal experiences? *I am affected by dramatically beautiful scenery and was quite moved by the scenery the first time I visited Sedona (in the early Seventies). Likewise, part of the spiritual/emotional experience of visiting Two Bunch Palms was gazing across the valley at majestic Mt. San Jacinto. I probably would have credited the vortex back then, but after living here for ten years, I'm no longer affected the same way by the now very familiar beautiful local scenery.*
- Are you satisfied, unsatisfied or dissatisfied with the overall living environment within Desert Hot Springs? *Quite satisfied. I like the small town feel. The lack of noise and traffic. I like the people who I know in the community. I like the wide open spaces and the convenience to the nearby upscale desert cities.*
- Do you plan to live out the remainder of your life in Desert Hot Springs? *I don't really know. I don't look more than a year or two ahead and right now my children and young grandchildren live nearby (just two or three minutes away) so I'm not interested in moving.*

- If you were King, what would you do to improve/change the living environment of Desert Hot Springs? *I would redistribute the wealth to alleviate the grinding poverty in Desert Hot Springs and other impoverished communities. I would prefer the social organization one finds in Western Europe where everyone's health care and education through college are provided by the state, where all workers are paid a living wage, where there's help for the homeless and the hungry. The very rich in America are under-taxed and far too much national treasure is wasted on war and "defense."*
- Other comments: *I look forward to reading your book. Good luck and fond regards, Lane*

―――――

Council Member Russell Betts: Questions for Book Interviews

- When did you move to Desert Hot Springs? *March 28, 2003 at 5:30 p.m.*
- How did you hear about the city? *Real estate agent.*
- Why did you choose Desert Hot Springs over all of the other Valley cities? *The value of the homes compared to other cities and a belief that Desert Hot Springs was the next city to be on par with the other Coachella Valley cites.*
- Do you believe in the medicinal value of the Mineral Springs? *The medicinal value of the mineral springs is well established. Even skeptics can't deny that a soak in a hot mineral water pool will make you feel much better.*
- How often do you go to one of the Spas in DHS? *I visit our spas one to four times per month depending on my schedule.*
- How often do you go to one of the Spas in other Valley Spa Cities? *I visit the spas in the other valley cities occasionally.*
- Where do you do most of your shopping for Household goods & Services? *Most of my shopping*

439

for household goods and services is done in Desert Hot Springs. Some items must be purchased outside the city due to lack of availability be generally I find most of what I need is available.

- Where do you do most of your grocery shopping? *In Desert Hot Springs.*
- What organizations do you belong to in Desert Hot Springs? *City council*
- How often do you attend council meetings? Planning meetings? *I have attended all city council meetings as a council member with the exception of a couple of meetings. Prior to serving on the city council, I regularly attended council meetings and planning commission meetings.*
- If you attend church, which do you attend?
- Do you believe in the powers of the Energy Vortex? *I am not so spiritually inclined to believe in things like an energy vortex.*
- If the answer is yes to the above, have you had any personal experiences?
- Explain
- Are you satisfied, unsatisfied or dissatisfied with the overall living environment within Desert Hot Springs? *Out of a belief that one should never give up on trying to improve, I will never be satisfied with the living environment in Desert Hot Springs. In the short term, the city needs work on beautification.*
- Do you plan to live out the remainder of your life in Desert Hot Springs? *My wife and I will likely always maintain a home in Desert Hot Springs but we plan to travel extensively in the coming years.*
- If you were King, what would you do to improve/change the living environment of Desert Hot Springs? *The first proclamation as "king" would be to limit a king's rule to two terms of office with any second term requiring reaffirmation through re-election. As in Australia, voting would be compulsory in Desert Hot Springs.*
- Other comments

Council member Karl Baker: Questions for Book Interviews
- When did you move to Desert Hot Springs? *1995*

- *H*ow did you hear about the city? *I WAS TEACHING SCHOOL IN Palm Springs and visited here several times and decided it was a place where community members had no pretenses, unlike what I experienced in Palm Springs.*

- Why did you choose Desert Hot Springs over all of the other Valley cities? *See above*
- Do you believe in the medicinal value of the Mineral Springs? *Yes*
- How often do you go to one of the Spas in DHS? *Never—I have a spa in my back yard.*
- How often do you go to one of the Spas in other Valley Spa Cities? *Never*
- Where do you do most of your shopping for Household goods & Services?
- Where do you do most of your grocery shopping? *Half in Desert Hot Springs and half at CostCo in Palm Desert*
- What organizations do you belong to in Desert Hot Springs? *Rotary; Coachella Valley Mountain Conservancy; Bug Board (Mosquito Abatement district)*
- How often do you attend council meetings? Planning meetings? *NA*
- If you attend church, which do you attend? *I play the piano as a volunteer for the First Community Baptist Church*
- Do you believe in the powers of the Energy Vortex? *I believe there is enough evidence that there is something to it*
- If the answer is yes to the above, have you had any personal experiences? *No*
- Explain
- Are you satisfied, unsatisfied or dissatisfied with the overall living environment within Desert Hot Springs? *I am pleased with the direction the city is heading*

- Do you plan to live out the remainder of your life in Desert Hot Springs? *Yes*
- If you were King, what would you do to improve/change the living environment of Desert Hot Springs? *I would rehab all of the houses and buildings in the entire city that need repair and painting*
- Other comments *NA*

———

Council member Scott Matas Questions for Book Interviews

- When did you move to Desert Hot Springs? *Born 8/13/71 in Palm Springs California – Mother and Fathers family were living in DHS my parents rented a small apartment in Palm Springs until I was about 6 months old. My parents bought their first home early 1972 in DHS.*
- How did you hear about the city? *NA*
- Why did you choose Desert Hot Springs over all of the other Valley cities?
- Do you believe in the medicinal value of the Mineral Springs? *Yes*
- How often do you go to one of the Spas in DHS? *Couple times a year*
- How often do you go to one of the Spas in other Valley Spa Cities? *Never*
- Where do you do most of your shopping for Household goods & Services? *We always try local first, but end up on the south side of the freeway quit often*
- Where do you do most of your grocery shopping? *VONS, Sam's Club (have growing teenage child Sam's Club have better values)*
- What organizations do you belong to in Desert Hot Springs? *Rotary, Chamber, DHS Volunteer Fire Company, Little League*
- How often do you attend council meetings? Planning meetings? *NA*

- If you attend church, which do you attend? *Christ Lutheran Church*
- Do you believe in the powers of the Energy Vortex? *Yes*
- If the answer is yes to the above, have you had any personal experiences? *Have used the hot and cold water many times for healing*
- Explain
- Are you satisfied, unsatisfied or dissatisfied with the overall living environment within Desert Hot Springs? *Satisfied but as a community leader we can do better, the quality of life is 10,000% better then it was 10 years ago, but we still have issues to fix.*
- Do you plan to live out the remainder of your life in Desert Hot Springs? *Not sure*
- If you were King, what would you do to improve/change the living environment of Desert Hot Springs? *I believe DHS is a unique and wonderful place, if I was to change anything it might be more of a focus on our resources, such as, our water. Capitalize on this resource and DHS will be a shining star.*
- **Other comments** *NA*

Karl Furrer Owner, Swiss Spa Resort Questions for Book Interviews

- When did you move to Desert Hot Springs? *May 01, 1992.*
- How did you hear about the city? *From our relatives.*
- Why did you choose Desert Hot Springs over all of the other Valley cities? *Hot mineral Water, view*
- Do you believe in the medicinal value of the Mineral Springs? *Absolutely. It is one of the most curative waters in the world*
- How often do you go to one of the Spas in DHS? *I own one.*
- How often do you go to one of the Spas in other Valley Spa Cities? *Never.*

- Where do you do most of your shopping for Household goods & Services? *50% DHS 50% valley*
- Where do you do most of your grocery shopping? *Costo in Palm Desert & Vons in DHS.*
- What organizations do you belong to in Desert Hot Springs? *Rotary Club, Hotelier's Assocoation, Chamber of Commerce.*
- How often do you attend council meetings? Planning meetings? *Rarely*
- If you attend church, which do you attend? *None, have our own meditation group in our home.*
- Do you believe in the powers of the Energy Vortex? *Absolutely.*
- If the answer is yes to the above, have you had any personal experiences? *I see the effects every day at our resort*
- Explain *Guests soaking in our water feel so much better afterwards. They get rid of pains and discomfort.*
- Are you satisfied, unsatisfied or dissatisfied with the overall living environment within Desert Hot Springs? *satisfied except sometimes with the vortex "wind"*
- Do you plan to live out the remainder of your life in Desert Hot Springs? *Probably will move closer to the coast*
- If you were King, what would you do to improve/change the living environment of Desert Hot Springs? *I am glad that I am not King here. I would do pretty much what the present city manager and council are doing.*
- Other comments *None.*

————

Dr. Paul Ross Questions for Book Interviews

- When did you move to Desert Hot Springs? *May 14, 1980*
- How did you hear about the city? *Friends retired here*

- Why did you choose Desert Hot Springs over all of the other Valley cities? *Dr. Henry Brown died, his practice was for sale.*
- Do you believe in the medicinal value of the Mineral Springs? *Yes*
- How often do you go to one of the Spas in DHS? *Once every three months.*
- How often do you go to one of the Spas in other Valley Spa Cities? *Once every six months.*
- Where do you do most of your shopping for Household goods & Services? *Local Markets*
- Where do you do most of your grocery shopping? *Stater Bros. & Vons*
- What organizations do you belong to in Desert Hot Springs? *Chamber of Commerce.*
- How often do you attend council meetings? Planning meetings? *Rarely*
- If you attend church, which do you attend? *Temple Negvy Shalom until it closed in 1997.*
- Do you believe in the powers of the Energy Vortex? *Yes*
- If the answer is yes to the above, have you had any personal experiences? *I've seen people throw away their crutches , canes etc. after bahtig in our healing waters.*
- Explain
- Are you satisfied, unsatisfied or dissatisfied with the overall living environment within Desert Hot Springs? *Satisfied*
- Do you plan to live out the remainder of your life in Desert Hot Springs? *Yes until I retire. The clean air and water makes it a healthy place to live.*
- If you were King, what would you do to improve/change the living environment of Desert Hot Springs? *Attract more middle income people and businesses to town.*
- Other comments *None*

Linda Burke: Questions for book Interviews

- When did you move to Desert Hot Springs? *July 1, 2008*

- How did you hear about the city? *I lived in Morongo Valley for eight years prior to moving here and had become familiar with the area.*

- Why did you choose Desert Hot Springs over all of the other Valley cities? *DHS has senior communities and is near shopping and medical facilities.*

- Do you believe in the medicinal value of the Mineral Springs? *No...DHS Spa claims to have medicinal powers, but I spent many hours in their pools, back when they still had classes for arthritics. Entry for the day was only $2 if you paid early in the morning to go to the class, so that was far from a hardship, but I don't believe the waters helped, beyond being comforting through their warmth.*

- How often do you go to one of the Spas in DHS? *No longer often since I have spas available at Hidden Springs. My son and his family, though, go to DHS Spa frequently. They enjoy the atmosphere and restaurant/bar.*

- How often do you go to one of the Spas in other Valley Spa Cities? *Never.*

- Where do you do most of your shopping for Household goods & Services? *DHS Kmart, occasionally Costco.*

- Where do you do most of your grocery shopping? *DHS-Stater, Rancho and Vons.*

- What organizations do you belong to in Desert Hot Springs? *Hidden Springs HOA and GSMOL (I'm secretary); VFW and American Legion but temporarily inactive.*

- How often do you attend council meetings? *Planning meetings? Never.*

- If you attend church, which do you attend? *Occasionally...St. Anthony's.*

Do you believe in the powers of the Energy Vortex? *No*.

- If the answer is yes to the above, have you had any personal experiences?
- Explain
- Are you satisfied, unsatisfied or dissatisfied with the overall living environment within Desert Hot Springs? *Almost satisfied. The crime level has intimidated many of us older people from shopping at the local malls during evening hours because of the serious crime in the area. It is uncomfortable to be hit on for money from drug addicts and homeless persons regardless of the hour.*
- Do you plan to live out the remainder of your life in Desert Hot Springs? *I live here because my son settled in Morongo Valley because that's where I was living when he needed a home. I'm in a nice, older manufactured home that he bought for me in Hidden Springs. It's a nice place to live. I like the atmosphere and have made many, many friends. I'll probably die here because I have no place else to go that I could afford. I spent years helping my husband in his career, moving at ever whim of his and losing my retirement funds. Now he has the property we accumulated in Mexico and a nice retirement that I helped him achieve...oh, plus Social Security because he was married to me for more than 10 years. Now, THAT's irritating.*
- If you were King, what would you do to improve/change the living environment of Desert Hot Springs? *Keep arresting the drug sellers and repeat offenders...even if we have to put a pink tent city out in the desert. These people are destroying our youth. Our elementary school is not doing very well. Our HOA volunteered to aid in the school and never received a response, even after the president and another person went personally to offer our services in whatever capacities were needed. Finally, we withdrew our offer. Which is sad...I had had my TB test and fingerprints taken and was ready to roll. I*

447

know I'm good at teaching reading. Our president was a retired principal and we had several retired teachers and many experienced grandparents.

- Other comments *Somebody really blew it when designing those angled curb projections into the street. They aren't particularly attractive...nor admittedly unattractive...but on first viewing them, they immediately screamed "Hit me." They are a bad design, and many of us fear that they will cause accidents or, at best, tire damage.*

Bill, when you get your book put together, if you need a proofreader/editor, please keep me in mind.

Linda Burke

Bill Effinger (answering my own questions)

- When did you move to Desert Hot Springs? *May 30, 2005.*
- How did you hear about the city? *From our friend Cheryl.*
- Why did you choose Desert Hot Springs over all of the other Valley cities? *New homes were less expensive.*
- Do you believe in the medicinal value of the Mineral Springs? *Somewhat.*
- How often do you go to one of the Spas in DHS? *Very rarely-we had our own spa at our home.*
- How often do you go to one of the Spas in other Valley Spa Cities? *Never.*
- Where do you do most of your shopping for Household goods & Services? *When we lived there, mostly "down valley".*
- Where do you do most of your grocery shopping? *When we lived there, Costco in Palm Desert & Vons in DHS.*
- What organizations do you belong to in Desert Hot Springs? *When we lived there, I belonged to the DHS*

- *Rotary Club, Chamber of Commerce and was the City appointed board member of the Coachella Valley Economic Partnership on five committees.*
- How often do you attend council meetings? Planning meetings? *Never missed one, beginning in 2003, 18-months before moving there.*
- If you attend church, which do you attend? *None*
- Do you believe in the powers of the Energy Vortex? *I'm a skeptic, but willing to be proven wrong.*
- If the answer is yes to the above, have you had any personal experiences? *Other than my references in this book, no.*
- Explain
- Are you satisfied, unsatisfied or dissatisfied with the overall living environment within Desert Hot Springs? *We were dissatisfied & unsatisfied*
- Do you plan to live out the remainder of your life in Desert Hot Springs? *We moved back to the coast in 2009*
- If you were King, what would you do to improve/change the living environment of Desert Hot Springs? *Most of what I have written about in over 300 articles; what I have said on these pages and spoken about for the past eight-years on what is needed to bring Desert Hot Springs into the 21st Century. As I see it, the last available hope for the city is to capitalize on the newly annexed 4000-acres by zoning and promoting the area as being the closest to Las Angeles, the gateway to Coachella Valley and the largest composite Industrial manufacturing site in the entire Valley, with major power facilities that can offer reduced power rates, that is ripe for development, in a city willing to incentivise businesses to locate in their city.*

Eleven: And it just doesn't seem to stop

Unfortunately for Desert Hot Springs, just days before we were ready to publish this book, several negative issues again surfaced, once again shedding a dark shadow over the city and its attempt to rise up in the eyes of its citizens and neighbors.

We know when election time roles around, it becomes the "silly season". However, in DHS, it tends to get quite bizarre as you will see:

Alex Bias (you remember him—he's the former mayor of DHS who's wife recently robbed two banks?) well he's once again running for mayor. How typical is that? There goes that Vortex again!

And council member Karl Baker not to be outdone has been exposed (literally) by recent news accounts complete with pictures published on You Tube. Baker is posing semi-nude on a gay publication page where he purportedly trolled for sexual favors. Why not? It's a free country—right? And what's the difference if Karl is a city council member? Who need s decorum in Desert Hot Springs anyhow?

The above issue not being enough, now Baker is involved in an investigation where his house-mate has a $15 Thousand contract with the city to install and maintain alarm systems on city-owned and private residences.

Baker of course denies any wrong doing, but this kind of publicity won't do him any favors in his run for re-election I would think.

Surely the Vortex made Karl Baker do these things. What other reason could explain these situations?

And now the following article continues this unbelievable tale of misfortune, misconduct, mistakes and petty crimes in the desert community of Desert Hot Springs where the Vortex again casts its spell on citizens and leaders alike.

Desert Hot Springs city councilman endorsed checks

City says it forwards case against Karl Baker to district attorney's office

5:50 PM, Oct. 28, 2011

Written by **Kate McGinty**

The Desert Sun

Desert Hot Spring City Councilman Karl Baker's name is signed on the back of nearly $15,000 in checks the city wrote to a local businessman.

Baker appears to have endorsed all 22 checks paid to Chryss Home Automation, as recently as a $1,200 check dated Oct. 6.

The owner, Pete Chryss, rents a room in Baker's house and has worked on Baker's Nov. 8 re-election campaign.

"I was shocked at what I found. I recognized a familiar signature on the back of the checks for pretty much every check to Chryss Home Automation," Finance Director Jason Simpson told The Desert Sun.

Simpson said he forwarded the checks and other evidence this week to the Riverside County District Attorney, citing a state law that addresses conflict of interest.

District attorney spokesman John Hall said he could not confirm or deny an investigation.

State law says any elected leader or government employee who could have a financial tie, direct or indirect, cannot participate in securing a contract with that business. Financial ties include landlord-tenant relationships, the state specifies.

The council did not vote on the contract.

Baker did not return email or phone messages Friday, and Chryss declined comment.

"I don't know anything about that business," Baker told The Desert Sun in a phone interview Oct. 14. "He (Chryss) does his business. I do mine."

The checks were part of an internal review into how city staff approved a business license and a series of contracts with the company, which is not licensed by the state as required to install alarms.

That report, with 734 pages of supporting documents, was released Friday.

It is the second time this year Desert Hot Springs has come under fire for not conducting background checks on the people it pays.

In March, the city fired Tony Clarke after paying him $250,000 to produce the Wellness and World Music Festival, which was canceled.

The city did not solicit bids before hiring Clarke in December 2009 and did not verify his claims of being an internationally known producer.

City Manager Rick Daniels took responsibility for any mistakes made in City Hall.

"It all ends up here, and I am responsible for all of it," Daniels said.

Since December 2010, the city has paid Chryss $15,328 for security and monitoring services at city-owned homes and buildings.

It was "sloppy" of the city not to verify the license before hiring the alarm company, said Bob Stern.

He is president of the Center for Governmental Studies, a Los Angeles-based nonprofit research and civic engagement group that closed this month.

"Ultimately, the City Council is accountable for that, but the city manager is the one who should be minding the store," he said.

Ties to the city

On his Dec. 28 business application to the city, Chryss listed Baker's name and cell phone number as his emergency contact.

The address where the city sent the checks is the same as Baker's home address.

Daniels and Simpson said they were aware of the living arrangement before public scrutiny began in early October, but could not say when they met Chryss or how they were introduced.

Daniels said he thinks he met Chryss at a party and hired Chryss to install a security system at his home shortly after, in March 2010.

He paid Chryss, then working with American Alarm Co., $298 to install the system.

Daniels said he did not see any ethical or legal problems for the city signing business deals with a councilman's housemate.

"It's not illegal," Daniels said. "Is it unethical? No. Would living with, being a roommate or renting a room from a city councilor disqualify somebody from certain types of business? No."

453

When asked whether Baker's name being the emergency contact raised any red flags, the city's finance director questioned how The Desert Sun knew that.

"That information should have been redacted for all emergency contacts, so I don't know if you saw something or you just heard about it," Simpson said.

The business application was provided to The Desert Sun by the city as part of a request under the state's open records law.

Simpson, who signed the contracts with Chryss, said he also did not find any ethical or legal problem with hiring someone who is a tenant of a councilman.

"On surface, it's not an issue," Simpson said. "It could be, but they, you know, talking to Pete, he's said repeatedly, 'Karl has nothing to do with my business.' Are we going to put a camera in their house and see what's going on? How do you monitor that?"

The relationship between Baker and Chryss is unclear, though those who know Baker say he rents rooms to several people.

The allegations against Baker of violating conflict of interest laws suggest "a very serious violation," Stern said. He said such violations are rare because council members are warned of the law.

"That could be a problem. Why would he be endorsing the check? That's the $15,000 question," Stern said.

Stern — who co-wrote the state's 1974 Political Reform Act, one of several conflict of interest laws — said the investigation should also address whether Baker pushed for the contract behind the scenes or recommended Chryss to city staff.

No license

Neither Chryss nor Chryss Home Automation has a license with the state as required by law to install alarms, California Department of Consumer Affairs spokesman Russ Heimerich said.

He's asked the Bureau of Security and Investigative Services, which investigates reports of unlicensed business activity for alarm companies, to look into the case.

Daniels said Thursday the city does not contract with businesses that are not properly licensed.

"(When) there is a license required, if you don't have it, we will not contract with you," he said.

However, on his Dec. 28 business application to the city, Chryss left blank several fields, including his state license number, license type and expiration date.

"I don't know what our business license clerk did, but in my discussions with my staff, it's not that they didn't ask the questions," Simpson said.

Daniels said the business license clerk relied on the word of Chryss, who explained that he was covered under the license of another company.

The clerk, who is in charge of processing about 1,500 business applications each year, has worked for the city for about five years.

Daniels declined to say whether he would face any discipline.

"Our objective is to protect the public interest, which includes the dollars that are spent, and we are diligent in that. So what we can't do is act in haste with incomplete information, and as a result, cause personal harm," Daniels said.

When asked if the city acted with incomplete information when approving the license, Daniels responded: "We believed it to be true at the time, that he was covered."

Daniels said he will ask the council to review and consider updating its purchasing policy within the next 30 days.

City Attorney Ruben Duran met with the council in closed session Thursday to discuss a potential lawsuit.

Baker did not attend the closed-door meeting, during which council did not take any votes.

The city did not know Friday how much it would be charged by Duran for his review, which included looking into what business activity requires a state license.

Duran generally bills $175 an hour, Simpson said.

Kate McGinty is a reporter for The Desert Sun. She covers public safety and the city of Desert Hot Springs. She can be reached at (760) 778-6451, kate.mcginty@thedesertsun.com, or @TDSKateM.

Council, residents react

At least some of the council members and residents distance themselves from Baker on Friday, but voiced mixed views on how well city staff is performing.

Councilman Scott Matas, who had publicly endorsed Baker for reelection, said Friday he no longer supported Baker after "the information that was given to us" about the checks.

Matas called awarding the festival and security contracts "just two incidents" and said he maintains the city has moved in a positive direction.

"I think our staff does a really good job, and there might have been oversight at this time, but I think all the measures have been taken to make sure this is corrected," he said.

Mayor Pro Tem Russell Betts, who is also up for election Nov. 8, said he could not support Baker after the allegations surfaced.

Betts, who did not vote for the music festival contract, said he expects a report to council on how the city intends to better vet its vendors.

"Mistakes will happen in any system, but after it's happened once or twice it's clear something needs to be done to shore up whatever is causing these problems," Betts said.

"Ultimately, the city manager is responsible for it, and he has got to go in and find out what's causing these problems and make sure the systems are put in place that they get caught."

Mayor Yvonne Parks and Councilwoman Jan Pye did not immediately return phone messages from The Desert Sun.

Adam Sanchez, who is challenging the two incumbents for a seat on council, called the checks frustrating and said it reflects poorly on the city.

The council lacks oversight and too often delegates all its responsibility to the city manager, Sanchez said.

"They've been speaking a lot about accountability and transparency, and I think that this proves right here that's been lacking at City Hall," he said.

Longtime resident Dave Hoopes, who has volunteered on city commissions, said he has supported the council's progress but the conflict of interest allegations against Baker will likely factor into his voting decision.

"I think at election time, I think people are looking for daggers to shoot," he said. "But Karl's business life and his personal life should be kept separate."

City Manager Rick Daniels took responsibility for any mistakes made in City Hall.

"It all ends up here, and I am responsible for all of it," Daniels said.

Since December 2010, the city has paid Chryss $15,328 for security and monitoring services at city-owned homes and buildings.

It was "sloppy" of the city not to verify the license before hiring the alarm company, said Bob Stern.

He is president of the Center for Governmental Studies, a Los Angeles-based nonprofit research and civic engagement group that closed this month.

"Ultimately, the City Council is accountable for that, but the city manager is the one who should be minding the store," he said.

Ties to the city

On his Dec. 28 business application to the city, Chryss listed Baker's name and cell phone number as his emergency contact.

The address where the city sent the checks is the same as Baker's home address.

Daniels and Simpson said they were aware of the living arrangement before public scrutiny began in early October,

458

but could not say when they met Chryss or how they were introduced.

Daniels said he thinks he met Chryss at a party and hired Chryss to install a security system at his home shortly after, in March 2010.

He paid Chryss, then working with American Alarm Co., $298 to install the system.

Daniels said he did not see any ethical or legal problems for the city signing business deals with a councilman's housemate.

"It's not illegal," Daniels said. "Is it unethical? No. Would living with, being a roommate or renting a room from a city councilor disqualify somebody from certain types of business? No."

When asked whether Baker's name being the emergency contact raised any red flags, the city's finance director questioned how The Desert Sun knew that.

"That information should have been redacted for all emergency contacts, so I don't know if you saw something or you just heard about it," Simpson said.

The business application was provided to The Desert Sun by the city as part of a request under the state's open records law.

Simpson, who signed the contracts with Chryss, said he also did not find any ethical or legal problem with hiring someone who is a tenant of a councilman.

"On surface, it's not an issue," Simpson said. "It could be, but they, you know, talking to Pete, he's said repeatedly, 'Karl has nothing to do with my business.' Are we going to put a camera in their house and see what's going on? How do you monitor that?"

The relationship between Baker and Chryss is unclear, though those who know Baker say he rents rooms to several people.

The allegations against Baker of violating conflict of interest laws suggest "a very serious violation," Stern said. He said such violations are rare because council members are warned of the law.

"That could be a problem. Why would he be endorsing the check? That's the $15,000 question," Stern said.

Stern — who co-wrote the state's 1974 Political Reform Act, one of several conflict of interest laws — said the investigation should also address whether Baker pushed for the contract behind the scenes or recommended Chryss to city staff.

No license
Neither Chryss nor Chryss Home Automation has a license with the state as required by law to install alarms, California Department of Consumer Affairs spokesman Russ Heimerich said.

He's asked the Bureau of Security and Investigative Services, which investigates reports of unlicensed business activity for alarm companies, to look into the case.

Daniels said Thursday the city does not contract with businesses that are not properly licensed.

"(When) there is a license required, if you don't have it, we will not contract with you," he said.

However, on his Dec. 28 business application to the city, Chryss left blank several fields, including his state license number, license type and expiration date.

"I don't know what our business license clerk did, but in my discussions with my staff, it's not that they didn't ask the questions," Simpson said.

Daniels said the business license clerk relied on the word of Chryss, who explained that he was covered under the license of another company.

The clerk, who is in charge of processing about 1,500 business applications each year, has worked for the city for about five years.

Daniels declined to say whether he would face any discipline.

"Our objective is to protect the public interest, which includes the dollars that are spent, and we are diligent in that. So what we can't do is act in haste with incomplete information, and as a result, cause personal harm," Daniels said.

When asked if the city acted with incomplete information when approving the license, Daniels responded: "We believed it to be true at the time, that he was covered."

Daniels said he will ask the council to review and consider updating its purchasing policy within the next 30 days.

City Attorney Ruben Duran met with the council in closed session Thursday to discuss a potential lawsuit.

Baker did not attend the closed-door meeting, during which council did not take any votes.

The city did not know Friday how much it would be charged by Duran for his review, which included looking into what business activity requires a state license.

Duran generally bills $175 an hour, Simpson said.

Kate McGinty is a reporter for The Desert Sun. She covers public safety and the city of Desert Hot Springs. She can be reached at (760) 778-6451, kate.mcginty@thedesertsun.com, or @TDSKateM.

Council, residents react

At least some of the council members and residents distance themselves from Baker on Friday, but voiced mixed views on how well city staff is performing.

Councilman Scott Matas, who had publicly endorsed Baker for reelection, said Friday he no longer supported Baker after "the information that was given to us" about the checks.

Matas called awarding the festival and security contracts "just two incidents" and said he maintains the city has moved in a positive direction.

"I think our staff does a really good job, and there might have been oversight at this time, but I think all the measures have been taken to make sure this is corrected," he said.

Mayor Pro Tem Russell Betts, who is also up for election Nov. 8, said he could not support Baker after the allegations surfaced.

Betts, who did not vote for the music festival contract, said he expects a report to council on how the city intends to better vet its vendors.

"Mistakes will happen in any system, but after it's happened once or twice it's clear something needs to be done to shore up whatever is causing these problems," Betts said.

"Ultimately, the city manager is responsible for it, and he has got to go in and find out what's causing these problems and make sure the systems are put in place that they get caught."

Mayor Yvonne Parks and Councilwoman Jan Pye did not immediately return phone messages from The Desert Sun.

Adam Sanchez, who is challenging the two incumbents for a seat on council, called the checks frustrating and said it reflects poorly on the city.

The council lacks oversight and too often delegates all its responsibility to the city manager, Sanchez said.

"They've been speaking a lot about accountability and transparency, and I think that this proves right here that's been lacking at City Hall," he said.

Longtime resident Dave Hoopes, who has volunteered on city commissions, said he has supported the council's progress but the conflict of interest allegations against Baker will likely factor into his voting decision.

"I think at election time, I think people are looking for daggers to shoot," he said. "But Karl's business life and his personal life should be kept separate."

Then some good news pops up:

Desert Hot Springs' new Hotel Lautner featured on Today Show

11:22 AM, Nov. 2, 2011 |

The Desert Sun
SUBSCRIBE NOW!

Bill Effinger

Hotel Lautner, a Desert Hot Springs hotel designed by famed architect John Lautner, was featured on a Today Show travel segment. / Dan Chavkin Photography

Desert Hot Springs' new Hotel Lautner made the Today Show's list this morning of the Top 5 spots in the nation that are affordable and close to a major city.

The city's new Hotel Lautner was profiled on the Today's Travel segment as an affordable road trip.

Getting the second berth behind Kinderhook Farm near New York City was the John Lautner-designed boutique hotel.

It made the mark for its accoutrements, affordability, closeness to hiking and the geothermal hot springs.

Only to be overshadowed by the following:

Desert Hot Springs City Councilman Karl Baker makes first public appearance

His presence follows city's allegations Baker violated conflict of interest laws

8:32 PM, Nov. 1, 2011

Written by Kate McGinty

464

The Desert Sun

What Baker had to say

Desert Hot Springs City Councilman Karl Baker spoke Tuesday during his first public appearance since the city asked for an investigation into whether Baker violated conflict of interest laws.

His two-minute speech read as follows:

"I'm sure I don't need to say this has been the most agonizing two or three weeks I've experienced in my life. I feel like I have really given above and beyond to this council and this community to help bring us forward.

"Unfortunately, because things have been turned over to the DA, my attorney advises me to shut up. But I can say that the opera ain't over until the fat lady sings, and I'm not even vocalizing yet. There have been no charges, and I've seen nothing except what's in the newspaper.

"It hurts. It hurts a bunch when you don't want to walk out your front door, when you don't want to be seen in the community for fear that people are thinking evil of you when there was never an evil intent in anything I ever did. To see someone on TV say he's a thief really hurts. It really hurts.

"I hope we get through this completely and soon, I hope that no other people are drawn into this, and that's a distinct possibility. I hope that we as a city will have an opportunity to explain exactly what's gone on, and also have an opportunity to continue the good work that has been going on, I'm proud of what I have been able to do on this council, and I would sincerely like to continue. However, having been as tarnished as I have, it's pretty difficult to wake up in the morning and smile.

"So I can't go into specifics, but that's all I have to say. Thank you."

Desert Hot Springs City Councilman Karl Baker made his first public comments today since the city asked prosecutors to investigate whether Baker violated the state's conflict of interest laws.

During a two-minute speech at the council meeting tonight, Baker said he has been afraid to leave the house since the allegations surfaced.

"I'm sure I don't need to say this has been the most agonizing two or three weeks I've experience in my life. I feel like I have really given above and beyond to this council and this community to help bring us forward," he said.

Baker hinted other people could be implicated as the district attorney investigates.

"I hope we get through this completely and soon, I hope that no other people are drawn into this, and that's a distinct possibility," he said.

Baker's appearance at the council meeting follows intense scrutiny of the city's $15,000 business deal with Chryss Home Automation, which is not licensed by the state as required by law.

On his Dec. 28 business application to the city, Pete Chryss left blank several fields, including his state license number, license type and expiration date.

He rents a room from Baker, who is up for election Nov. 8, and listed Baker as his emergency contact on his application to the city.

The city also concluded last week that Baker endorsed nearly $15,000 in checks the city wrote to the company.

The Riverside County District Attorney's office has agreed to investigate whether Baker violated the state's conflict-of-interest laws, Finance Director Jason Simpson told The Desert Sun.

More than 50 people filled into the council meeting, which began at 5 p.m. at the Carl May Community Center, 11-711 West Drive.

Thirteen people asked to speak during public comment, and Parks said she would allow all speakers time, despite the council's policy to allow only up to 10 speakers.

Only one comment so far has hinted at the scrutiny of the city during the last three weeks since the city ended its contracts with Chryss.

Resident Adam Sanchez, who is the single challenger to the two incumbents in the Nov. 8 election, said the city needs to be more transparent in its business deals.

He proposed that the city create a commission that focuses on transparency in government.

"I want, one day, for people to say that Desert Hot Springs has those high standards because it's going to speak well of the city," Sanchez said.

****

Where Desert Hot Springs is concerned "Transparency in Government" is an oxymoron in that many of its leaders seem to be openly conducting illegal activities right in front of their constituents with impunity. Such is the power of the negative Vortex on all citizens of the city it would seem. And then one day later, this:

Baker Busted Driving on Expired Tags

November 3, 2011 Desert Star Weekly <u>Desert Hot Springs,News,Riverside County</u>

Councilman Threatens Retribution for Latest Exposure

Councilman having a little chat with police officer about his driving his vehicle with expired tags.

Desert Hot Springs, CA - The Never Ending Story of Karl Baker never ceases to amaze and amuse. Jaws dropped at the noon Rotary meeting at the Aqua Soleil Hotel when the embittered and politically battle weary councilman attended today. It was what happened afterwards in the parking lot that sent media tongues wagging for those hungry for latest chapter of The Baker Story.

The councilman has been driving a vehicle with expired tags for the last four months after the registration expired. The old Cadilac the councilman was driving has expired tags from July of 2011, parking his vehicle at city hall on a regular basis.

Since busting up his diesel pick-up truck earlier this year, Baker has been driving the distinctive Cadilac of a pewter color. Many months ago the wreck of Baker's damaged pick-up truck was spotted at the city public works yard.

Karl's BakerMobile

City Attorney Rubin Duran stonewalled this newspaper by denial of our Public Records Act requests attempting to get public documents relating to storage of Baker's personal vehicle wreck on city property, how it got there, and where did it go. This afternoon Baker was exposing his new vehicle for all to see it was not currently registered.

Baker was caught this afternoon trying to talk his way out of his predicament. When Baker spotted us taking pictures he shouted threats to have us arrested.We hung around for a while as Baker waved a handful of papers around and overheard Baker telling a code enforcement officer his lack of registration was all the fault of Sacramento.

469

Baker tries to talk his way out of his problems again

As we departed Baker was facing the possibility of having his vehicle impounded. The vehicle code requires vehicle owners to pay registration fees within thirty days of vehicle transfer. Vehicles of violators are to be impounded for thirty days. The Desert Hot Springs Police Department has been tough on violators, frequently clearing unregistered vehicles from private property and impounding them even though the vehicles are not moving.

A spokes person for the Desert Hot Springs Police Department said there is no law giving council members special favoritism to drive vehicles that are not properly registered.

Time wore on and we didn't have all day to listen to Baker argue with the code enforcement officer. As we left, a black and white, driven by another officer in full uniform, rolled into the parking lot to provide back-up to prevent the situation from getting out of hand.

(a special tip 'o the hat appreciation to the eagle-eyed citizen who spotted the elusive BakerMobile)

Baker Mobile's expired license

What can possibly be next for Desert Hot Springs?

With three open seats in the election just days away, one wonders what changes will be in store for the citizens of the "Shinning City on the Hill"? We are sure that whatever happens, the Vortex will have made them do it!

So, rather than wrap this tale up, I will close with the results of the November 8th city council election and an endnote or two.

However, a new light is being shown on Desert Hot Springs' political antics by a well seasoned editor now living in the city: Ms. Michelle Eaton. Eaton's introductory column and her observations are worth reading, particularly when you consider all of what has been documented in previous pages of this book. So here is what I hope to be the beginning of a very bright light being concentrated on DHS city hall until the shenanigans cease and progress begins for the betterment of its citizenry:

Speaking Volumes at DHS City Council Meeting

November 7, 2011 | Filed under: Columns,Desert Insider,News |

Posted by: Michelle Eaton

(Introducing Michelle Eaton, our new editor with a new column, Desert Insider. Look for Desert Insider to be examining our desert cities and public agencies)

Desert Hot Springs, CA - I attended the **Desert Hot Springs** (DHS) City Council meeting last Tuesday night (Nov. 1) night to find out what the council members and city staff had to say for themselves about the latest scandal to unfold at city hall. I was also anticipating hearing testimony from the outraged members of the public who have been blogging on the matter nearly non-stop for more than a week. I half expected to find the council chambers to be overflowing with angry citizens carrying pitchforks, picketing with "Throw the Crooks Out" signs, and demanding answers. Instead, I found a sea of well-behaved aloha shirt-wearing and sandal-clad residents quietly seated inside the council chambers waiting in anticipation for something to happen. In spite of the veneer of calm, the tension and anxiety in the room was palpable.

Thirteen people signed up to deliver public comments. Each was allotted the usual 3 minutes. The first to touch upon the "elephant in the room" was DHS city council candidate **Adam Sanchez**. He was the fourth speaker to step up to the podium. Sanchez began by focusing on the positive aspects of living in Desert Hot Springs. He praised the abundance of mineral water, mountain views, and spa hotels. Sanchez then politely pointed to an area he believes is badly "in need of improvement," and called for an increased transparency in city government. He said he wants members of the community to be able to say with confidence that DHS has "high standards" and wants everyone here to be "proud" of their city.

Next up was the DHS Police Officer Association (POA) President **Paul Tapia**, who used his time to plead with the city council to hire more police officers. He explained the department is currently undermanned and working excessive amounts of overtime to ensure residents are safe. Tapia credited "the system of checks and balances, the chain of command, and the code of ethics" upheld by the members of law enforcement in town for enabling the DHS police department to function so effectively in spite of the challenges it currently faces. It was surely not lost upon those watching and listening to him that these very elements of good governance are sorely lacking at DHS city hall.

The last speaker was a woman named **Dot Reed**. After talking about the DHS Community & Cultural Affairs Commission (CCAC) she launched into a tiresome and cliche condemnation of journalists; using the old "blame the messenger" tactic of criticizing those who deliver the "bad news" instead of correctly focusing upon the bad news itself. Apparently referencing the adage "those who live in glass houses should never throw stones," Reed began complaining about "stones being thrown" at elected officials and city staff, and wanted to know if the "stone thrower" was "squeaky clean." (She also disturbingly wondered aloud if this person should "have stones thrown" at him or her.) It was a strange and disjointed rant. She closed by saying that she doubted the aforementioned "stone thrower" was present.

If Reed was specifically defending Councilman **Karl Baker**, I want to know how and why she expects any of us to accept his aberrant and abhorrent behavior. Should we ignore the "full frontal nudity" photos of himself he posted on internet sex sites while clearly identifying himself as a city representative? Whitewash his racial slurs? Tolerate his bullying of investigative reporters daring to ask questions about city business? Allow his defense of a local sex spa that admittedly provides rooms for orgies, "complimentary" condoms, and "lube"? Permit him to have an unlicensed city contractor operate a business out of his home? Say nothing while he cashes the city checks written to a convicted felon?

The DHS city council members and mayor next took turns commenting on city business. All four council members addressed the latest scandal involving Baker in one way or another. However, Mayor **Yvonne Park**s inexplicably chose to ignore it. Her silence spoke unfavorable volumes about her.

Councilwoman **Jan Pye** went first. She referenced an article in The Desert Sun noting the reporter had asked her who she blamed for the problems at city hall, and admitting she had answered "**Rick Daniels**" because the city manager "reports to the city council." She then addressed Daniels directly, saying: "I have no issue with you. You have given me no reason to raise an eyebrow. I believe we are hearing the bad part, and not hearing the good." Pye told Daniels she believed he had "had recognized his error" in losing $250,000 of city money due to the World Music Festival debacle. She then said she was "glad the allegations were being brought up," but said she questioned the timing. (When the facts were revealed?) She wondered aloud if this was an effort to improve the city or if there was a "different agenda" in motion. Like Reed, Pye seems to want to brush problems under the proverbial rug and hope they disappear for good. Pye closed by saying "I am going to choose to not unknowingly impede the District Attorney's investigation, and so there will be no more conversations (with me) about any of this."

Councilman **Scott Matas** followed Pye. He commented the least on the topic. At the conclusion of his activity report, he jokingly noted that he thought "the lynch mob was going to be here" at the city council meeting, and then laughed nervously. I found his glib handling of such a serious matter to be surprising and inappropriate. I knew he and his colleagues were breathing a collective sigh of relief over not having to be confronted by protesters. It seemed the absence of public acrimony had emboldened all of them.

Councilman **Russell Betts** then took his turn. Betts used the bulk of his time to focus on what he found to be most troubling at city hall. He first declared that "it is a serious matter when bonds are not executed properly" and addressed what he believes to be Daniels' failure to properly monitor the situation. Betts next chastised those who blamed the media for reporting on the "bad news."

"How do we get good news?" asked Betts. "We do good things. It is not about just about looking good. It is doing good. I cannot ignore the problem areas in this city, and I cannot blame the print and TV media for pointing out the problems here."

Betts continued by stating that "something is not right about the system of checks and balances" in city government, and called for an outside audit of the management system. "It needs to get fixed now," said Betts. "I do not want any more of these episodes. There is nothing wrong with us taking a more serious look at how we do things here. We need to operate like a well-oiled machine to get done what needs to be done." It was a welcome idea. Meeting attendees applauded loudly, and I could hear a few cheers of "hear, hear" being shouted from the back of the room. I then wondered when the city council would be voting on this idea. I hoped Betts could make it happen very soon.

Mayor Parks followed Betts. She regaled the audience with her busy social calendar. I soon stopped taking notes, and almost fell asleep as she droned on about attending this party and that fundraiser. I waited for her to talk about something of importance, especially the political scandal at hand involving the city council member slouched in his seat to her immediate left. But she said nothing about the latest problems with Baker. Her silence was both deafening and embarrassing. She appeared to be either clueless about the gravity of the situation, or just unwilling to deal with a difficult topic. My impression? Parks is a vacuous place-filler at city hall. She has no business "playing" mayor and I hope she is ejected soon. The citizens of DHS need authentic leadership, not an overgrown sorority president.

Councilman Karl Baker spoke next. In a nutshell he was rude, defensive and whiny. It was shocking, especially considering his precarious circumstances. I expected him to demonstrate at least a touch of humility, or to offer some sort of apology to the people he was elected to serve regarding his countless failures. But he did not. As usual, Baker displayed a distasteful arrogance about his bad behavior.

"Unfortunately, because things have been turned over to the (Riverside County) D.A., my attorney advises me to shut up," stated Baker. And, with the repulsive swagger of one who believes he is above the law, Baker continued with this statement: "But I can say that the opera ain't over until the fat lady sings, and I'm not even vocalizing yet."

I was stunned at the offensive metaphor. Was he hinting that he might "squeal" on the others at city hall who might have turned a blind eye to his exploits? Worse yet, those who may have collaborated with him? Barely concealing what struck me as a threat to those who have wisely decided to distance themselves from him in recent weeks, Baker next announced: "I hope that no other people are drawn into this, and that's a distinct possibility. I hope that we as a city will have an opportunity to explain exactly what's gone on." I wondered why Baker felt "the city" needed to explain his actions. I was even more curious about the "what's going on" part. "What's going on" in DHS is still the burning question.

City Manager Rick Daniels was the last to speak. He began by saying "every one" of the DHS alarm contracts in question were put out to bid and three quotes had been secured for each one. Daniels said, therefore, the city purchasing policy had been "complied with" in every case. As he said this, I recalled one comment posted on an article in The Desert Sun (http://www.mydesert.com/comments/article/20111029/NEWS01/110290315/Desert-Hot-Springs-city-councilman-s-name-checks) by a reader who had reviewed all of the city documents and had characterized the second and third bids as "looking like notes from home." This along with all I have been learning about the matter makes me skeptical about Daniels' insistence that he had indeed adhered to the city purchasing policy in this case or others.

Daniels soon launched into what he called an "uncomfortable subject." He claimed that when he took the job four years prior he found the "practices, procedures and culture" of Desert Hot Springs to be "a mess," and said he had been working "diligently" to change things. Like Baker, Daniels was highly defensive, not apologetic. He made no mention of his costly on-the-job missteps that have angered so many. Daniels next announced that the people of DHS are "entitled to know if I am honest." Then, like Baker, he assumed the victim posture. Daniels said recent newspaper articles have "slandered him and spread malicious lies" in an attempt to "harm my reputation, me, my family and my ability to provide for my family." He took no responsibility for exercising any lack of judgment, intentionally making any unwise choices, or failing in any way to do his job over the years.

Daniels next described how he had purchased from American Alarm (**Pete Chryss**) a "simple alarm" for $258, and pays a monthly monitoring fee of $39.95. He said he had also hired American Alarm (Pete Chryss) to install a $6000 home entertainment system at his residence. Daniels noted he had provided the city council and city attorney with receipts showing he had personally paid for both. Daniels closed by saying, "My life is an open book. Ask any one who knows me. I operate in a transparent manner. I want residents to know their city manager is honest."

Daniels certainly made a show of being concerned about repairing his professional reputation at the meeting. But the only way we will know if he is serious about any of this is if he joins Betts in calling for an outside probe of DHS city finances, policies, procedures, management systems, etc. right away.

The final speaker for the evening was DHS mayoral candidate **Robert Bentley**. He stepped up to the podium, faced the city council members and staff, and began pointing fingers at those he says are bringing the city to ruin. The sparks soon started flying. Bentley expressed his ongoing frustration at city council members for "doing a bad job." Matas and Parks alternately banged their gavels to silence him. City Attorney Ruben Duran came to Bentley's defense, stating that according to a "policy of decorum" members of the public were indeed allowed to criticize elected officials. Bentley then told Mayor Parks that it was illegal for her to silence him because his freedom of speech was Constitutionally protected. Parks banged her gavel again and interrupted Bentley. He objected loudly, and Duran said to Parks: "The speaker is correct. He cannot be stopped if he makes his comments in a respectful way."

Duran then instructed Bentley to direct his comments to the mayor, and told him that he could be critical but not "personally attack" any council members or staff. Bentley continued with his comments, citing his Constitutional rights to speak at a public meeting and said to Parks: "I can state my complaints any way that I want, and you cannot stop me." Parks banged her gavel again and responded in saying to him in a tone laden with sarcasm and contempt, "I know you have taken some law courses online, and so you think you are very knowledgeable about all of this."

Bentley again stated to Parks, "The law allows me to criticize you." He then announced that he had filed a Grand Jury complaint against the City of Desert Hot Springs and had specifically requested an investigation into the Karl Baker check cashing scandal. He closed in saying "There is an absolute prohibition for what he did. It is completely illegal for Baker to have failed to disclose his conflict of interest in this matter."

I was disgusted at the way Mayor Parks tried to belittle Bentley when he challenged her. Making fun of his educational pursuits was a cheap shot, and attempting to silence him an ugly power play. Parks actually embarrassed herself because it is apparent Bentley has a firmer grasp of the law than she does.

There are many who might doubt Bentley's ability to serve as the mayor of Desert Hot Springs. He is not polished or smooth. And, he has difficulty tempering his frustration at times. But Bentley seems to be passionate about fighting corruption. I give him a lot of credit for taking concrete actions to try to right the wrongs he believes have occurred in his city. Bentley was the one person who took the strongest stand against the status quo at the city council meeting that night. He was bold enough to directly confront the individuals he holds responsible for what is wrong with DHS, and deal with the unwarranted verbal abuse he received for doing so. I believe Bentley is an earnest and honest person who could help take the city in a completely different direction than it is currently headed if elected.

We need those who will not stand by and allow political corruption to take root and flourish on their watch. The newly-paved streets and the construction of the Wellness Center in Desert Hot Springs are among the welcome additions to the city to be celebrated. But the bright and shiny new construction that represents the promise of a better future here cannot cover the stench of what is rotten at city hall. Too many citizens have been trained to be grateful for the crumbs they receive from their elected officials instead of demanding a high level of performance, accountability and integrity. In closing, I want to encourage more voters to raise their expectations and push for the much-needed change in

478

leadership in Desert Hot Springs on Election Day and beyond. My advice? Never stop fighting for good government. Imagine the tremendous growth possible in this city when it is not hobbled by deceit and self-interest.

****

Michelle Eaton's last sentence is an admonition for every current and future citizen of Desert Hot Springs and places a highlight on my may published articles in the Desert Sun; Desert Local News; Desert Valley Star and my book "I Told you So". As writers, we can get the issues out in the open, but it takes action by citizens to make things change.

And it appears that some change is what DHS voters want as the results of the election show. Adam Sanchez will be taking the place of besmirched council member Karl Baker by a wide margin, as one would hope. The crude antics, pompous attitude and downright lewd internet postings of Baker's nude body was way over the top, even for Desert Hot Springs.

But one new council member will not create a sea-change in the politics of Desert Hot Springs, I am sure. While the dynamics of council decisions may lean a bit differently at times, current mayor Yvonne Parks seemingly will retain the troika of required votes to get her agenda passed when push comes to shove.

The content of this book has been stretched well beyond my original expectations, but to capture the full flavor of the mystery and history of this truly dysfunctional community and its leaders, I felt it was necessary.

Whether we are to believe there is an unexplainable metaphysical pull of an unseen but powerful Vortex causing strange behavior of the city's inhabitants or a circumstantial in migration of citizens bent on self destruction is for you the reader to decide.

Diana and I remain friends with several of Desert Hot Springs residents, most of which have been and remain outside of the political mayhem paying it no mind and are the better for it. They pay their taxes and entertain themselves outside of the city limits "down Valley" as the natives refer to the other valley cities.

My effort to record the history and mysteries of Desert Hot Springs has been an interesting undertaking to say the least. Surprises have been abundant but not unexpected. I hope one day to be able to revisit the city when it has finally reached its potential of becoming the health and wellness center of Coachella Valley, if not all of California.

I hope you have found the information informative and are empathetic to the good citizens of Desert Hot Springs and their wish to one day truly become that "Shining City on a Hill".

About The Author

Bill Effinger lived in Desert Hot Springs from May 2005 to November of 2008 and was active in civic affairs and local politics for the duration of his time living in Desert Hot Springs. Bill's wife Diana worked for the city of Desert Hot Springs as assistant to the deputy city Manager from early 2005 to late 2007.

Bill began writing a regular column for the "Valley Breeze" the local bi-weekly paper in 2005 and continued for two-years. He also wrote Op-Ed pieces for the Desert Sun, the Gannett-owned daily for all of Coachella Valley and authored more than 300 articles for the online local paper the Desert Local News.

Bill has been successful in a number of areas, including developer, home builder, mortgage lending, sales and land acquisition specialist. He served as the Mayor of Buena Park, CA and is a long time member of the National Association of Home Builders, where he was appointed to the National Marketing Committee. His writings have appeared in many building industry journals and he has Authored four books on a variety of subjects.

Bill has lectured on entrepreneurism at leading colleges and universities, such as Babson College, Massachusetts Institute of Technology, Arizona State and National University. He is much in demand as a building industry seminar leader; his "How to Survive, Succeed and Grow in the Building & Contracting Business" continues to win him friends and clients as a business coach and marketing consultant. Bill is active in community and civic affairs serving on a number of boards and advisory groups, including the Escondido Housing Commission, http://www.linkedin.com/profile/view?id=22240172&trk=tab _pro - name#nameSan Marcos Community Development Agency and the San Marcos Unified School District Community Oversight Commission.http://www.linkedin.com/profile/view?id=222401 72&trk=tab_pro - name#name